THE
VICTORIA HISTORY
OF THE COUNTIES
OF ENGLAND
NORTHAMPTONSHIRE

THE BOROUGH OF NORTHAMPTON

REPRINTED FOR

NORTHAMPTONSHIRE
VICTORIA COUNTY HISTORY TRUST
1998

First published 1998

ISBN 0 9532959 0 7

Published by the
Northamptonshire Victoria County History Trust
Northamptonshire Record Office
Wootton Hall Park
Northampton
NN4 8BQ

Published by arrangement with the
Institute of Historical Research
University of London

© Copyright University of London and in this edition, including new Introduction,
Northamptonshire Victoria County History Trust, 1998

Original text and illustrations reprinted from Volume III of
The Victoria History of the County of Northampton
(St. Catherine's Press, 1930; reprinted by Dawson of Pall Mall, 1970)

Plates facing pages 8, 18 and 30 reproduced by permission of
Northamptonshire Libraries and Information Service

Printed by
Hillman Printers (Frome) Ltd
Handlemaker Road
Marston Trading Estate
Frome, Somerset
BA11 4RW

INTRODUCTION TO NEW EDITION

This extended essay on the borough of Northampton, originally published in Volume III of the Northamptonshire *Victoria County History* (1930), merits reissue in the form in which it now appears on two grounds. First, it remains the only connected account based on a detailed investigation of primary evidence of one of the more important county towns of medieval England; second, it is a substantial, but somewhat neglected, piece of work by one of the greatest medieval historians of her generation.

Helen Maud Cam was born in 1885 at Abingdon (Berks.), the fourth of nine children of the Revd. William Herbert Cam and his wife Katherine.[1] In 1893 her father, who had taken a first in Greats at New College, Oxford, in 1873, became rector of Birchanger (Essex), and in 1911 moved to Paulerspury, a wealthy New College living serving a large village close to Watling Street two miles south of Towcester, where he remained until his retirement in 1926. Helen was educated at home until the age of nineteen, when she became a college scholar at Royal Holloway College, London, from where she graduated with a first in 1907. After a year at Bryn Mawr College in the United States, Miss Cam returned to England to teach for three years at Cheltenham Ladies' College before securing a post at Royal Holloway, where she remained until 1921, when she succeeded Eileen Power as director of studies in history at Girton College, Cambridge. From 1929 she was also a university lecturer. In 1948 Miss Cam resigned both her college and university appointments to take up a chair at Harvard, which she held until her retirement six years later. She remained active as an historian until her death in 1968.

No evidence appears to survive to explain why Miss Cam accepted an invitation to write an account of Northampton for *V.C.H.*, whereas her only other contribution to the *History*, a much longer essay on Cambridge, written in 1951 but not published until 1962,[2] formed part of a longstanding interest in the history of that city, in which she lived, worked and was active in public life for more than a quarter of a century.[3] Nor is it clear when the piece was written, since some of the material published by *V.C.H.* during the lean years between the two World Wars had been assembled before 1914.[4] Internal evidence, however, points to revision, if not compilation, during the early 1920s,[5] not long before the work was published, and a few years after its author moved to Cambridge. Neither in this period nor any other did Miss Cam publish anything else on the history of Northampton, and it may be that she agreed to write the essay, which embodies extensive research in primary sources, well beyond the range normally searched by *V.C.H.* writers in this period, from a sense of duty towards the county in which she had spent most of her youth. Fragmentary evidence of at least a casual interest in the history of Northamptonshire at a slightly earlier date survives in the form of notes she made in 1914 correcting and amplifying the text of a pamphlet history of Paulerspury, written by the curate of a neighbouring parish, a task she took sufficiently seriously to spend a day in the British Museum Library.[6] Her only article on Northamptonshire was published in 1934.[7]

Whatever its origins, Miss Cam's essay stands out, not merely from the rather brief accounts of rural parishes which fill the rest of the third and fourth volumes of the Northamptonshire *V.C.H.*, but also from the much slighter articles on county towns published before the First World War. During the period in which Vol. III of *Northamptonshire* appeared, few other towns of similar size were treated by *V.C.H.* and only the studies of Durham (published in 1928) and Chichester (1935), both the work of several authors, none of them of the same stature as Miss Cam, are even remotely comparable with the work republished here.[8] An essay on Worcester by Sir Frank Stenton, although published in 1924, was among work for the *History* completed before 1914 and delayed 'owing to the war and other reasons'.[9] Miss Cam's study of Northampton is thus one of the few contributions to the inter-war *History* by a major scholar from outside the small circle which kept the project alive during these years. It is true that, for the architectural descriptions of churches and other buildings, she was joined by one of the early *V.C.H.* stalwarts, Frank Haliday Cheetham, who contributed to eleven other volumes, and Prof. Alexander Hamilton Thompson, who wrote extensively on ecclesiastical history for *Yorkshire*, Vol. III,[10] but this does not lessen her achievement in providing a rounded account of Northampton's history, topography and institutions, especially in the middle ages, which remains useful to the present day.

To the modern reader, used to generously illustrated town histories in which the text is arranged under helpful subheadings, Miss Cam's essay may at first sight appear offputting. Like all her work, it is uncompromisingly scholarly, based on the rigorous use of published and unpublished primary evidence, and it concentrates on aspects of urban history which interested her and her generation of medievalists, which may seem far removed from the concerns of local historians today. At the same time, the text is laid out in the equally formidable manner followed by *V.C.H.* from its inception, with twin columns of closely printed type, and a forest of references full of abbreviations at the foot of each page. But those who make the effort to read Miss Cam's essay will also

---

[1] C.R. Cheney, 'Helen Maud Cam 1885–1968', *Proc. Brit. Acad.*, lv (1969), 293–309, which is the source for all the biographical details here not otherwise acknowledged. Even this very full memoir fails to mention its subject's contribution to *V.C.H. Northants*.

[2] *V.C.H. Cambs.* iii. 1–149.

[3] *Dict. Nat. Biog.* 1961–70, 167.

[4] *V.C.H. General Introduction*, ed. R.B. Pugh (1970), 31–3.

[5] Below, 19 (a reference to Margaret Bondfield as M.P. for Northampton in the Parliament of 1923–4), 23 (the acreage of municipal parks and open spaces in 1921), 33n. (Thomas H. Mawson's proposals of 1925 for a town planning scheme for Northampton). The account of charities (below, 62–7), which includes a note of the income of some charities for the year ending 31 March 1926, was written by an official of the Charity Commission, rather than Miss Cam, and may have been supplied after the main text was finished.

[6] Northants. Record Office, ROP 752; ZB 190.

[7] 'The Hundreds of Northamptonshire', *Journ. Northants. Nat. Hist. Soc. & Field Club*, xxvii. 99–108.

[8] *V.C.H. Durham*, iii. 1–190; *V.C.H. Sussex*, iii. 71–169. The general history of Durham city was written by Henry Gee, dean of Gloucester, with contributions by several others, none of them university teachers; much of Chichester was by William Page, the general editor of *V.C.H.* until his death in 1933, published posthumously.

[9] *V.C.H. Worcs.* iv. 376–420; *General Introduction*, 33.

[10] *General Introduction*, 276, 281.

A HISTORY OF NORTHAMPTONSHIRE

find that it has all the qualities normally associated with both its author and the series for which it was written. The text is concise, written with absolute clarity and precision. It presents the facts, with a complete absence of the speculation that so often accompanies attempts to reconstruct the early history of any community, urban or rural. Sources are cited in the same way, with only occasional additional comments as to their reliability. Such a text may not be easy to read but it is rewarding, and forms a solid starting point for more detailed investigation of almost any aspect of Northampton's history, at least in the period before about 1660.

Despite the small number of subheadings, or other signposts, the text is arranged in a series of sections dealing with different aspects of the town's history, even if this is not immediately apparent on a first reading. The essay opens with a description of Northampton's geographical position and stresses how this contributed to the town's importance on the national political stage in the middle ages. The constitutional history of the borough from the 11th century is discussed next (pages 3-15), and this leads naturally to the history of the mayoralty and other offices, the various borough courts, and the nature of the gild merchant and town assembly in the middle ages. This section ends (pages 15-17) with the stagnation of the corporation after the Restoration, before the period of statutory reform began in 1835. Miss Cam deals next (pages 17-19) with Northampton's parliamentary representation from the time of Edward I down to the era of Charles Bradlaugh and Margaret Bondfield, before turning (pages 19-26) to the topography of the medieval town and the history of the borough estate. Under the subheading 'Trades' (pages 26-30) she stresses that wool, not leather, was the basis of Northampton's medieval economy, the emergence of tanning and boot- and shoemaking as major industries coming only in the 16th and 17th centuries.

The next section (pages 30-40) is headed 'Description' and deals with the town walls and gates, the market place, castle, town halls, county hall and gaols, as well as the more important private houses to survive from before the fire of 1675. Modern institutions, such as the library and museum, the hospital and the barracks, are described, and there is a short section of local biographies (page 40). The remainder of the text deals, on a much larger scale than for a rural parish, with three standard *V.C.H.* topics: the churches and other religious institutions of the borough (including dated plans of the four medieval parish churches) (pages 40-61), the older secondary schools (pages 61-2, supplementing the account in *Northants.*, Vol. II), and the town's charities (pages 62-7, a section supplied by the Charity Commission and not the work of Miss Cam herself).

Were *V.C.H.* to tackle Northampton today, it would do so on a much larger scale than was contemplated in the 1920s, dealing with a wider range of topics, and drawing on far more sources, especially for the modern period. Indeed, a town the size of Northampton would now be accorded a whole volume to itself, whereas in 1930 it was allotted less than 70 pages out of book of 280. More maps and other illustrations would also be included, although it should be said that even in 1930, when the *History* was dependent for its continued publication in Northamptonshire on the munificence of James Manfield, a local shoe manufacturer who died in 1925 (and of his executors),[11] and photographs were far more expensive to reproduce than today, Miss Cam's essay was quite generously illustrated. As well as the church plans and line drawings of a number of surviving secular buildings in the town, the text is enhanced by about a dozen half-tone plates and also three maps of the early 17th, mid 18th, and early 19th centuries.[12]

It is also important to appreciate that Miss Cam had far less material on which to draw in the 1920s than would be the case today. In particular, although the Northamptonshire Record Society, founded in 1920, had begun to collect private muniments from around the county, there was evidently nothing then in their custody of any value to her. She does, however, acknowledge the help of Joan Wake, the society's founder, in connection with the use of county quarter sessions papers. Miss Cam was also able to draw on records then in the custody of the town clerk, while relying (not wholly uncritically) for most medieval material on a published edition of the older borough records which Northampton, like many towns, had issued at the turn of the century.[13] Apart from this, the most extensively used secondary sources are the histories of the town's four medieval parish churches written before the First World War by the Revd. R.M. Serjeantson,[14] who died in 1916,[15] and who, with Sir William Ryland Dent Adkins (1862-1925),[16] was one of the original editors of the Northamptonshire *V.C.H.*[17]

Northamptonshire in this period lacked a county antiquarian society with its own journal, which might have provided a further source of reliable published material; similarly, although Miss Cam occasionally drew on John Bridges's county history, written in the 1720s, and Morton's account of its natural history of 1712, George Baker's much larger-scale county history of the early 19th century foundered before it reached Northampton.[18] For all these reasons, apart from the general policy of *V.C.H.* to rely as far as possible on primary evidence, the footnotes to Miss Cam's essay cite for the most part items from the public records, manuscripts in the British Museum or Bodleian Library, or published transcripts and calendars of archival sources.

---

[11] P. Stamper, 'Northamptonshire', in *English County Histories. A Guide*, ed. C.R.J. Currie and C.P. Lewis (1994), 300; *V.C.H. Northants.* iii, p. xvii.

[12] For this reissue, we are indebted to Northamptonshire County Libraries and Information Service for making available modern facsimiles of the maps of 1746 and 1810 facing pages 18 and 30 below, from which it has been possible to secure a higher standard of reproduction than that achieved in 1930 from the same originals. The map originally published facing page 8, a reconstructed medieval town plan derived from Speed's bird's eye view of 1610 (which cannot now be traced), has been replaced by a copy of Speed's own drawing, also kindly supplied by the library.

[13] C.A. Markham and J.C. Cox (ed.), *The Records of the Borough of Northampton* (1898-1901). Miss Cam draws attention to several errors by Cox in his part of this work; she also makes a number of comparisons between Northampton and Leicester, quoting from Mary Bateson's edition of that town's early records.

[14] *A History of the Church of the Holy Sepulchre, Northampton* (1897, written jointly with J.C. Cox); *A History of the Church of All Saints, Northampton* (1901); *A History of the Church of St. Peter, Northampton, together with the chapels of Kingsthorpe and Upton* (1904); *A History of the Church of St. Giles, Northampton* (1911).

[15] Stamper, 'Northants.', 300.

[16] *Who's Who of British M.P.s 1919-45*, 3.

[17] *V.C.H. Northants.* iii, p. xvii.

[18] Stamper, 'Northants.', 292-9.

INTRODUCTION TO NEW EDITION

Despite the passage of almost seventy years, and a great growth of interest in urban history in the last two or three decades, much of what Helen Cam wrote about Northampton for *V.C.H.*, especially in the middle ages, remains unchallenged. The main thrust of more recent work has been concerned with the topography of the early settlement, drawing on archaeological evidence completely lacking in her day. Interest in this topic first arose during the period of reconstruction after the Second World War, when a local planning officer raised questions concerning the layout of the early town.[19] The debate was reopened during the campaign of excavation sponsored by the Northampton Development Corporation in the 1970s in a series of publications by the corporation's chief archaeologist.[20] In the same period the Royal Commission on Ancient and Historical Monuments for England devoted one volume of its Northamptonshire inventory to the borough.[21] More recently, John Blair has argued for a different interpretation of some of the archaeological evidence.[22]

Northampton finally acquired its own historical journal in 1948 when the Record Society began the publication of *Northamptonshire Past and Present*, which has served as an outlet for numerous contributions on the history of the borough.[23] For the middle ages these include accounts of both the battles of Northampton,[24] as well as a reconsideration of parish boundaries within the town,[25] early borough administration, and the medieval guildhall.[26] R.J.B. Morris has extended Miss Cam's references to local Acts of Parliament relating to the town,[27] and Northampton's bridges, both in the middle ages and later, have been studied afresh.[28] For the early modern period, Alan Dyer has examined the evidence of the 1524 lay subsidy for Northampton,[29] P. Thomas the problem of soldiers in the Elizabethan town,[30] Glenn Foard the town's Civil War defences,[31] and R.L. Greenall the demolition of its walls after the Restoration.[32] D.L. Bates has amplified Miss Cam's account of an early cotton mill at Northampton,[33] D. Paton has examined the parliamentary election of 1734 in the borough,[34] Jeremy Black has drawn attention to a short-lived local newspaper,[35] and V.A. Hatley has discussed several other aspects of the town's 18th- and early 19th-century history.[36] Hatley and others have also continued the debate, mentioned briefly by Miss Cam, as to why the London & Birmingham Railway's main line, opened in 1838, by-passed Northampton by several miles.[37] Jack Simmons has compared Northampton with two of its neighbours,[38] while others have considered education in 19th-century Northampton,[39] the new police,[40] local politics,[41] suburban development south of the Nene,[42] a visit by the Royal Agricultural Society,[43] and the boot and

---

[19] F. Lee, 'A new theory of the origins and early growth of Northampton', *Archaeological Journal*, cx (1954), 164–74; idem, 'Northampton's town centre', *Journ. Northants. Nat. Hist. Soc. & Field Club*, xxx (1942), 41–53.

[20] J.H. Williams, 'The early development of the town of Northampton', in A. Dornier (ed.), *Mercian Studies* (1977), 135–52; idem, *St. Peter's Street, Northampton: Excavations, 1973–1976* (1979); idem and H. Bamford, *Northampton. The first 6,000 years* (1979); J.H. Williams, *Saxon and Medieval Northampton* (1982); J.H. Williams, M. Shaw and V. Denham, *Middle Saxon Palaces at Northampton* (1985).

[21] *R.C.A.H.M. Northants.* v (1985).

[22] J. Blair, 'Anglo-Saxon Minsters: a Topographical Review', in J. Blair and R. Sharpe (ed.), *Pastoral Care before the Parish* (1992), 226–66; idem, 'Palaces or Minsters? Northampton and Cheddar reconsidered', *Anglo-Saxon England*, xxv (1996), 97–121. See also T. Welsh, 'Geographical reconstruction: an alternative interpretation of early Northampton', *Environment and Society*, iii (1) (1997), 73–87.

[23] Joined since 1974 by *Northants. Archaeology*, which grew out of the *Bulletin of the Northants. Federation of Archaeological Socs.*, first published in 1966.

[24] R.F. Treharne, 'The Battle of Northampton, 5th April 1264', *Northants. P. & P.*, ii. 73–90; R.I. Jack, 'A Quincentenary: the Battle of Northampton, July 10th, 1460', Ibid., iii. 21–25. Cf. below, 3.

[25] J.H. Williams, 'Northampton's Medieval Parishes', *Northants. Archaeology*, xvii (1982), 74–84.

[26] J.H. Williams, 'The Forty Men of Northampton's First Custumal and the Development of Borough Government in late twelfth-century Northampton', *Northants. P. & P.*, vii. 215–34; idem, 'Northampton's Medieval Guildhall', Ibid., vii. 5–10. Cf. below, 3–4.

[27] R.J.B. Morris, 'Northampton's Local Legislation: 1430 to 1988', *Northants. P. & P.*, viii. 73–82.

[28] A.V. Goodfellow, 'The Bridges of Northampton', *Northants. Archaeology*, xv (1980), 138–55.

[29] A. Dyer, 'Northampton in 1524', *Northants. P. & P.*, vi. 73–80.

[30] P. Thomas, 'Vagabond Soldiers and Deserters at Elizabethan Northampton', *Northants. P. & P.*, ix. 101–10.

[31] G. Foard, 'The Civil War Defences of Northampton', *Northants. P. & P.*, ix. 4–44.

[32] R.L. Greenall, 'The Demolition of Northampton's Walls, July 1662', *Northants. P. & P.*, vi. 83–4.

[33] D.L. Bates, 'Cotton-spinning in Northampton: Edward Cave's Mill, 1742–61', *Northants. P. & P.*, ix. 237–52. Cf. below, 29–30.

[34] D. Paton, 'National Politics and the Local Community in the Eighteenth Century: the Northamptonshire Election of 1734', *Northants. P. & P.*, vii. 164–72.

[35] J. Black, 'A Missing Northampton Paper', *Northants. P. & P.*, vii. 339–42.

[36] V.A. Hatley, 'Locks, Lords and Coal: a Study in eighteenth-century Northampton History', *Northants. P. & P.*, vi. 207–18; 'The Headless Trunk: a Study in Northampton Politics, 1795–1796', Ibid., viii. 105–20; 'Literacy at Northampton, 1761–1900', Ibid., iv. 379–81 and v. 81, 347–8; and 'Some Aspects of Northampton's History, 1815–51', iii. 243–53.

[37] Below, 1; see J. Wake, *Northampton Vindicated: or why the main line missed the town* (1935); V.A. Hatley, 'Northampton Re-vindicated. More light on why the main line missed the town', *Northants. P. & P.*, ii. 305–9; idem, 'Northampton Hoodwinked?', *Journ. Transport History*, iii. 160–72; J. Lovell, 'Why the Railway missed Northampton: some further thoughts', *Northants. P. & P.*, ix. 80–4. For the railway's eventual arrival see A. and E. Jordan, 'Northampton's First Railway Station', *Northants. P. & P.*, ix. 133–46.

[38] J. Simmons, 'Three Midland Towns. Northampton, Leicester, Nottingham', *Northants. P. & P.*, iii. 136–40.

[39] J. Lawes, 'Voluntary Schools and Basic Education in Northampton, 1800–71', *Northants. P. & P.*, vi. 85–91.

[40] R. Etheridge, 'Nineteenth-century Northampton: the Nature of the New Police, Change and Power', *Northants. P. & P.*, ix. 175–90.

[41] N. Goddard, '"A Sensation almost with Parallel"?: Reflections on the third Earl Spencer's Northampton Speech, November 1843', *Northants. P. & P.*, ix. 265–72.

[42] A. Lovell, 'The Northampton Freehold Land Society and the Origins of Far Cotton', *Northants. P. & P.*, viii. 299–305.

[43] T. Hold, 'The Royal Agricultural Society in Northampton in the year 1847', *Northants. P. & P.*, vii. 434–6.

A HISTORY OF NORTHAMPTONSHIRE

shoe industry.[44] The town's 20th-century history has also begun to receive attention.[45]

Since 1930 no writer has attempted a general history of Northampton, although the period since 1835, not covered in any detail by Miss Cam, has been well served,[46] and a popular history first published in 1912 has been reprinted.[47] Among numerous more specialised studies, those on working class society,[48] two local hospitals,[49] higher education,[50] theatre history,[51] and the work of W.J. Bassett-Lowke, the model engineer,[52] are among the more substantial. The career of the Northampton Development Corporation, which between 1968 and 1985 supervised a rapid expansion of the population and built-up area, has also been chronicled.[53] As in most towns, several albums of old photographs have been published.[54]

PHILIP RIDEN
County Editor

CHARLES INSLEY
Assistant Editor

March 1998

---

[44] J.H. Porter, 'The Northampton Arbitration Board and the Shoe Industry Dispute of 1887', *Northants. P. & P.*, iv. 149–54; idem, 'Northampton Boot and Shoe Arbitration Board before 1914', Ibid., vi. 93–9; K. Brooker, 'The Northampton Shoemakers' Reaction to Industrialisation: some thoughts', Ibid., vi. 151–9.

[45] M. Dickie, 'Liberals, Radicals and Socialists in Northampton before the Great War', *Northants. P. & P.*, vii. 51–4; G.H. Bennett, 'The Northampton Labour Party and the Abyssinian Crisis of 1935: the Resignation of Cecil L'Estrange Malone', Ibid., ix. 287–92.

[46] C. Brown, *Northampton 1835–1985. Shoe Town, New Town* (1990), which has a good bibliography.

[47] A.P. White, *The Story of Northampton* (1912; repr. 1986).

[48] J. Seabrook, *The Unprivileged* (1967); idem, *The Everlasting Feast* (1974).

[49] F.F. Waddy, *History of Northampton General Hospital, 1743–1948* (1974); A. Foss and K. Trick, *St. Andrew's Hospital, Northampton. The First One Hundred and Fifty Years (1838–1988)* (1989).

[50] D. Walmsley (ed.), *An Ever-Rolling Stream: the on-going story of the Development of Higher Education in Northampton and Northamptonshire* (1989).

[51] R. Foulkes, *Repertory at The Royal. Sixty-five years of theatre in Northampton 1927–92* (1992). See also A. Dias, *Adventure in Repertory. Northampton Repertory Theatre 1927–48* (1948), L. Warwick, *Death of a Theatre. A History of the New Theatre, Northampton* (1960) and idem, *Theatre Un-Royal. Or 'They called them Comedians'* (1974).

[52] R. Fuller, *The Bassett-Lowke Story* (1984).

[53] H. Barty-King, *Expanding Northampton* (1985).

[54] For which see Brown, *Northampton*, 229–31.

The Victoria History of the County of Northampton

Volumes already published

VOLUME ONE (1902)

Natural History, Early Man, Romano-British Remains, Anglo-Saxon Remains, Introduction to the Northamptonshire Domesday, Text of the Northamptonshire Domesday, The Northamptonshire Survey, Monumental Effigies, Domesday Index.

VOLUME TWO (1906)

Ecclesiastical History, Religious Houses, Early Christian Art, Schools, Industries, Forestry, Sport Ancient and Modern, Ancient Earthworks. Topography: Soke of Peterborough, Willybrook Hundred.

VOLUME THREE (1930)

Northampton Borough, Polebrook Hundred, Navisford Hundred, Huxloe Hundred, Borough of Higham Ferrers.

VOLUME FOUR (1937)

Higham Ferrers Hundred, Spelhoe Hundred, Hamfordshoe Hundred, Orlingbury Hundred, Wymersley Hundred.

NORTHAMPTONSHIRE FAMILIES (1906)

The Landed Houses of Northamptonshire, Cartwright of Aynhoe, Cecil Marquess of Exeter, Dryden of Canons Ashby, Elwes (now Cary-Elwes) of Billing Hall, Fane Earl of Westmorland, FitzRoy Duke of Grafton, Isham of Lamport, Knight of Fawsley, Langham of Cottesbrooke, Maunsell of Thorpe Malsor, Palmer of Charlton, Powys Lord Lilford, Robinson of Cranford, Rokeby of Arlingworth, Spencer Earl Spencer, Thornton of Brockhall, Wake of Courteenhall, Willes of Astrop, Young of Orlingbury, List of Sheriffs of Northamptonshire, Lists of Members of Parliament for the County, Northampton, Peterborough, Brackley and Higham Ferrers.

Volumes in preparation

VOLUME FIVE

Transport and Communications; Industry in the 20th century; Table of Population, 1801–1991.

VOLUME SIX

Cleley Hundred.

TOPOGRAPHY

THE BOROUGH OF NORTHAMPTON

Ham tune (x cent.); Nordhamtune, Northantone (xi cent.); Norhthamtune, Norhanthon, Norhantuna, Norhantona (xii cent.); Norhamptone (town seal) (xiii cent.).

Northampton, the county town, lies mainly to the north and east of the River Nene, the oldest part of the town being on a hill which rises from 194 ft. above sea level at the west bridge near Castle station to 294 ft. at the prison near the site of the old north gate. The road from London and Old Stratford, joined south of the river by the road from Oxford and Towcester, runs due north through the town towards Market Harborough and Leicester, and is intersected at right angles in the middle of the town, at All Saints' Church, by the road from Daventry to Little Billing. From here also, roads run to Kettering and to Wellingborough, and it is in this direction that the chief expansion in the 19th and 20th centuries has taken place. West of the river lie the suburbs of Duston and Dallington, extending from the medieval suburb of St. James' End; to the south of the river, and west and east of the London Road lie the rapidly expanding suburbs of Far Cotton and Hardingstone, beyond the medieval suburb of St. Leonard's End. To the north, along the Market Harborough road, the municipality now includes Kingsthorpe, an independent royal manor in the Middle Ages, and outside the parliamentary boundary until 1918. The remains of the town fields are seen in the Race Course, once Northampton Heath, between the Kettering and Market Harborough roads, where the freemen had grazing rights down to 1882, and in Cow Meadow, Calvesholme and Midsummer Meadow, lying along the river to the south of the town.

The first plans for a railway, deposited in 1830, show the line passing through Ashton, Roade and Blisworth, avoiding Northampton. In 1831 the Corporation of Northampton, who owned an estate at Bugbrooke, took up the same attitude as other local landowners in opposing the project for a railway.

BOROUGH OF NORTHAMPTON. *Gules on a mount vert a castle with three towers supported by two leopards rampant or.*

Later, however, they were acting with a committee of inhabitants of the town in pressing for the line to be brought as near to Northampton as possible. Stephenson reported against the route through the town. The bill for the railway was thrown out in 1832, it was thought by the opposition of the landowners, but a subsequent bill received the Royal assent on 6 May 1833. The London Midland and Scottish Railway now runs from London through Northampton to Rugby and the north; lines run also to Leicester, Kettering, Peterborough, Market Harborough and Bedford. The station in Cotton End, known as Bridge Street, was opened in 1845, the Castle Station in 1859, the latter being enlarged in 1881 so as to become the chief station. The station in St. John's Street was opened in 1872. The Grand Junction Canal joins the Nene at Northampton, this branch having been completed in 1815. Tram lines were first laid down in the town in 1881 and were electrified in 1903. An early omnibus service was run to Wellingborough, and since 1919 motor omnibus services have run to the villages round the town and bring in thousands of both buyers and sellers to the market.

The earliest reference to Northampton in writing occurs in 914, and though the archaeological evidence clearly indicates occupation of the castle site in the Romano-British and Anglo-Saxon periods,[1] no settlement of any importance seems to have existed at Northampton before the time of the Danish conquest. The Danes appear to have made it a centre for military and administrative purposes during the thirty years of their undisturbed occupation (877-912); by 918[2] it had a jarl and an army dependent upon it, whose territory extended to the Welland.[3] Thus, after its reconquest by Edward in 918 it naturally became the centre of one of the new shires organised in the district recovered from the Danes, and in 940 it successfully resisted the invading forces of Anlaf Guthfrithson, the Danish ruler of Northumbria.[4] As in the case of other Danish towns, however, the military centre seems to have rapidly become a trading centre, for in 1010 it is described as a 'port,' and in spite of the burning in that year by Thorkil's Danes[5] and the ravages of Edwin's and Morcar's forces in 1065,[6] it possessed about 316 houses in 1086, and ranked between Warwick

---

[1] *Assoc. Arch. Soc. Rep.* 1882, pp. 243-251. On the evidence here given, the castle-mound itself cannot be pre-Norman; *V.C.H. Northants.* i, 219.

[2] Accepting the chronology of W. J. Corbett, *Camb. Med. Hist.* iii, 364.

[3] *Angl. Sax. Chron. s.a.* 921. (Parker MS.)

[4] Simeon of Durham, *Opera* [Rolls Ser.], ii, 93 (*s.a.* 939).

[5] *Angl. Sax. Chron.* (Laud. MS.)

[6] *Angl. Sax. Chron.* (Cott. MS. Tib. B iv.).

A HISTORY OF NORTHAMPTONSHIRE

and Leicester in size.[7] It may have possessed three churches, for Anglo-Saxon sculptured stones have been found both at St. Sepulchre's and St. Peter's churches,[8] and the early reference to All Saints' fair[9] suggests that this church also may be pre-Norman.

In Domesday[10] Northampton has the marks of an old county borough. It is extra-hundredal, being rated in the Northants Geld Roll[11] at a quarter of a hundred. It is characterised by heterogeneity of tenure, containing 87 royal burgesses holding their burgages of the King, whilst some 219 other houses belong to 34 different lords. Of these lords, 24 hold other lands of the King in the county, and the 21 houses of Swain the son of Azur are explicitly said to pertain to his rural manor of Stoke Bruerne. To the old borough, which held 60 royal burgesses under Edward the Confessor, a new borough containing 40 royal burgesses had been added. Unlike the majority of county boroughs, Northampton appears to have no mint;[12] on the other hand, it is unique among Domesday boroughs in having its farm assessed at a fixed sum (£30 10s. 0d.), payable by the burgesses to the sheriff. There is mention of a 'Durandus prepositus,'[13] who may well have been the town reeve and have acted in this matter as the sheriff's subordinate. The 'portland' mentioned on folio 219b seems on a balance of evidence to belong rather to the carucated Stamford than to the hidated Northampton.[14] There is no mention of a castle; its creation was to be the work of the first Norman earl, and the Countess Judith, lady of 16 houses, had not yet given place to her daughter's husband. The other chief tenants were the Bishop of Coutances (23 houses), the Count of Mortain (37 houses), and William Peverel (32 houses). The 'waste' condition of 35½ houses is probably attributable to the raid of 1065.

With the Norman Conquest Northampton became a town of national importance. Its geographical situation, 'in the middle of the kingdom,' as Geoffrey le Scrope said in his opening speech at the Eyre of Northampton in 1329,[15] made it a valuable strategical point for a government which was determined to control the north and west as well as the south and east, and even before the line of Senlis earls had died out, the castle built by the first of them had been taken over as a royal residence and fortress.[16] The neighbourhood of the royal hunting lodges of Silverstone and Kings Cliffe and the royal palace of Geddington accounts, no doubt, for a large number of brief royal visits,[17] but its general convenience as a meeting place is attested by the number of political, social, ecclesiastical and military events that occurred here. Among the long series of councils and parliaments held at Northampton, from the time of Henry I to that of Richard II, may be mentioned the council of 1131, at which the barons of Henry I swore fealty to Maud;[18] that of 1164 at which Becket was condemned by the King's court and appealed to the Pope;[19] that of 1176, at which the assize of Northampton was published;[20] that of 1211, in which John and the Legate Pandulf had their famous debate;[20a] that of 1232, in which the lands of the Earl of Chester were partitioned;[21] that of 1318, at which Edward II and Thomas of Lancaster came to terms for the time being;[22] the parliament of 1328, at which peace was made with Scotland and the statute of Northampton was passed;[23] and the parliament of 1380, at which the imposition of the Poll Tax was decided on.[24] The importance of the fairs of Northampton is noticed below, and the town was also a favourite centre for tournaments from the time of Henry III to Edward III.[25] Many church councils and chapters were held here,[26] and at least three crusades launched. In February 1214, according to the chronicle of St. Andrew's priory, 300 persons of both sexes took the cross here;[27] in November 1239, Richard of Cornwall and nobles too many to enumerate, swore on the altar of All Saints' that they would lead their troops that year to the Holy Land;[28] in June 1268 the two sons of Henry III, with 120 other knights and many others, took the cross at Northampton.[29]

To its geographical position is due the part played by Northampton in the various civil wars. It commanded one of the main roads from London to the North, and was a good base for movements against the west or south-west. In 1173 it was one of the strongholds that held out for Henry II, and next year William of Scotland made his submission there.[30] In 1215 the first move of the insurgent barons was to besiege Northampton,[31] and the castle was one of four which were to be given into their hands as a

---

[7] V.C.H. Northants. i, 276.

[8] Cox and Serjeantson, Hist. of Ch. of the Holy Sepulchre, Northampt. p. 30; R. M. Serjeantson, Hist. of Ch. of St. Peter, Northampt. p. 12.

[9] See below, under Fairs.

[10] V.C.H. Northants. i, 301.

[11] Ellis, Gen. Introd. to Domesday, i, 186.

[12] W. H. Stevenson suggested that coins minted here may have been credited to Southampton, whose Saxon name was identical in form. Eng. Hist. Rev. xiv, 590.

[13] Gilbert, son of Durand, acted as reeve in 1189–90 (Pipe Roll), and put his name to the first town custumal. Bateson, Boro. Customs, i, xli.

[14] V.C.H. Northants. i, 278. It should be observed, however, that carucates are found at Northampton in 1274 Rot. Hund. ii, 1.

[15] Eng. Hist. Rev. xxxix, 250. A similar expression, Tanquam in regni medio, is used in 1338 at a Provincial Chapter of the Benedictines (Wilkins, Concilia, ii, 628).

[16] By 1130. R. M. Serjeantson. The Castle of Northampt. p. 2.

[17] For John's 30 visits see Rot. Litt. Pat. I. (Rec. Com.), Itinerary of King John. For Henry III's constant visits see below under The Castle; Edward II was here in 1307, 1308, 1310, 1311, 1317, 1318. (Chart. R.)

[18] William of Malmesbury, Historia Novella. (Rolls Ser.) (Gesta Regum), ii, 534.

[19] Chron. Rog. de Hovedon (Rolls Ser.), i, 224–8.

[20] Ibid. ii, 89.

[20a] Annal Mon. (Rolls Ser.), i, 209–219, not in 1210, as stated V.C.H. Northants. ii, 9.

[21] Bracton's Notebook, case 1273.

[22] Parl. R. i, 453.

[23] Ibid. ii, 28.

[24] Ibid. iii, 88.

[25] Tournaments arranged to be held at Northampton were forbidden in 1218, 1219, 1227, 1228, 1233, 1234, 1237, 1241, 1247, 1249. [See Cal Pat. and Matthew Paris, Chron. Maj. (Rolls Ser.), iv, 88,

647; v, 54]. For tournament of 1265 see below; for that at which Geoffrey le Scrope was knighted under Edward II see Harris Nicolas, Scrope and Grosvenor Roll, i, 142, 144; for one in 1342, Murimuth [R.S.], p. 124.

[26] At least 46 Benedictine chapters were held here, and 20 chapters of Augustinian canons. See below under St. Andrew's Priory and St. James' Abbey. The first general chapter of the Cistercian order in England met here (between 1400 and 1404), and Dominican chapters were held here in 1239, 1271, 1272, 1234, 1312, 1362. (Eng. Hist. Rev. xliv, 386. Serjeantson, The Black Friars of Northampt.)

[27] Corpus Christi Coll. Camb. MS. 281 (2) s.a. 1214.

[28] Matthew Paris, Chron. Maj. (Rolls Ser.), iii, 620.

[29] Annal Mon. (Rolls Ser.), iv, 217.

[30] Chron. Rog. de Hoveden (Rolls Ser.), ii, 64.

[31] Walter of Coventry (Rolls Ser.), ii, 219.

2

BOROUGH OF NORTHAMPTON

pledge for keeping Magna Carta.[32] It served as a base in the siege of Bedford in 1224.[33] Its pivotal position comes out most strikingly in the campaigns of 1264-6. The Royalist forces mustered by Henry at Oxford, at the end of March 1264, marched against Northampton, which was held by the younger Simon de Montfort and 'a great multitude '[34] of knights and squires. In the Cow Meadow adjoining the town William Marshall, keeper of the peace, and Walter Hyldeburn, assembled the community of the county and addressed them, on behalf of the Earl of Leicester, on the iniquities of the King's party.[34a] The Prior of St. Andrew's, a Frenchman, whose priory occupied the north-west angle of the town fortifications, facilitated the entry of the King's troops through a breach in the garden wall,[35] and the town was taken and sacked ruthlessly by the Royalists, who, according to Wykes, reduced a most flourishing town to a most wretched state.[36] Fifty-five knights, including Sir Hugh Gobion and Sir Baldwin Wake, were taken prisoners[37] and sent to various castles for safe keeping, and at a later date to have been against the King at Northampton was the measure of a man's disloyalty.[38] The story of the King's threat to hang the students of the ephemeral university of Northampton[39] for their resistance to him occurs only in a 14th century chronicle.[40] The town was, however, deprived of its mayor and committed to the keeping of a royal *custos*,[41] Ralph de Hotot, who was to keep in touch with the constable of the castle. In the autumn that followed Lewes, when the King's government was controlled by Leicester, the levies were assembled at Northampton,[42] and a tournament was planned here by the younger de Montforts for Easter 1265, which was cancelled because of Gilbert de Clare's refusal to come.[43] Later, when the younger Simon was marching from the south to join his father in the west, he went out of his way to go through Northampton, counting, it would seem, on the warm support of the town.[44] Again, after Evesham, Henry and his son made Northampton the rendezvous for the troops going against the isle of Axholm,[45] and held a council here at Christmas, at which the younger Simon surrendered himself.[46] Northampton was also the King's headquarters from April to June 1266.[47] With the town held in turn by the rival parties, it is not surprising that the Jews took refuge in a body in the castle,[48] and that the priory suffered both from want and from failure to maintain order.[49]

Edward I made little use of Northampton as compared with his father, though four parliaments were held there by Edward II, and both parliaments and assemblies of merchants[50] by Edward III. The parliament of 1380, however, some of whose sessions were held in St. Andrew's Priory,[51] was the last to meet here, and in the 15th century Northampton ceases to be a centre of national importance. Its strategic significance was illustrated again in 1460. In June of that year Warwick had landed from France and been welcomed enthusiastically by London. The forces of Henry VI moved from Coventry and took up a position at Northampton to cut off London from the north. On July 10 they were routed by the forces of Warwick and March, marching from London through Towcester, in the meadows south-east of the town, between the river and Delapré Abbey. Henry VI was taken prisoner, and his queen fled to Scotland. We are told that the flight was watched by the Archbishop of Canterbury from the hill of the Headless Cross, which indicates that the Eleanor Cross on the London Road outside the abbey grounds had already had its top broken off.[52] Not till 1642 was Northampton to be as prominent again in national politics.

Between the record of Domesday Book and the first royal grant to the borough, almost exactly a hundred years elapsed. In 1185 the burgesses of Northampton made a fine of 200 marks to hold their town in chief,[53] and it is probably to this grant by Henry II that John's charter refers.[54] The constitutional history of the intervening period is largely conjectural, but for some of the time, at least, it must have been bound up with that of the earls of Northampton.[55] No earl is mentioned in Domesday; it is supposed that Simon de Senlis became earl after his marriage with Waltheof's daughter Maud about 1089, and died on his return from the Holy Land some time between 1111 and 1113.[56] He was the founder of the Cluniac priory of St. Andrew's, the builder of the first castle, the Norman churches of the Holy Sepulchre and All Saints, and, according to tradition, of the town wall. In 1113 his widow married David of Scotland,[57] who probably acted as guardian to his stepson, the second Simon, the founder of Delapré Abbey. By August 1138 Simon II had been rewarded with the earldom for his loyalty to Stephen, whom David was opposing.[58] In 1153, when Simon II died, his son, Simon III, the builder of St. Peter's Church, was under age, and he only held the earldom from 1159 to 1183 or 1184, when he died without heirs.[59] Various charters of the Senlis earls are preserved in the cartulary of St. Andrew's priory. One of the charters of Simon I is addressed to ' his reeve of Northampton,' and those of Simon II are addressed to ' his reeves and burgesses of Northampton

---

[32] Matthew Paris, *Chron. Maj.* (Rolls Ser.), ii, 603. It seems likely that it never was handed over in fact. A royal garrison was holding it in October 1215. *Mem. Walt. de Coventria* (Rolls Ser.), ii, 226.
[33] *V.C.H. Beds.* iii, 10.
[34] C.C.C.C. MS. 281 (2) s.a. 1264.
[34a] Hunter, *Rot. Selecti*, 194.
[35] *Annal. Mon.* (Rolls Ser.), iii, 229-30.
[36] Ibid. iv, 145.
[37] W. Rishanger, *Chronica* (Rolls Ser.), p. 21.
[38] *Cal. Pat.* 1258-66, pp. 311, 314, 316, 318, 323, 472, 555; 1266-72, pp. 66, 248.
[39] *V.C.H. Northants.* ii, 15-17.
[40] Walter of Hemingburgh, *Chronicon Eng. Hist. Soc.*), i, 311.
[41] *Cal. Pat.* 1258-66, p. 315 (26 April 1264).
[42] *Annal. Mon.* (Rolls Ser.), iii, 234.
[43] Ibid. iv, 162.
[44] Ibid. 170.
[45] *Cal. Pat.* 1258-66, pp. 520, 549.
[46] Corpus Christi Coll. Camb. MS. 281 (2) s.a. 1265.
[47] *Cal Pat.* 1258-66, pp. 581, 595, 664.
[48] Ibid. p. 320-1.
[49] Ibid. p. 403.
[50] *Cal. Close.* 1333-37, p. 677; p. 517.
[51] *Parl. R.* iii, 88.
[52] *Northants. Nat. Hist. Soc.* March 1907; R. M. Serjeantson, *The Battle of Northampton*.
[53] Pipe R. 31 Hen. II.
[54] *Rot. Cart.* (Rec. Com.), p. 45-6. The grant to the burgesses of Lancaster in 1199 refers to all the liberties which the burgesses of Northampton had on the day that King Henry died. *Rot. Cart.* (Rec. Com.), p. 26.
[55] R. M. Serjeantson, *Origin and History of the de Senlis Family* (Assoc. Arch. Soc. Rep. xxxi, 504 ff.)
[56] Wm. Farrer, *Honors and Knights' Fees*, ii, 296.
[57] *Dict. Nat. Biog.* This is probably the date at which the castle became royal.
[58] Dugdale, *Angl. Mon.* v, 356; Round, *Geoff. de Mandeville*, 285.
[59] *Dict. Nat. Biog.*

A HISTORY OF NORTHAMPTONSHIRE

and to all his ministers of Northampton.'[60] These formulae are lacking from the charters of Simon III. They indicate, as Dr. Tait has shown,[60a] that for part of the 11th and 12th centuries Northampton was a mesne borough, dependent, like Leicester, upon its earl, and not directly upon the King. Granted by Rufus to Simon I with the earldom, the town was retained by Henry I on his death, and was being farmed by the Crown in 1130.[61] Stephen restored it to Simon II with the earldom, but Henry II resumed it in 1154,[61a] and it was farmed by a royal official—from 1170 onwards, by the sheriff [61b]—up to 1185. The death of Simon III may have made the King the readier to grant the burgesses' request in that year to farm the borough themselves, though the concession was terminable. This farm had risen from the £30 10s. 0d. of Domesday to £100 in 1130, and from 1185 onwards it was £120 down to the 15th century.[62] The right to pay the farm directly at the Exchequer logically involved the right to elect reeves or *prepositos*, and this right is expressly granted in the first charter extant, that of 18 November 1189, which is preserved in the town archives at Northampton.[63] From 1185 to 1197 the names of the two town reeves are to be found on the Pipe Roll;[64] after that year the formula runs 'the burgesses of Northampton,' giving no names.

Besides the grant of the *firma burgi* in fee-farm, which made the concession of Henry II a permanency, and the licence to choose their own reeve freely every year, the privileges granted to the burgesses of Northampton in 1189 included the ratification of established customs, the tenurial privileges of warranty of lands, freedom from scotale and such exactions, freedom from billeting; the jurisdictional privileges of freedom from external pleas, freedom from the duel, and preservation of established judicial customs, a weekly court of husting to be held in the town, and exemption from *miskenning*; also freedom from the murder fine and from arbitrary amercements; the commercial privileges of freedom from toll throughout England, and the right of retaliation on any borough which infringed this custom. The privileges granted to Northampton were explicitly modelled on those of London. It falls into that group of boroughs, others of which were Norwich, Lincoln and Oxford, which looked to London for forms and precedents,[65] and on several occasions it definitely and consciously copied London customs,[66] if in some other respects, as will be shown, it had affinities with its neighbour, the mesne borough of Leicester. The clause confirming ancient custom, grants to the burgesses 'all other liberties and free customs which our citizens of London have had or have ... according to the liberties of the city of London and the laws of the borough of Northampton.' [67] This last phrase is almost certainly to be associated with the oldest town custumal, which, as Miss Bateson has shown,[68] belongs to much the same date as the charter of Richard I. The town custumals throw so much light on the constitutional history of the borough that it will be well to describe them here. The *Liber Custumarum* preserved at Northampton, and printed in the 'Records of the Borough,' is the last of four versions of the town customs. The two oldest are in Latin and are preserved in a 14th century manuscript in the Bodleian Library.[69] The first, containing 24 clauses, is headed by a list of the forty burgesses who authorised the custumal and swore to preserve it.[70] Nine of these appear on the Pipe Rolls as accounting for the farm of the borough between 1184 and 1196, and it seems certain that the custumal was drawn up in connection with the grant of the *firma burgi*, between 1185 and 1190. The second custumal, containing 42 clauses, is headed by a list of 24 burgesses, most of whom can be identified as having flourished 1228-1264. Two of the clauses of this custumal are dated and belong to 1251 and 1260; it may thus be assigned to round about 1260. The next version is French, and is in a manuscript now at the British Museum,[71] but belonging to the town of Northampton as late as 1769, and uniform in binding with the *Liber Custumarum*, still in the possession of the corporation. It contains 58 articles, the first 56 adapted from those of the two earlier custumals, the two last new. The latest is dated 7 October 1341. From this French version was made an English translation, seemingly about 1461,[72] supplemented by further regulations and ordinances, enrolled from time to time, as they were carried in the town assembly or council, the whole forming the *Liber Custumarum*, now preserved at Northampton, the latest entry in which is dated 11 October 1549.[73]

The first custumal (c. 1190) refers to bailiffs who take distresses on behalf of the King,[74] to reeves or *prepositi* who intervene with an apparently higher authority and can give a man entry, together with the bailiff,[75] and to the *probi homines de placitis*—the suitors of a court at which transfers of land take place for which the witness of these suitors is sufficient warrant.[76] There is no reference to a mayor; the reeves seem to be the highest officials. Nor is there any reference to a mayor in John's charter. Of this charter, granted to the town in April 1200, there are two versions differing from each other at the precise point where both differ from Richard's charter. This is with regard to the election of officials. The

---

[60] Cott. MS. Vesp. E xvii; fo. 6 *prefecto suo de Northampt.; omnibus prepositis suis et burgensibus Northampt.; Ricardo Grimbaud et G. de Blosseuile et omnibus suis ministris de Northampt.* The charters of the Scottish Kings in this MS. never describe them as Earls of Northampt.

[60a] *Engl. Hist. Rev.* xlii, 335.

[61] Pipe R. 31 Hen. I.

[61a] The exact moment when the change occurs is recorded in the Pipe Roll Account at Michaelmas, 1155. *Red Bk. of the Excheq.* (Rolls Ser.), ii, 655. I owe this reference to the kindness of Dr. Tait.

[61b] *Eng. Hist. Rev.* xlii, 352.

[62] Pipe R. 31 Hen. II.

[63] See *Records of the Boro. of Northampt.*, ed. Markham and Cox (cited henceforth as *Boro Rec.*), frontispiece, for facsimile of charter.

[64] Ibid. i, 21-23.

[65] Gross, *Gild Merchant*, i, 254. Northampton itself served as a model to Grimsby and Lancaster.

[66] E.g. Bowbell in 1391 (*Boro Rec.* i, 252), orphans' custody in 1599 (ibid. i, 124); common council in 1649 (ibid. ii, 21).

[67] *Secundum libertates Londoniarum et leges burgi Norhamtonie.*

[68] Bateson, *Borough Customs*, I, xli.

[69] Douce MS. (Bodl. Lib.), 98. fo. 158, *et seq.*

[70] *Isti sunt subscripti qui providerunt leges Norhampton' et iuraverunt eas observandas.*

[71] Add. MS. 34308.

[72] *Boro. Rec.* i, 208-236.

[73] Ibid. i, 341.

[74] Cl. 19.

[75] Cl. 13.

[76] Cl. 1, 4, 16.

BOROUGH OF NORTHAMPTON

version on the charter roll[77] provides that two burgesses were to be elected by the common counsel of the vill and presented to the sheriff, who should select one of them and present him to the chief justice at Westminster at the time of rendering his account, to be *prepositus* of the town. The version of the *Cartae Antiquae*[78] provides that the two burgesses elected should be presented to the chief justice at Westminster and should serve as *prepositi*. Both versions say that the officials so elected should only be removable by the common counsel of the town, and provide also for the election of four coroners[79] to keep the pleas of the Crown and to see that the reeves treat rich and poor alike justly. There is some difficulty in deciding between the merits of the two charters.[80] On the whole, the version of the *Cartae Antiquae* seems the more likely to be correct.[80a] Its form was followed by Henry the third's charter of 1227,[81] which merely adds that the two *prepositi* shall be presented to the chief justice by the letters patent of the vill, and this procedure was presumably followed down to the charter of 1299, though the early Exchequer rolls do not record the presentations.

The *prepositi* of 1227 are certainly the bailiffs of a later date; indeed, as early as 1222 the Exchequer addresses a writ to 'the mayor and bailiffs' of Northampton.[82] Two *prepositi*, as we have seen, appear on the Pipe Roll accounting for the farm as early in 1185. This is an additional reason for preferring the version of the *Cartae Antiquae*. Dr. Cox assigns the first mayor to the reign of Richard I, but there appears to be no evidence for the existence of a mayor, so-called, save the handwriting of certain undated deeds.[83] As late as 1212 John addressed to the reeve and good men of Northampton a command to lead the armed forces of the town, which is directed in the cases of London and Lincoln to the mayors of those cities.[84] But three years later an unequivocally dated document mentions what may well be the election of the first mayor of Northampton. On 17 February 1215 John, then at Silverstone, addressed a writ to his good men (*probi homines*) of Northampton: 'Know that we have received William Thilly to be your mayor. We therefore command you to be intendent to him as your mayor, and to cause to be elected twelve of the better and more discreet of your town to expedite with him your affairs in your town.'[85] From this date onwards commands directed to the mayor, coupled sometimes with the reeves or bailiffs and sometimes with the good men of the town, occur upon the Close and Patent Rolls,[86] though the reeves are addressed by themselves on matters connected with the Exchequer,[87] and under Henry III the title of bailiff soon displaces that of reeve altogether in the royal commands whether on judicial or on financial matters.[88]

William Tilly, the first mayor of Northampton, is also mentioned in a letter of Faukes de Bréauté to Hubert de Burgh, which must fall between 1215 and 1224.[89] He held land in Flore:[90] he, or a relation of the same name, is mentioned in the 1260 custumal as one of the burgesses appointed for levying a duty on the sale of cloths to foreign merchants,[91] and his name occurs in several early town deeds.[92] He probably held office for many years, as was usual among his successors in the 13th century.[93] The next mayors mentioned by name are Robert de Leycester, who occurs in a lawsuit in 1229,[94] and Robert le Especer, who accounts at the Exchequer in 1231.[95] Six other mayors are named, from 1249 to 1272,[96] and six from 1273 to 1299.[97] Under the charter of 1299, now preserved at Northampton,[98] the burgesses were to present the mayor-elect at the Exchequer every year within the octave of Michaelmas, that he might there take the oath pertaining to his office. From 1299 onwards the name of the mayor is enrolled on the Michaelmas *Presentationes* of the Memoranda Roll in the Exchequer, often accompanied by the names of the burgesses who signed the letters patent presenting him.[99] The same names recur from year to year, and are clearly those of the leading burgesses—the mayor's colleagues and councillors. In 1478 Edward IV granted by letters patent that the mayor might henceforth be sworn in before the town recorder at Northampton, without coming up to Westminster.[1] The re-election of the mayor, usual in the 14th century, was restricted in the 15th. In 1437, during the fourth mayoralty of John Sprygy, it was

---

[77] Printed Stubbs' *Select Charters* 306-7; *Rot. Cart.* p. 45-6.

[78] *Cartae Antiquae* G. 15; *Boro. Rec.* i, 30-31.

[79] In 1329 the burgesses said that this unusually large number had been granted them for the convenience of merchants (*pur ese de merchauntz*), presumably that they might serve in rotation. Egerton MS. (B.M.) 2811, fo. 250. The same number had, however, been granted to Lincoln, Gloucester, and Ipswich in the same year. Ballard, *Borough Charters*, i, 247.

[80] The copy on the *Cartae Antiquae* roll follows on a charter dated 1206, so it cannot be strictly contemporary. It is dated at Windsor 17 April, and that on the Charter Roll at Westminster 20 April. None of the three witnesses to the C.A. version appears on the Charter Roll, which gives only one witness. The version on the Charter Roll has *Salopesbir'* written for Northampton at one point, and then corrected; the charter, as far as the election of officials is concerned, is identical with one to Shrewsbury, dated 20 April, entered next but one on the roll. See *Rot. Cart.* (Rec. Com.), p. 46.

[80a] This is the opinion of Dr. Tait. It seems probable that the Chancery clerk assimilated the date and this clause of the Northampton Charter to that of Shrewsbury, which he was about to copy. The retention of permission to elect *one* reeve from the charter of 1189 may have contributed to the confusion.

[81] Chart. R. 11 Hen. III, Part I, m. 17.

[82] Mem. R. (K.R.) 5, m. 4.

[83] *Boro. Rec.* ii, 548. All the deeds which I have examined bearing the name of William Tilly appear to belong to the 13th century.

[84] *Rot. Litt. Claus* (Rec. Com.), i, 123b.

[85] Ibid. i, 188. If John meant by this grant to secure the loyalty of the townsmen he failed, for in April they attacked the royal garrison in the castle, which later burnt half the town in revenge. *Mem. Walt. de Coventrie* (Rolls Ser.), ii, 219.

[86] *Rot. Litt. Claus.* i, 227b, 233b, 367, 383, 431.

[87] Ibid. i, 100b, 112, 152, 155, 222.

[88] Ibid. i, 517, 550, 567, 586.

[89] *Anct. Corresp.* (P.R.O.) vol i, 66.

[90] *Rot. Litt. Claus.* (Rec. Com.), i, 511b.

[91] Cl. 38 (fo. 162 v).

[92] Northampt. Corp. Deeds, Press c. 7; Harl. Ch. 85, c. 1; Anct. D. (P.R.O.) B 2484; Cott. MS. Tib. E.V. 147, fo. 16.

[93] e.g. Robert le Spicer, thrice; Robert, son of Henry, five times; Pentecost de Kershalton, four times.

[94] *Bracton's Notebook*.

[95] Mem. R. (K.R.) ii, *Adventus Vicecomitum Mich*.

[96] Roger, son of Theobald, 1249-50 (deed at Lichborough); Benedict Dod. (Pat.); William Gaugy (*Rot. Hund.*); Thomas Ken (Mem. R.); John le Specer (*Rot. Hund.*); William, son of Thomas.

[97] William le Pessoner (*Rot. Hund.*); John de Staunford (Add. Ch.); Robert, son of Henry (Corporation Deeds); John le Megre (Add. Ch.); Philip de Horton (Assize R.); and Peter de Leycestre (Anct. D.).

[98] *Boro. Rec.* i, 57.

[99] One such presentation is printed by Madox, *Firma Burgi*, p. 153, and gives the usual formula.

[1] *Boro. Rec.* i, 93.

A HISTORY OF NORTHAMPTONSHIRE

ordained that henceforth no mayor who had held office for a whole year should be re-elected till seven years had passed.[2] In 1558 the assembly confirmed this, adding that none should be chosen mayor oftener than thrice,[3] whilst in 1570 this was reduced to twice.[4] The election of the mayors, to be held before Michaelmas under the charter of 1299, took place about St. Matthew's Day (21 September) in the 14th century,[5] about St. Giles' Day (1 September) in the 16th,[6] and was directed in 1618 to be held within ten days of the first of August.[7] The mayor-elect was known as 'the mayor's joint' till Michaelmas, when he assumed office.[8]

The charters of 1200 and of 1227 had stated that the bailiffs, if well conducted, were only to be removable by the common council of the town. All the evidence indicates that they were elected annually and served for a year only, rarely being re-elected. They were the chief administrative officials, sharing the judicial duties of the mayor,[9] and acted within the borough as the sheriff did outside, with additional duties, as the custumals show, in connection with the industrial regulations. As the officials who executed the king's writs, before 1257 by custom and after 1257 by charter, they were the king's bailiffs and are sometimes so described.[10] They were personally responsible for the payment of the fee farm of the town at the Exchequer, and the office, like the sheriff's, thus entailed financial risks. 'Every year the men of the town who are bailiffs are impoverished and made beggars by reason of the aforesaid farm,' says the petition of 1334.[11]

The 13th century custumal refers to the mayor's clerk as issuing the mayor's summons,[12] but the earliest mention of a clerk by name is in connection with the records. Ralph Barun witnesses deeds as clerk under the first and third mayors,[13] and John, son of Eustace, who had the customs of Northampton recorded for the information of those who should come after, is described in this second custumal as clerk of Northampton,[14] and witnessed a deed as such in the mayoralty of John le Especer.[15] The town farm is occasionally paid in at the Exchequer by a clerk.[16] In the 14th century the town clerk is called the *clericus memorandorum*,[17] which indicates his duty of keeping the records of pleas and enrolments, and in 1419 John Lauendon is called the common clerk.[18]

The letters close of 17 February 1215 had commanded the 'good men' to elect twelve of their number to assist the mayor in the government of the town. This was not then a general custom in English boroughs, in spite of the statement in the Little Domesday of Ipswich regarding the election of 12 portmen there in 1200. But if the number of the mayor's advisers was twelve in the first half of the 13th century, by the second half we already seem to trace the Twenty Four who were sharing the work of government with him in the later middle ages. Leicester, which offers both parallels and contrasts to Northampton, had by 1225 set up its body of 24 sworn men or jurats who were bound to come at the summons of the alderman to give him help and counsel in the affairs of the town.[20] The second Northampton custumal (c. 1260) is headed with the names of 24 *jurati* who passed the regulations,[21] and whose consent is later mentioned as necessary if a stranger wishes to set up his stall in the market.[22] In spite of the gaps in the records, ten out of the twenty-four can be identified as having held office as bailiff or mayor before 1255. Moreover, the first regulation that follows provides for a 2s. amercement of those who fail to come at the mayor's summons. It would seem that these are the Twenty Four who in the 14th century act as the mayor's colleagues in official transactions.[23] In 1401 they are described as the Twenty Four sworn of the Mayor's council[24] and in 1415 as the Twenty Four *comburgenses*;[25] in 1473 they are called *his* Twenty Four.[26] The form of the oath taken by the Twenty Four suggests that it was re-administered each year.[27] In 1442, at a husting held in the council house at the Guildhall, it was agreed by the Mayor and several of the Twenty Four that heavy penalties should be imposed on those sworn 'as well to the mayor's counsel as to the secret counsel (*secretum consilium*) of the town of Northampton' who divulged discussions held therein.[28] There is no other reference to any privy council, and the resolution probably refers to emergencies when there was a special need of secrecy. It was re-enacted in 1557 with altered penalties.[29] In 1531 two mercers of the town were said to be 'for ever put out of the Court and Councell of the seid toun of Norhampton, and never to be sommoned ne takyn for any of the Company of the xxiiij[ti] Comburgesses of the same toun . . . and never have place ne seit within the Court of the same toun whereas other the xxiiij[ti] Comburgesses do alweise sitt, that is to sey within the barris comynly called the Chequer of the seid Court.'[30] This, like

---

[2] *Boro. Rec.* i, 275-6.
[3] Ibid. ii, 30.
[4] Ibid ii, 31. This new order was transgressed in 1575, and frequently later.
[5] See the dates of the letters patent of the town enrolled on the Memoranda Roll under *Presentationes*.
[6] *Boro. Rec.* i, 122.
[7] Ibid. i. 128.
[8] Ibid. ii, 33, 35, 548.
[9] See below, under Town Courts.
[10] E.g. Assize R. 619, m. 75.
[11] *Parl. R.* ii, 85.
[12] Douce MS. (Bodl. Lib.) 98, fo. 160.
[13] Anct. D. (P.R.O.) B 2484; Add. Ch. 22353, 34251.
[14] Bateson, *Borough Customs*, I., xli.
[15] Add. Ch. 22347.
[16] Mem. R. (K.R.) 14, 17, 18, 20, under *Adventus Vicecomitum*.
[17] William de Burgo, Add. Ch. 22355.
[18] Add. Ch. 732 (1). Other town clerks mentioned are William de Flore (c. 1292), William de Bray (1319), Honorius Saucee (1351), John Molyner (1358), William Lichebarwe (1406), Lawrence Quenton (1408), and John Towcester (1460–69).
[19] Gross, *Gild Merchant*, ii, 116; cf. Dr. Tait in *Eng. Hist. Rev.* xliv, 183.
[20] Bateson, *Records of the Borough of Leicester*, I, xxxi, 34.
[21] *Consideraciones facte per xxiiij juratos Northampton.* Douce MS. 98, fo. 160.
[22] Ibid. fo. 160 v°. (Cl. 11).
[23] See Bridges, *Hist. of Northants.* i, 364. *Robert le Spicer maior North' et ejusdem xxiiij burgenses* (1358); and the petition of Richard Stormesworth in 1393, mentioning "the 24 chief men." *V.C.H. Northants.* ii, 29.
[24] *Boro. Rec.* i, 245, *xxiiij de consilio suo iurati.*
[25] Ibid i, 243.
[26] Ibid i, 405. Dr. Cox suggests that the mayor's council numbered twelve in 1341, judging from the list of names on *Boro Rec.* i, 235. The French original, however, gives only eleven names; Adam fiz Adam Garlekmongere is only one person. The number of leading burgesses mentioned in official transactions varies from the sixteen addressed by Henry III in 1264, to the ten, six, four or two who sign the letters patent presented annually at the Exchequer. The burgesses mentioned can, however, be always shown to be ex-mayors or ex-bailiffs.
[27] "Ye shall gefe good and trew councell to your meire all this yere ensuyng," *Boro. Rec.* i, 393.
[28] Ibid. i, 276–8.
[29] Ibid. ii, 20.
[30] Ibid i, 425.

BOROUGH OF NORTHAMPTON

another expulsion in 1544, is authorised by the mayor and ex-mayors, who bind themselves not to recall the expelled but by the consent of all the mayors and ex-mayors. By this time, then, an inner ring existed in the town government, and though the act of 1489, hereafter to be mentioned, had sanctioned the privileges of the ex-mayors, it seems unlikely that it created them. The 'twenty four co-burgesses' of the 16th century town assembly books become from 1595 onwards 'the bailiffs and ex-bailiffs,' of varying numbers, who wore distinctive gowns, and still occasionally acted with the mayor and aldermen apart from the rest of the assembly up to 1835,[31] but had resigned the control of town policy to 'the mayor's brethren'—soon to be called the aldermen. In the 15th century, however, the mayor's council seems to have had considerable powers as the effective town executive. A number of ordinances for the crafts were issued by its authority, after consultation with the craft concerned.[32] The wardens and searchers of the crafts reported before the mayor and his council;[33] they had some standing in the Court of Husting, which is said on one occasion to have been regularly summoned by the mayor, the coroner and the Twenty Four.[34] They acted with the mayor in exercising patronage and in assigning guardians to minors in the mayor's custody.[35] The council met like the husting on Mondays, at the Guildhall.[36] In fact, in the 15th century, the mayor's council, like the king's, was a body exercising legislative, administrative and judicial functions, and effectively directing the supposedly popular assembly which met from time to time at St. Giles'.

In addition to the officials already mentioned the 13th century custumal mentions a mayor's serjeant, or executive official, to whom the 15th century records add four bailiffs' serjeants,[37] later to be known as serjeants-at-mace. In the 15th century also appear the two chamberlains who have custody with the mayor of the common chest and of the town property[38] and pay the mayor his allowance of twenty marks.

As at Exeter and Norwich, whose constitutions were likewise modelled on that of London, there is no trace of the existence of a merchant gild; the *prepositura* or provostry regulate all industrial matters. Freemen were, however, sharply distinguished from other residents. The second custumal (*c.* 1260) provided that every native merchant who wished to enter the freedom must pay 5s. 4d., whoever he was,[39] and this rate held good till 1341, when it was reduced to 6d. for sons of townsmen at lot and scot of the town.[40] It is probable that freemen and *probi homines* were the same; sons of *probi homines* had to pay only a halfpenny to be enrolled in a tithing, where strangers had to pay 5d.[41] In view of the high payment for the freedom, one clause of the 13th century custumal is of special interest: 'That no commune be made henceforth by which the government (*prepositura*) may lose its rights. If anyone be convicted of this he shall incur the amercement of the town of 40s. without remission.'[42] There is other evidence of the existence of an aristocracy envied by their less well-to-do fellow-townsmen. The only original return extant to the inquest of 1274-5[43] is described as being made by the lesser folk of the town,[44] and it complains bitterly that the wealthier burgesses escape the burdens of citizenship. 'Divers burgesses holding many and great rents in the town refuse to make common cause with the community in tallages and other things, with the result that a large number of craftsmen (*menestralli*) have left the town because they are too grievously tallaged.'[45] Some of the exemptions from tallage to which the jurors refer are enrolled upon the Patent Roll.[46] They complain further that when poor townsmen are put on assizes and have to go to London and elsewhere on the business of the town, it is at their own charges, whilst the rich men, if they have to do business abroad on behalf of the town, have all their expenses allowed them and the poor have to pay for it.[47] This kind of complaint was arising from many towns in the 13th century,[48] notably from Oxford,[49] and it has recently been suggested that it forms part of the wave of anti-aristocratic feeling expressed in 1259 by the *communitas bachelerie Angliae*.[50] There is no record in Northampton of the proclaiming of a commune as at London in 1262-3[51] or at Bury St. Edmunds in 1264,[52] but we are told that the bad example of the *bachelarii* of those towns infected others,[53] and it would seem that such a demonstration was apprehended by the drafters of the second custumal. The ruthless sacking of the town by the royalists in 1264 suggests that if the priory was for the King, the townsfolk, like the scholars, were for the barons, and the attribute of Northampton in the medieval list of towns preserved in the same manuscript with the custumal echoes the term associated with turbulent democracy—'Bachelerie de Norhampton.'[54] Already in the 13th century it looks as if the town government was in the hands of an oligarchy, closed by custom, if not by ordinance.

Freedom in Northampton was probably the equivalent of membership of the gild merchant in towns where such existed; its essence lay in the right to 'marchaundizen' in the town itself, and to claim the town's chartered privileges of exemption from toll and custom elsewhere.[55] In 1396 it was ordered that no freeman need pay stallage, unless he had more than one stall in the market.[56] A petition of 1433

---

[31] *Boro. Rec.* ii, 19.
[32] Ibid i, 237, 245, 269, 273, 265, 294, 309 (1401–1467).
[33] Ibid. i, 238.   [34] Ibid. i, 260.
[35] Ibid i, 242.
[36] Ibid i, 260–276 *passim*.
[37] Ibid. i, 244, 250, 257.
[38] Ibid i., 250, 251, 255–7.
[39] Douce MS. (Bodl. Lib.) 98, fo. 160 Clause 2). The same fee is payable for purchase of a stall. No stranger can have a stall but by consent of the 24 *jurati*, fo. 160 v°. (Clause 11).
[40] *Boro. Rec.* i, 235.
[41] Douce MS. (Bodl. Lib.) 98, fo. 160 v° (clause 12).
[42] Ibid. fo. 161 (clause 20).
[43] *Rot. Hund.* ii, 1–5. There are three returns at Lincoln, made by the greater, the lesser and the 'secondary' burgesses. *Rot. Hund.* i, 309, 315, 322.
[44] Ibid. ii, 5.
[45] Ibid. ii, 3.
[46] *Cal. Pat.* 1258–66, pp. 532, 603.
[47] *Rot. Hund.* ii, 5.
[48] York, Carlisle, Bristol, Lincoln, King's Lynn, Norwich; see E. F. Jacob, *Studies in Baronial Reform*, p. 136, n.5. Stamford, Grimsby, Gloucester, Winchester; see *Eng. Hist. Rev.* v, 644–7.
[49] *Cal. Inq. Misc.* i, no. 238.
[50] Jacob, pp. 127, 134.
[51] *Liber de Ant. Leg.* (Camden Soc. p. 55.)
[52] *Engl. Hist. Rev.* xxiv, 313–7.
[53] *Annal. Mon.* (Rolls Ser.) iv, 138.
[54] Douce MS. (Bodl. Lib.), 98, fo. 194 v° (printed *Engl. Hist. Rev.* xvi, 502). It is possible, however, that the expression has a purely economic significance. See below, on Trades of the Town.
[55] See *Boro. Rec.* i, 378–80 for letters of exemption from toll, according to the privileges of the borough, to be presented by Northampton merchants when trading elsewhere.
[56] *Boro. Rec.* i, 262.

A HISTORY OF NORTHAMPTONSHIRE

shows that non-residents held the freedom as well as residents.[57] Certain judicial privileges of freemen are mentioned; the right to wage a single-handed law,[58] and exemption for the first year from service on juries.[59] Further regulations are found on the assembly books when these begin. All members of crafts could be made free of the borough by paying 20s.[60] From 1606 there are lists of freemen from year to year, as they were enrolled, down to 1833,[61] and from these it would appear that the fee for a freeman's son was 3s. 4d., for an apprentice who had fulfilled his term 10s., and for an outsider £5, in 1606. The fee for outsiders was raised later. The freedom was granted free to various deserving persons, and outsiders marrying freemen's widows were admitted at a reduced fee. In 1835[62] the commissioners found that freedom could be acquired in five ways: by birth—fee £1 2s.; by marriage—fee £8 4s.; by apprenticeship—fee £1 15s. 6d.; by purchase—fee £15 4s.; and by gift. The freeman's oath, of loyalty to the King, obedience to the mayor, contribution to town charges, and keeping of the peace, is given in a 16th century form in the *Liber Custumarum*.[63] The assembly books of 1568 give examples of the enforcement of these duties on persons who had failed to keep their oaths 'taken at the time of their admission to the freedom of the town.'[64] A 17th century version of the oath in the British Museum custumal adds the words 'You shall take no apprentice for any less term than seven years, by indenture, which indenture you shall cause to be made by the town clerk . . . and enrolled at the next court of hustings after his binding.'[65] This clause was cut out of the freeman's oath by a resolution of the assembly on 2 May 1778. From 1660 to 1733 freemen, whether resident or not, had the parliamentary vote; after 1733 only residents could vote. Up to 1796 the freemen still had the monopoly of trade, but the privilege was dropped in the new charter of that year. In 1835 the town clerk estimated the number of freemen at about 400.[66]

The town assembly, consisting presumably of the whole body of freemen or *probi homines*, was held from very early times, according to Henry Lee,[67] in the churchyard of St. Giles for the election of the town officials, and in St. Giles' church, according to the *Liber Custumarum*, for the passing of municipal legislation.[68] It was apparently summoned by the mayor, and met on any day of the week except Saturday, the market day, and only rarely on Monday, the meeting day. As at Leicester and Chester,[69] the meeting about St. Denys' day seems to have been especially important for craft business.[70] In the 14th century the assembly is described as a congregation, consisting of the mayor, the Twenty Four, and the whole commonalty of the town.[71] In the 15th century it is also called a *colloquium generale* and a *comyn semble*.[72] In one case it is said that the mayor and the Twenty-Four made certain provisions and ordinances at the special petition of the commonalty,[73] and it seems probable that the 'commonalty' did not retain much initiative. On another occasion the commonalty confirms in December an ordinance made by the mayor in September.[74] Important craft ordinances were passed by the mayor and his council without reference to the assembly.[75]

The assembly was to lose its popular character on the pretext of its disorderly conduct, but there is evidence of disputes within the town government itself at an earlier date. In the eyre of 1329 complaint was made that William de Tekne (mayor 1309–10 and 1314–15)[76] and William de Burgo, the town clerk, had by colour of their office levied sums of money from certain ex-bailiffs, broken into the common chest, taken the common seal and sealed with it the quittances which they gave to the bailiffs, thus defrauding the whole community. The jury, however, acquitted the accused, saying that they had opened the chest by the consent of the whole town because of important affairs touching the welfare of the whole community, and had not converted any of the town funds to their own use.[77] Again in 1326 or 1327 a number of burgesses, some of whom were later mayors of the town, making a confederacy with a convicted clerk and a man in process of being outlawed, attacked the mayor, Walter de Pateshull, who was also a coroner, dragged him by the hair of his head out of his house, and made him, in full court of Northampton, forswear the office of coroner henceforth.[78] Public opinion seems to have been on the side of the rioters, for though the deed was not denied, their substantial fellow burgess John de Longueville[79] stood pledge for five of the offenders and a royal pardon was forthcoming for another.[80]

The medieval phase in the borough's constitutional history ends not so much with the incorporation of the town by the charter of 14 March 1459, by the name of the mayor, bailiffs and burgesses of Northampton,[81] as with the passing of the act of 1489. This act was almost certainly the result of the concerted action of Leicester and Northampton. There is much to make such joint action natural. There are several later instances of the one borough seeking the other's advice.[82] Commercial intercourse was close; payments for entering the Leicester gild merchant were made in Northampton fair, and Northampton merchants traded at Leicester.[83] Leicester, like Northampton, had 24 jurati originally elective;[84] it had a weekly portman moot with competence similar to the Northampton husting; its common hall corresponded to the Northampton assembly.[85] By the

---

[57] *Boro. Rec.* i, 274.　[58] Ibid. i, 236.
[59] Ibid. i, 263.
[60] Assembly Book, 13 Oct. 1559.
[61] *Boro. Rec.* ii, 314–20.
[62] *Parl. Papers* 1835, vol. xxv, p. 1968.
[63] *Boro. Rec.* i, 352.
[64] Ibid. ii, 313.
[65] Add MS. 34308, fo. 12 d.
[66] *Parl. Papers*, 1835, vol. xxv, p. 1969.
[67] Top. MS. (Bodl. Lib.) Northants, c.9. Collections of Henry Lee, Town Clerk of Northampton 1662–1715, p. 94. Cited henceforth as Lee, Coll.
[68] *Boro. Rec.* i, 237, 247, 249, 261, etc.

[69] Bateson, *Rec. Boro. of Leics.* i, xxx.
[70] *Boro. Rec.* i, 235, 290, 307.
[71] Ibid. i, 261, etc.
[72] Ibid. i, 300, 291.
[73] Ibid. i, 275 (1437).
[74] Ibid. i, 264.　[75] Ibid. i, 269.
[76] Mem. R. (K. R.) 83, m. 79 d; 88, m. 169.
[77] Assize R. 635, m. 66 d.
[78] Ibid. m. 68 d.
[79] Mayor in 1333, 1334, 1340.
[80] Various other riots in the town are mentioned about this date: in March 1314 an attempt to disturb the holding of an Assize of Novel Disseisin, (*Cal. Pat.* 1313–17, p. 141); in Jan. 1328 a free fight between the townsmen and Mortimer's Welshmen (*Cal. Pat.* 1327–30, p. 423, Assize R. 635, m. 66d.); in March 1332 resistance to justices of oyer and terminer, headed by the mayor and bailiffs (*Cal. Pat.* 1330–34, p. 291).

[81] *Boro. Rec.* i, 85–8.
[82] Bateson, *Rec. Boro. of Leics.* iv, 134, 438, 471. *Boro. Rec.* ii, 498.
[83] Bateson, *Rec. of Boro. of Leics.* i, xxix, 250.
[84] Ibid. i, 40–42.　[85] Ibid. ii, xlvi.

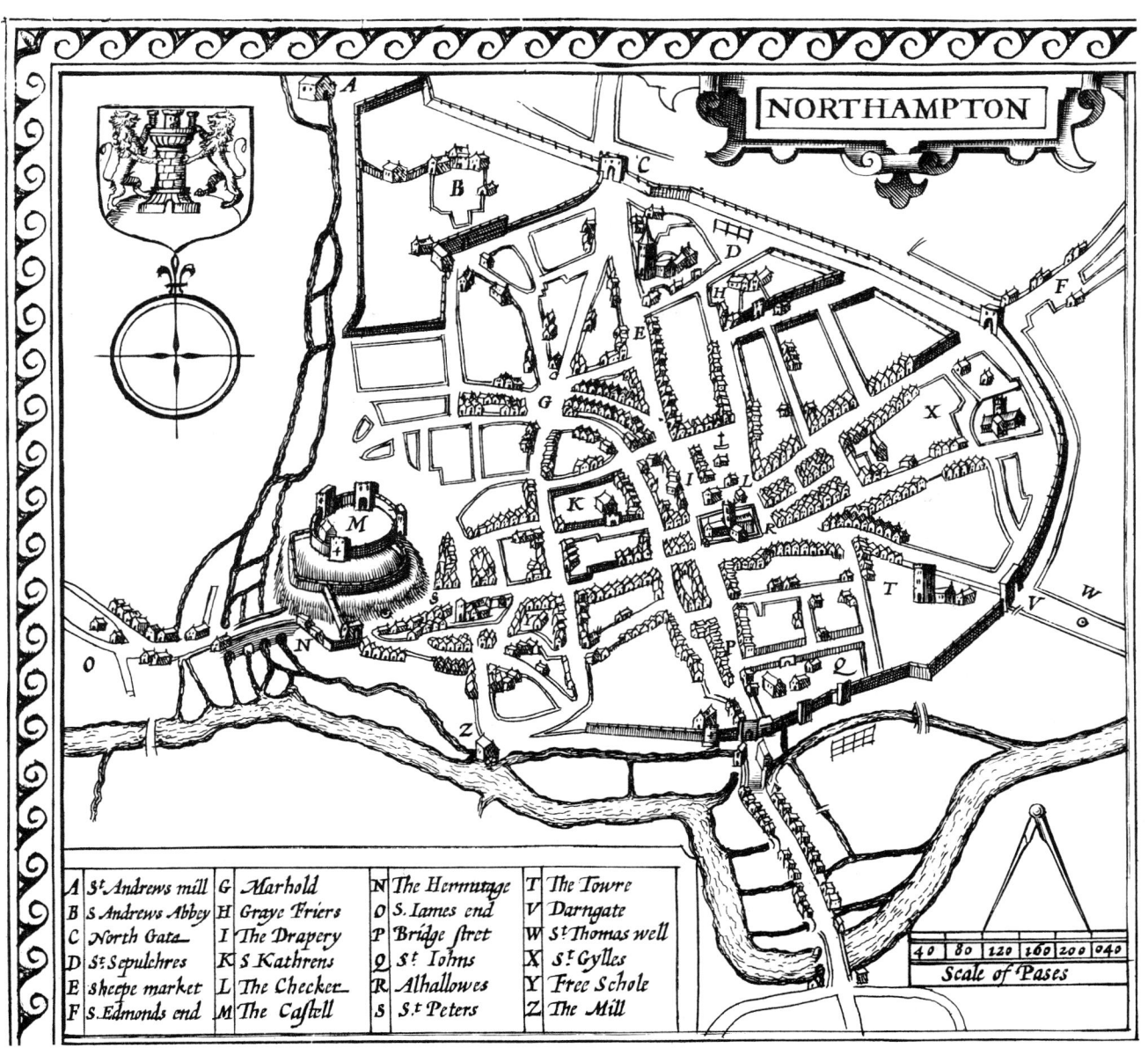

JOHN SPEED'S VIEW OF NORTHAMPTON IN 1610
(Reproduced by permission of Northamptonshire Libraries and Information Service)

BOROUGH OF NORTHAMPTON

14th century its twenty-four jurati had become a close body, the last election having occurred in 1273,[86] and in the 15th century they also were called the comburgesses. In 1466 and 1467 orders were carried excluding the common folk of Leicester who were not gildsmen from meetings of the common hall, especially at the time of the election of the mayor.[87] As in the county courts, it would seem that the unenfranchised were crowding in and claiming an equal share in elections with those worthy and substantial burgesses who had for the last two hundred years been effectively controlling the town government. The corporations of Northampton and Leicester fell back on Parliament to support their vested interests, and in response to their petition or petitions two acts were passed in the Parliament of Jan.-Feb. 1489, which created in each town a body of 48 burgesses who were henceforth to exercise the powers possessed till then by the assembly at Northampton and the common hall at Leicester. The wording of the two acts was not identical, but their interpretation was very similar. The act for Northampton opens 'Forasmoche as of late greate divisions, dissentions and discordes have growen and been had as well in the Townes and Boroughes of Northampton and Leycester as in other dyvers Townes . . . amongst the Inhabitauntes of the same, for the election and choyse of Mayres, Bailles and other Officers within the same, by reason that such multytude of the said Inhabitauntes, beyng of lytil substaunce and haveour, and of no sadnes, discretion, wisdome ne reason, whiche oft in nombre exced in their Assembles other that been approved, discrete, sadde and well disposed persones, have by . . . their Bandys, Confederacys, Exclamacions and Hedynesse, used in the seid Assembles, caused great trobles, divisions and discordes among theym selfe, as well in the seid Ellections, as in Assessyng of other lawfull Charges and Imposicions amongst theym, to the subversion of the gode Rule, Governaunce, and old Politik demenyng of the seid Burghes, and oft tymes to the greate breach of the Kyngs Peace within the same, to the fere, drede and manyfold perills that thereby may ensue'[88] . . . and provides that henceforth the Mayor and his brethren the ex-Mayors shall nominate 48 persons who have not hitherto been mayors or bailiffs who shall, in conjunction with the mayor, the ex-mayors and the ex-bailiffs, henceforth yearly elect the mayors and bailiffs for the town. The Mayor and ex-mayors shall have power to change the personnel of the 48 at will, and shall also appoint all other town officials, the mayor having a casting vote if the votes are equal.[89] The council of the borough followed up this act by an order as to the procedure to be followed in holding the elections of mayors and bailiffs. 'Fyrst the day of the seide eleccion acustomed all tho that have voyces in the same eleccions to mete at all halowe Chirche att a convenient houre bi fore none and ther to here a masse of the holy goste. And at the ende of the same to departe and goo to the Gylde halde And ther to take every man ther setes be the Assigment of the Meire and of his brethern As schall Accorde with theire discrecions And then the Joyntes to be made Accordyng to the olde Custome. And the parsones named in the Joyntes severyally to be sette in sondry papyrs. And then the same papers to be borne abowte bi the town Clerke and the Comen serieant for the tyme beyng to every of the parsones thatt shall geve voyces. As stylly as maybe. And every voyce to be entred bi the seide Clerk to the names of the seide parsones to Whom they geve their voyces. And whan the hole voyces be geven and passed then the seide clerke and serieant to bryng the papers to the Meire for the tyme beyng. And to his brethren that have ben meyres. And ther bi the sight of the more parte of the seide voyces to puplisshe and make opyn the persones uppon whom the eleccions rest. And thys ordur to be folowed and thus done withoute noyse or crye.'[90] The council also issued an order early in 1490 inflicting penalties on those who should use seditious or slanderous words against the mayor, his brethren, or the Twenty Four,[91] clinching it by an ordinance in 1495–6 which declared disobedience to the mayor to be perjury or breach of the freeman's oath, and gave the mayor,' the King's chancellor' for his year in Northampton, power to determine such perjury and disobedience.[92] The act had probably provoked opposition here at Leicester, where the commonalty elected a rival mayor in opposition to that chosen by the Forty Eight.[93]

From this time onwards the government of the town was in the hands of a closed body; the mayor and ex-mayors (called aldermen from 1618),[94] the Twenty Four (called ex-bailiffs from 1595),[95] and the company of Forty Eight, who made up with the others what was called from 1599 the common council of the town.[96] An oath, pre-reformation in form, to be administered to the aldermen, indicates that they were at first supposed roughly to represent the five wards of the town.[97] The charter of 1599 further declared that the Eight and Forty should hold office for life, unless removed according to the custom of the town, and that the bailiffs could only be elected from among the number of the Forty Eight.[98] This finally closed the ring.

Throughout the middle ages only one town court is named: the court of husting which the charter of 1189 provided should be held once only in the week. Whether the various jurisdictions acquired by the town were all exercised at this weekly court, or whether other sessions were held with other names it does not seem possible to say. The charter of 1189 provided that no burgess should plead outside the walls save in pleas of foreign tenures; that right should be done concerning lands and tenures within the city according to its own customs; and that pleas of debt within the town should be held there. The first custumal (c. 1190) is mainly concerned with

---

[86] Bateson, *Rec. of Boro. of Leics.* i, ii. xlv.
[87] Ibid. ii, 285–6.
[88] *Parl. R.* vi, 431.
[89] The letters patent exemplifying the act, dated 28 March, 5 Hen. VII, are enrolled in the Brit. Mus. Custumal. Add. MS. 34308 fo. 15 d–17.
[90] Ibid. fo. 17.
[91] *Boro. Rec.* i, 312–4.
[92] Ibid. i, 338–9.
[93] Bateson, *Rec. of Boro. of Leics.* ii, 326–7.
[94] *Boro. Rec.* i, 127.
[95] Ibid. ii, 19.
[96] Ibid. i, 121.
[97] 'Ye shall swere that ye do name persones other then have ben meires and bailliffs of this borowe parte of them to be dwellyng severalli in every of the V. quarters of this borough, and moste convenient nombre of them to be appoynted dwellers in every of the seide quarters.' Add. MS. 34308, fo. 15.
[98] *Boro. Rec.* i, 122.

A HISTORY OF NORTHAMPTONSHIRE

matters of land tenure; 16 out of its 24 chapters deal with customs of inheritance, alienation and the rights of the feudal lord. The witness of the 'men of the pleas' is frequently mentioned[1] as necessary for transfers of land in the town court (undoubtedly the husting), while the bailiffs and coroners seem to be needed to authorise seisin.[2] No records of the court survive, but a large number of deeds, at Northampton and elsewhere, register transfers of land that took place in it, and illustrate the special customs of the town. If a kinsman wished to assert his right of first purchase, he had to make his offer before three court days had passed, after the feoffment of the stranger.[3] In one early 13th century deed the court in which the plea of land had been held is called the *porthimoth' de Norhant'*.[4] No other instance of the use of this term at Northampton has been found; at Leicester and Ipswich the court at which transfers of land took place was called the *portmannmot*.[5] Both bailiffs and *prepositi* are mentioned in connection with the court,[6] and John's charter appoints coroners to see that the *prepositi* do justice. At the end of the 12th century, then, the weekly court was a court of record for land cases and a court for the collection of debts and probably enforcement of contracts,[7] at which the *prepositi* presided, royal writs were pleaded,[8] and the 'good men of the pleas' made the judgments.

The charter of 18 Jan. 1257 authorised a number of jurisdictional privileges, some of which had certainly been exercised before without express sanction.[9] In consequence, probably, of the general enquiry into royal rights in 1255, Thomas Kin, mayor of Northampton, appeared at the Exchequer and declared that the burgesses of Northampton had always had the return of writs, and the sheriff of Northants said that he had found the town in possession of that right.[10] It was this, probably, that led to the burgesses purchasing their new Charter, in which, in common with some seventeen other boroughs in the years 1255 to 1257,[11] they obtained the right to exclude the sheriff from executing summons or distresses in the town and to serve writs and summons of the Exchequer by their own officials. Henceforth the bailiffs took the sheriff's place in the borough, and he could only intervene if they neglected their duties. The charter also granted that burgesses should not be convicted by strangers in any trespass, appeal or criminal charge brought against them, but only by their fellow-burgesses, unless concerning matters touching the borough community. Infangthef was also granted. Thus the town courts now had jurisdiction over criminal matters, excepting only those pleas of the crown which the coroners kept against the coming of the justices in eyre. The eyre roll of 1247 shows that even before this grant thieves who admitted their crime had been hanged by the judgment of the town court.[12] The eyre roll of 1285 mentions a case of appeal for defamation in the court of Northampton.[13] In 1274 the jurors said that the sheriff had never held his tourn in Northampton, and that the town had a free court with gallows, pillory, tumbril, assize of bread and ale and all other liberties belonging the crown by royal grant.[14] Both the custumal and the eyre rolls of 1253 and 1285 show that the frankpledge system was operative in the borough. The mayor and bailiff must have held what was later called a court leet,[15] whilst the rights of infangthef, etc., would constitute the town court a court baron. Both these names survived into the 19th century and are mentioned in 1835. The ordinary business of the town court is well illustrated by a cancelled account of its pleas and perquisites for one whole year,[16] which shows that payments were taken for trespass, for *hamsoken*, for hue unjustly raised, for contempt done to the bailiffs and their serjeants, for default, for false claims and for claims not prosecuted, for licence to agree, for unjust detention of chattels, for entering a tithing, for having a place to sell bread in, and for selling unsealed or badly baked bread. Judging by the names of the townsmen, the date of this estreat is between 1285 and 1300. It would seem to be the accounts of the court during a period when the liberty was in the king's hands, possibly after the eyre of 1285, when the borough was convicted of having exceeded its rights of infangthef by hanging a Dunstable man.[17] In 1329 a *custos* of Northampton was appointed for similar reasons. The second custumal, with its frequent references to the bailiffs' power of amercement,[18] and its numerous mercantile regulations,[19] which must have been enforced in the town courts, belongs to the same stage. A plea of 1307 shows that the bailiffs of Northampton had no jurisdiction in pleas of debt over 40s.[20] The court was described in 1315 as 'the King's court of Northampton.'[21] In the eyre of 1329 the mayor and commonalty claimed jurisdiction in a case of dower before the justices, asserting that by their charter no plea of tenements within Northampton ought to be held except before the mayor and bailiffs within the walls. This led to a long discussion as to the jurisdiction of the mayor, who soon shifted his ground, asking only that the justices should sit within the walls (as they had done in 1285) and not at the Castle. Justice Scrope and the King's Counsel, however, pointed out that the charter under which jurisdiction was claimed made no mention of a mayor, and asserted that the town had no mayor in the reign of Henry III. From the coroners' roll, also, it was clear that the king's lieges had been arraigned and put to death for felonies committed outside the town, the franchise of infangthef having thus been executed. The justice also condemned the irregularity of the coroners keeping a joint record, when each of the four

---

[1] Bateson, *Boro. Customs* (Selden Soc.), i, 245, 272–3; ii, 63, 102.
[2] Ibid. ii, 63–4.
[3] Ibid. ii, 63. Miss Bateson interprets this as referring to six-monthly 'great courts.' Ibid. ii, p. lxxxix.
[4] Harl. Chart. 86, D. 45 (1231–33 ?).
[5] Bateson, *Rec. of Boro. of Leics*. i, 8; Bateson, *Boro. Customs* (Selden Soc.), i, 254.
[6] Ibid. i, 103, 292–3.
[7] Ibid. i, 215.
[8] Harl. Ch. 86, D. 45.
[9] In 1221 the Exchequer was complaining that the burgesses had failed to execute Exchequer writs and summons, Mem. R. (K. R.), 4, *Visus Vic. Norhant*.
[10] Madox, *Firma Burgi*, p. 159.
[11] Ballard and Tait, *Boro. Charters*, ii, 155–60, 171–3.
[12] Assize R. 614 B. m. 48d.
[13] Ibid. 619, m. 75.
[14] *Rot. Hund.* ii, 2, 4.
[15] The petition of Richard Stormesworth in 1393 refers to indictments by the 'Dosouns' (*i.e.* tithing men) before the mayor. *V.C.H. Northants*. ii, 29.
[16] Ct. R. (P. R. O.), 195/57; printed *Northants N. and Q.* (New Ser.), vol. v, pp. 203–11.
[17] Assize R. 619, m. 75.
[18] Clauses 9, 14, 15, 21, 22.
[19] Thirty-three of its 42 clauses are concerned with trade.
[20] *Abbrev. Plac.* (Rec. Com.), p. 300.
[21] De Banc. R. 208 m. 62d.

BOROUGH OF NORTHAMPTON

ought to have had his own roll. For these various reasons the liberties of the town were seized into the king's hands, and the officials removed from their offices. The bailiffs and two of the coroners were reappointed and sworn in as the king's delegates, but a *custos* was appointed in place of the mayor.[22] From the deeds of the 13th and 14th centuries it appears that mayor, bailiffs and coroners were present at the court,[23] and in the 15th century the Twenty Four sometimes at least took part.[24] The pleas at which the freemen were sworn in must have been the husting.[25] In 1557 the assembly ordered that the mayor should be assisted by four ex-mayors and six ex-bailiffs every Monday at the court of husting, and that members of the Common Council might also be called upon to attend there.[26] The proceedings were enrolled by the town clerk on the *Rotulus Memorandorum*,[27] destroyed presumably in the fire of 1675, for no medieval court rolls are extant. Some legal formulæ are entered in the *Liber Custumarum*.[28]

The charter of Richard II of 14 June 1385 granted to the mayor and bailiffs cognizance of all pleas whatever arising within the town, to be holden before them in the guild hall of the town and to the mayor the right to keep the assize of bread, wine and ale, of measures and of weights, to inquire concerning forestallers and regraters, and to inflict the penalties and take the profits arising from this jurisdiction.[29] This charter again must have sanctioned existing practices; the mayor had the assize of bread and ale in 1274. The procedure and scope of his duties as clerk of the market are indicated by the formulæ in the *Liber Custumarum* and the charge administered to the jurors.[30] In 1621 the mayor was said to fine victuallers sitting as clerk of the market, at court-leet, as well as at quarter-sessions.[31] The charter of Henry VI of 11 June 1445, constituted the mayor for the time being the King's escheator in the town, its suburbs and fields, with the jurisdiction belonging to the office,[32] and his charter of 14 March 1459, which incorporated the town, appointed the mayor Justice of the Peace for the town.[33] In addition to these jurisdictions the mayor had the duty of registering recognizances of debt under the Statute Merchant, probably from 1283 and certainly from 1311.[34] This also was done in the court of husting.[35]

As elsewhere, the sessions of the Justices of the Peace absorbed the work of the older courts of Northampton. Under the charter of 1495 a recorder learned in the law and two other more honest and learned coburgesses were to be elected annually to sit with the mayor as justices of the peace.[36] The charter of 1599 provided that the late mayor should be one of the two burgesses.[37] By the charter of 1796 the bench was enlarged to consist of mayor, recorder, deputy-recorder, ex-mayor and three other aldermen, as the business was too heavy for the existing number.[38]

Thus down to 1835 all the magistrates were elective, and the majority were members of the corporation. The magistrates' sessions had absorbed all the criminal business, short of capital offences, and the court-leet and court-baron had purely formal duties.[39] The Northampton justices' abuse of their judicial powers, in combination with the town bailiffs' bias in empanelling juries, was singled out for condemnation in the general report of the Municipal Commissioners of 1835.[40]

The court of husting, still of importance in the 16th and 17th centuries,[41] had dwindled almost to vanishing point by the 19th century. It sat as a 'court of record' once in three weeks, and was held before the mayor and two bailiffs and the town steward, but had little business—in 1830 fifteen actions, in 1831 four, and in 1832 six.[42] An attempt to have a court of Requests established in 1818-19 was defeated in the House of Lords.[43] Enrolments of recognizances are extant for 1783-1803.[44] There was also, in the 16th and 17th centuries, an orphans' court, reorganised, if not originated by the charter of 1599,[45] which was held the first Thursday of Lent, at which the mayor and chamberlains inquired into the conduct of guardians and sureties.[46]

A special inquest was held at Northampton for inquiring into boundaries or party walls. A similar inquest was used in London from the 12th century onwards,[47] and in some other boroughs later, but the name by which it was known in Northampton—Vernall's inquest—appears to be unique. Its origin can be traced to clause 11 of the earliest custumal[48] (c. 1190), which provides for the holding of a jury to decide disputes over walls, gutters, or other boundaries. Records of the holding of such inquests are found in the assembly books as late as 1724, and the inquest was annually appointed down to 1768,[49] so that the institution has a history of some 570 years. The special local name has never been satisfactorily explained, in the absence of mediaeval forms of the word. It is possibly to be associated with the form *veiours*, *vayowres* or *aviewers*, as used for the jury that surveyed the boundaries in Bristol where, as in Northampton, it was the mayor's duty to adjudicate as to boundaries and gutters from the 13th century on.[50] The corruption would be no stranger than that of frith-borh to third borough, the Northampton term for the tithing man.

The closing of the corporation at Northampton,

---

[22] For reports of the Eyre of Northampt. see Egerton MS. (B.M.) 2811, ff. 248–50; Add. MS. 5924, f. 7, 12 d; see also Assize R. 635, m. 71 d. For appointment of *custos*, *Boro. Rec.* i, 64. A *custos* had also been appointed in 1227 and 1264.
[23] Add. Ch. 22354–7, etc.
[24] *Boro. Rec.* i, 309, 312.
[25] Ibid. i, 235.
[26] Ibid. ii, 20.
[27] Ibid. i, 384. Deeds were frequently enrolled upon it; see B.M. Add. Ch. 729, 730, 22368, 22371.
[28] Ibid. i, 382–391.
[29] Ibid. i, 367.
[30] Ibid. i, 373.
[31] *Cal. S. P. Dom. Add.* 1580–1625, p. 641.
[32] *Boro. Rec.* i, 77. The escheator's oath, from the Brit. Mus. custumal, is printed *Boro. Rec.* ii, 132.
[33] Ibid. i, 85.
[34] Ibid. ii, 120–1.
[35] Ibid. i, 382–3.
[36] *Boro. Rec.* i, 104.
[37] Ibid. i, 123.
[38] Ibid. i, 166; *Parl. Papers* 1833, vol. xiii, Minutes of Evidence, 1068.
[39] Ibid. 1344.
[40] Ibid. 1364–74, 1418; ibid. 1835, vol. xxiii, 40; vol. xxv, 1979–81.
[41] *Boro. Rec.* ii, 116, 118–9.
[42] *Parl. Papers* 1833, vol. xiii, 344, p. 52.
[43] Ibid. 1835, vol. xxv, 1970.
[44] Northampt. Corp. Rec. Press R. 101.
[45] *Boro. Rec.* i, 124.
[46] *Boro. Rec.* ii, 119–20.
[47] Bateson, *Boro. Customs* (Selden Soc.), i, 245–7.
[48] Ibid. i, 245.
[49] *Boro. Rec.* ii, 135–7.
[50] Bickley, *Little Red Book of Bristol*, ii, 134; Bateson, *Boro. Customs* (Selden Soc.), ii, 31.

A HISTORY OF NORTHAMPTONSHIRE

as at Leicester,[51] may not have involved any real injustice or caused any serious discontent in the 15th and 16th centuries. In the course of the 17th and 18th centuries, however, the situation was completely transformed, and this was due as much to political as to social developments. Northampton has been called the Mecca of English Nonconformists, and, less kindly, 'a nest of Puritans—malignant, refractory spirits who disturb the peace of the church.'[52] From the time when the students and 'bachelery' of Northampton supported Simon de Montfort against the King and the prior to the time when the borough persisted in re-electing Charles Bradlaugh, in the face of a House of Commons zealous for the conventions of religion, there is a recurring tradition of defiance of authority. The Lollardry of the 14th, and the prophesyings of the 16th century, the dissemination of Penry's Marprelate Tracts, stitched, if not printed, in Northampton; the obstinate resistance to Laudian reform in the 17th century,[53] are followed by the militant puritanism of the civil wars and the last stand of the Leveller Thompson;[54] the pioneer activities of Independent, Baptist, Quaker, Moravian and Wesleyan congregations, with their meeting houses at Castle Hill and College Lane, Doddridge's Academy and Ryland's School;[55] the iconoclastic free-thought of Thomas Woolston and Charles Bradlaugh; and the radicalism of Chartists like Gammage. The conservative influences come from the county; it was not a Northampton parson who preached the doctrine of 'Apostolic obedience' to the justices of Assize at All Saints' in 1632 so comprehensively that the Archbishop refused to license the publication of the sermon. In view of the proverbial relationship of cobbling and politics, it is interesting to notice that during these same centuries Northampton comes to take the first place in the shoemaking industry of England.

The irresolution of mayor and corporation as to their attitude on Elizabeth's death is vividly thrown up in Sir Thomas Tresham's account of his ride to Northampton in March 1603, and his threefold proclamation of James I (regarded as a potential patron of Papists) outside the south gate, on the steps of the mayor's house, and in the mayor's own chamber.[56] After these initial hesitations the town maintained the forms of loyalty in frequent welcomes to the first two Stuarts on their journeys through Northampton to or from Holdenby House,[57] but from 1632 overt acts of the corporation betray a growing opposition to royal policy. Troops were refused in that year,[58] shipmoney in 1636,[59] and the fees of the king's messengers were reduced in 1640.[60] In March 1641 the Assembly resolved to complain to Parliament of the renewed attempts to exact coat and conduct money from the town, and to take the trained bands out of the liberties.[61] In January 1642 a petition, signed at the Swan Inn, Northampton, against Papists and Bishops went up to the Commons.[62] From the outbreak of hostilities Northampton became one of the more important Parliamentary garrison towns, and the town government used every effort to strengthen it. Nicholas Wharton, one of the London volunteers in Essex' army, who entered the town in August 1642, describes the walls as 'miserably ruined, though the country abounds in mines of stones';[63] the town, with the assistance at first of the Earl of Manchester and later of the Parliamentary committee for the town and county set to work to organise the defences.[64] The assembly voted £100 in 1642 and another £160 in 1643, for improving the fortifications; a scheme for the provision of labour by the five wards in rotation on the first five days of the week was worked out.[65] Stores were laid up against a possible siege; the south and west bridges were turned into drawbridges,[66] and outlying houses in St. Edmund's end pulled down to make the east gate safer.[67] Besides occupying the castle, the troops were billeted on the townsmen, who further helped the forces by supplying 2,000 pairs of shoes to Cromwell's army.[68] From Northampton Fairfax marched out to Naseby in 1645, and after the battle the Northampton churches received the living as prisoners, and their churchyards the dead.[69] The Commonwealth reduced the parliamentary representation of the borough to one member, and it is possible that the town shared the dislike of the county for the government of Major-General Boteler,[70] though it does not seem to have joined in the county's Humble Address to General Monk on his arrival at Northampton on 24 January 1660.[71] Be that as it may, on 10 May 1660 Charles II was proclaimed 'by our Mayor and Aldermen in their scarlett, and the bayliffs and Forty-Eight burgesses in all their formalities, with a troop of Horse and three Companies of Foot, and Drums, Trumpets and the Town waitse.'[72] In spite of this show of loyalty, the corporation was drastically purged by the commissioners appointed under the Corporation Act of 1662. In September of that year, whilst the town-walls were being demolished under the supervision of the Lord Lieutenant, the mayor-elect, the bailiffs-elect, 8 aldermen, 14 ex-bailiffs and 32 of the Forty Eight were turned out,[73] and the town had to pay £200 for the renewal of its charter,[74] which was accompanied by the proviso that the appointments of recorder and town clerk were to be confirmed by the king, and that all the officials must take the oaths of allegiance and supremacy.[75] In 1672 there was some talk of a *quo warranto* against the town for the refusal to re-elect Peterborough as recorder,[76] and though the

---

[51] Bateson, *Rec. Boro. of Leics.* ii, liv.
[52] *Cal. S. P. Dom.* 1638-9, p. 588 (Humphrey Ramsden to Sir John Lambe).
[53] *V.C.H. Northants.* ii, 29, 43, 68 ff.
[54] Gardiner, *Commonwealth and Protectorate*, i, 54; Lee, Coll. p. 105. Note also the earlier Levellers of 1607, who opposed the enclosures. Serjeantson, *Hist. of Ch. of All Saints*, pp. 149-50.
[55] *V.C.H. Northants.* ii, 68-74.
[56] *Hist. MSS. Com. Rep.* Var. Coll. iii, 117-123.
[57] *Boro. Rec.* ii, 469-71.

[58] *Cal. S. P. Dom.* 1631-3, p. 278.
[59] *Boro. Rec.* ii, 435.
[60] Ibid. ii, 33.
[61] Ibid. ii, 437. For the town trained bands see ibid. ii, 444-453, and *Acts of the Privy Council* 1595, p. 392.
[62] *Cal. S. P. Dom.* 1641-3, p. 279.
[63] Ibid. p. 385.
[64] *Hist. MSS. Com. Rep.* viii, app. 2, p. 59.
[65] *Boro. Rec.* ii, 438-9.
[66] Bridges, *Hist. of Northants.* i, 431. (from T. Dust).

[67] Lee, Coll. p. 99.
[68] *Cal. S. P. Dom.* 1644, p. 285.
[69] R. M. Serjeantson, *Hist. Ch. of All Saints, Northampt.* p. 152.
[70] Lee, Coll. p. 109.
[71] Broadsheet, dated 24 Jan. 1659, 'The Humble Address of the Gentlemen, Ministers and freeholders of the county of Northampton.'
[72] Lee, Coll. p. 111.
[73] Ibid. 113.   [74] Ibid.
[75] *Cal. S. P. Dom.* 1663-4, p. 223.
[76] *Hist. MSS. Com. Rep.* xii, app. 7, p. 98.

BOROUGH OF NORTHAMPTON

king did not then insist, in 1681 the corporation were forced to accept him in place of the father of their sitting member, a prominent Exclusionist Whig, whom they had just elected to the office.[77] In 1683, following the example of a number of other boroughs who had been cowed by the fate of London, Northampton surrendered its charter and received a new one which nominated the town officials and entire corporation and 'according to the new mode of charters,'[78] reserved to the king the right to remove any official who should subsequently be elected.[79] This right was freely exercised by James II, who, between February and September 1688, removed a mayor, 8 aldermen, the town attorney, 16 ex-bailiffs, the acting-bailiffs, 23 common council men, and, in September, the mayor-elect.[80] The Earl of Peterborough, the recorder, also made a speech to the assembly, desiring them not to promise their votes at the coming parliamentary election till they had heard from him; 'but the Prince of Orange coming in a short time after, there was an end put to that request,'[81] and the mob broke into the earl's house and spoiled his chapel.[82] From 1688 the town supported the Crown loyally. In 1745, when the Duke of Cumberland was preparing to make a stand outside Northampton[83] against the advancing forces of Charles Edward, the recruiting efforts of Halifax were warmly backed up by Doddridge, and one of the pupils of his academy was standard-bearer to the regiment of 814 volunteers raised in Northampton.[84] This temporary rapprochement of church and chapel was not, however, lasting; the corporation grew steadily more exclusive in its Anglicanism and Toryism; and as the Liberal and Nonconformist element in the town became more wealthy and influential, the town government grew less and less representative. Of the 67 subscribers to the loan for the French war in 1757, more than half were members of the Castle Hill Church.[85] 'We term it a Tory Corporation,' said a leading Northampton dissenter, giving evidence before the Select Committee on Municipal Corporations in 1833,[86] and in 1835 'it was admitted by the mayor that he had never known an instance in which a person opposed to the politics of the corporation had been elected to the body.... Scarcely any of the master-manufacturers engaged in the staple trade of the town are members of the established church.... Since the repeal of the Test and Corporation Acts no dissenter has been admitted into the common council.'[87] The reform of the borough was long overdue in 1835.

The constitution of the corporation remained unchanged in substance from 1489 to 1835. As to its working we have evidence lacking for the medieval period. The records of the town assembly (latterly small enough to meet in the Guildhall)[88] are extant from 1553 to 1835;[89] the minutes of the Mayor and Aldermen's Court from 1694 to 1797;[90] the mayor's and chamberlain's accounts from 1675 to 1835;[91] the minute-books of the Committee of Accounts from 1800 to 1822,[92] and the Enrolments of Apprenticeship and admission of freemen, some in the first assembly book, and the rest separately enrolled from 1562 to 1835.[93] There is also a good deal of material on the parliamentary representation of the borough from 1732 to 1835.[94] There is also the chronicle of Henry Lee, town clerk from 1662 to 1715;[95] and the two

NORTHAMPTON : THE SWAN HOTEL

custumal books, at Northampton and at the British Museum, contain oaths of office, corrected and brought up to date from time to time,[96] which enable us to differentiate the functions and names of the town officials.

The mayor was generally chosen from among the ex-bailiffs, but sometimes (e.g., in 1702, 1762, 1817, 1819) from the members of the Forty Eight. In spite of a resolution of 1570 that no man should be mayor more than twice,[97] there are numerous instances of mayors serving thrice, and T. Cresswell served four times (1579, 1588, 1596, 1604). The mayor's allowance, 20 marks in the 16th, as in the

---

[77] Boro. Rec. ii, 109.
[78] Narcissus Luttrell, Diary, i, 278.
[79] Boro. Rec. i, 143–7.
[80] Ibid. ii, 476–7.
[81] Lee, Coll. p. 128.
[82] Hist. MSS. Com. Rep. xii, app. 7, p. 230.
[83] Letters of Cumberland to Wade and Newcastle, 4 Dec. 1745 (S. P. Dom.).
[84] Corresp. and Diary of Philip Doddridge, ed. J. D. Humphreys (1831), iv, 428–31, 436–9, 442–3.
[85] Ibid.

[86] Parl. Papers 1833, vol. xiii. Minutes of Evidence, 1400.
[87] Ibid. 1835, vol. xxv, pp. 1976, 1981.
[88] Boro. Rec. i, 329.
[89] Northampt. Corp. Rec. Press N. 2b, 3, 3a, 10, 5, 6.
[90] Ibid. Press N. 8, 9. 4.
[91] Ibid. Press H. 1–28, i–xvi ; Press O. 17–19b.
[92] Ibid. Press N. 11.
[93] Ibid. Press O. 13–16a.
[94] Ibid. Press H. ; Press I. 30–47 ; Press S. 33–35, 57–58.

[95] 'Memorandums of the Antiquities of the Town of Northampton and of severall remarkable things acted in this Kingdome of England Collected by Henry Lee in the Eighty Sixth Year of his Age who served the Corporacion of Northampton in the office of Town-Clerke Fifty and Three Years till August 1715.' Top. MS. (Bodl. Lib.), Northants, c. 9, pp. 89–163, cited as Lee, Coll.
[96] The pre-Reformation forms, adjuring 'the Saints' and 'the holydome' are cancelled.
[97] Boro. Rec. ii, 31.

14th century, varied according to the thrifty or festive tendencies of the times, but rose steadily in the 18th century from £30 in 1745 to £105 in 1801, £220 in 1814, and £350 in 1829, when the tide turned.[98] In 1835 it was £150. No doubt the increase was partly due to the difficulty of inducing members of the corporation to accept an office which entailed so much expenditure on 'treats' and 'feasts.'[99] The mayor and ex-mayors or aldermen had much the same functions as the mayor and his council had had before 1489.[99a] Under the charter of 1489 they nominated the Forty Eight, and thus completely controlled the personnel of the corporation.[1] They appointed all the corporation officials that were not elected by the assembly, such as coroners, chamberlains, constables, serjeants and beadles, searchers and tasters for the trades, collectors of rents, the town clerk and the steward. They administered a variety of charities, and their preferential treatment of candidates of their own political colour was noted severely in 1835.[2] Finally they decided when the assembly should be summoned. In the 17th century the court of the mayor and aldermen met fortnightly; in the 18th century less frequently, and the business was almost entirely confined to the filling of offices, the dealing with charity property, and the calling of assemblies.

The two bailiffs, elected annually from the company of the Forty Eight by the whole assembly, became members for life of the body of ex-bailiffs, from whom as a rule the mayor was chosen. They received as their allowance the rent of a river meadow known as the Bailiffs' Hook, which amounted in 1835 to £31 a year, and had then been recently supplemented by a grant of 50 guineas.[3] Their functions had come to be almost purely administrative and fiscal, as the Court of Record where they sat became less and less important. They were still responsible for the payment of the fee farm, for the arrangement of fairs and markets, and for the collection of tolls. They also supervised the keeping of watch and ward and the upkeep of the walls till 1662.[4] They impanelled juries and executed the writs of central and local justices, the corporation successfully upholding its right to exclude the sheriff's action in this matter.[5]

The Forty Eight, nominated for life by the mayor and aldermen from the body of freemen, served as a pool from which the bailiffs could be chosen.[6] They could be displaced by a vote of the assembly.[7] With the mayor and aldermen, the bailiffs and ex-bailiffs, they made up the common council or assembly, which elected the mayor, the recorder, and the bailiffs, and other corporation officials,[8] admitted freemen, leased corporation property, and passed ordinances or bye laws, though this form of activity practically ceased in the 18th century, when they had come to take very little thought for the general well-being of the town.[9] The contrast between the earlier and later Assembly Books well reflects the narrowing of interests.

Of the other town officials the Recorder was first in dignity. He is first mentioned in 1478 as the person before whom, with the coroners, the mayor was to be sworn in at Northampton, instead of going up to the Exchequer.[10] The charter of 1495 provided that the assembly should every year elect a discreet man learned in the law as Recorder, to serve as a justice of the peace for the borough, and be one of the quorum of three, with power to hear and determine all felonies and trespasses committed within the town.[11] The office was as a rule held for life, and the first recorded election (in 1568), was made by the mayor and aldermen.[12] As the influence of the county over the town increased, it became customary to appoint some neighbouring gentleman, who often served as knight of the shire or member for the borough. The first honorary appointment seems to have been the election in 1642 of the Earl of Manchester, a member of the family of Montagu of Boughton, 'for various favours shown by him to the town, and especially for having provided for its defence,'[13] and thenceforward the work of the office seems to have been done by a deputy-recorder. In 1671, the assembly elected the Earl of Peterborough as Recorder, but the next year the new mayor, a county gentleman, induced them to replace him by the Earl of Northampton.[14] For this discourtesy to a royal favourite the mayor was summoned before the Privy Council, and rebuked by the King, who, however, allowed the election to stand.[15] The Earl of Northampton was formally re-elected every year until his death, and was a most valuable friend to Northampton in forwarding the Bill for the rebuilding of the town after the fire of 1675. When the earl begged the King to delay the prorogation of parliament for half an hour or so that the Bill might pass, Charles observed : 'My lord, I do much wonder you should be so kind to the town of Northampton which in the time of the wars were so unkind to my lord of Northampton, your father.'[16] The earl replied : 'If it may please your Majesty, I forgive them,' and the King said : 'My lord, if you forgive them, I shall do the same.'[17] On Northampton's death, however, the town was forced to accept Peterborough until 1688, when the recordership became, in practice, hereditary in the Compton family, till the death of the last Earl of Northampton in 1828. The position then ceased to be honorary, and a working lawyer was appointed.[18] The most distinguished of the deputy-recorders of Northampton had been Spencer Perceval, who held the office from 1787–1807, gave legal opinion and advice to the

---

[98] *Boro. Rec.* ii, 41-2.

[99] In 1694 eight persons in succession were elected as mayor and paid the fine of £10 rather than serve. *Boro. Rec.* ii, 37.

[99a] For the mayor's oath see *Boro. Rec.* ii, 531, or Add. MS. Brit. Mus. 34308, fo. 10 d.

[1] For the aldermen's oath, see Add. MS. 34308, fo. 15.

[2] *Parl. Papers*, 1835, vol. xxv, p. 1978.

[3] Ibid. p. 1967.

[4] For the bailiffs' oath, see *Boro. Rec.* ii, 533, or Add. MS. 34308, fo. 11 d.

[5] Assembly Books, 20 April 1612, 10 May 1722.

[6] For oath of Forty Eight, see Add. MS. 14308, fo. 20.

[7] Assembly Book, 2 May, 1778.

[8] The distribution of patronage between the common council and the mayor and aldermen varied from time to time. See *Boro. Rec.* ii, 49.

[9] *Parl. Papers*, 1835, vol. xxv, pp. 1967, 1981.

[10] *Boro. Rec.* i, 94.

[11] Ibid. i, 104.

[12] Ibid. ii, 104.

[13] *Hist. MSS. Com. Rep.* viii, app. 2, p. 59a.

[14] Lee, Coll. p. 118.

[15] *Boro. Rec.* ii, 107.

[16] The second earl was killed in a skirmish in 1643, and the parliamentarians refused to give up his body to his son.

[17] Lee, Coll. p. 121.

[18] For the recorder's oath, see *Boro. Rec.* i, 392.

BOROUGH OF NORTHAMPTON

town on several important occasions, helped to secure the new charter in 1796, and represented the borough in Parliament from 1796 till his assassination in 1812.[19] His statue by Chantrey, erected by public subscription[20] and placed in All Saints' in 1817, was transferred to the council chamber of the town hall, where it now stands, in 1866.

The town clerk, common clerk or mayor's clerk acted also as clerk of the recognizances.[21] He was appointed as a rule by the mayor and aldermen and in practice held the office for life. He had a small stipend, but his income was mainly derived from fees. In 1652 it was put on record that he should have no voice in matters discussed in the assembly;[22] his importance as a permanent official is well illustrated by the story told by Henry Lee, town clerk from 1662-1688 and from 1690-1715, of the election of the mayor in 1694. Eight members of the corporation in turn had been elected and refused to serve. 'It being night, And the Mayor and Aldermen tired, the Mayor proposed to the Aldermen to adjourn the Court to the next day, And then I informed them That it was against the Express words of the Charter.' (If the mayor was not elected at one sitting, the existing mayor had to serve another year.) 'I told the present Mayor that . . . without speedy care taken they would all be gon, and thereupon he starts up from his Seat in the Councell Chamber and made hast to the Hall dore and lockt it and brought in the Keys and laid them before him upon the Table, and said: "Now I will stay here till to-morrow this time, but I will choose a Mayor." . . . It happened to be a wett night, and after nine of the clock.'[23]

The town steward, first mentioned in the 15th century,[24] acted as clerk to the bailiffs at the court of record, and mayor's clerk at the court leet.[25] He was appointed by the mayor and alderman and paid by fees only.

The coroners, according to the charter, should have been chosen by the assembly; in practice the mayor and aldermen often appointed. The election was annual, and it was usual to choose aldermen for the office.[26]

The chamberlains, elected annually, at first by the assembly and later by the mayor and aldermen, acted as the town treasurers. They kept the town accounts and had one of the keys of the common chest.[27] During the 17th century there were two, a senior and a junior chamberlain, each holding office for two years. Their accounts[28] are preserved in the corporation archives from 1554 onwards, with gaps, and are of great value, including as they do the rental of the town lands, receipts by fines and grazing fees, payments to town officials and beneficiaries, and all kinds of occasional expenditure. The increase in the amounts spent on feasting is well marked. From 1785 to 1835 the town chamberlain wore a distinctive badge of 'a respectable silver key in the gothic taste, double gilt.'[29] By 1835 the chamberlain's functions had become largely honorary, and the real work of accounting was done by a treasurer, also elected by the mayor and aldermen.[30]

The serjeants of the mayor and bailiffs, known, from the rods of office they carried, as mace-bearers from the 14th century[31] were five in number, one for each ward of the town. Four were reckoned as bailiffs' serjeants and called in the 17th and 18th centuries serjeants at mace; the fifth was known as mayor's serjeant or mace-bearer. According to the form of their oaths in the town custumal[32] they executed attachments and distresses and had custody of prisoners, whilst the mayor's serjeant also assized measures and weights and levied estreats. They were appointed by the mayor and aldermen. Besides the fees and perquisites of their office the bailiffs' serjeants received in 1833 a salary of 6 guineas each, and the mace-bearer £27.[33] Four small maces, one going back to the reign of James I, are preserved at Northampton, together with the great mace still in use, made probably, like that of Leicester, by Thomas Maundy of London under the Commonwealth.[34]

The duties of the serjeants had become largely formal by 1835; their police duties were being performed by the constables. The 15th century custumal gives the constable's oath which defines his duties, and also that of the tithing man or dozener,[35] whose office, at that period, is still mainly one of presenting at the leet. In the 17th century custumal a later form of the *sacramentum decenariorum* includes the duty of apprehension of wandering and idle persons of different kinds,[36] and can be taken as defining the duties of the third borough or head borough who in the 16th and 17th centuries assisted the constable. Each ward had one constable and two third boroughs, appointed from 1581 to 1690 by the assembly, and after that date by the mayor and aldermen.[37] In 1833 there were in all 23 constables and head boroughs, paid according to the work done, by piece rates, out of the town rates by authority of the magistrates.[38] Among other minor officials of the corporation were the town crier, the hallkeeper, and, from 1584 to 1698 at least, the town waits or musicians.[39]

The government of the close corporation appears to have been on the whole satisfactory down to the Restoration. From that date the town records give evidence of steady deterioration. Alongside of the growth of political exclusiveness went the tendency within the corporation of the mayor and aldermen to arrogate to themselves more power, and the diminution in the corporation as a whole of the sense of responsibility for the well-being of all the town. The borough revenues were regarded as a fund entirely at their disposal, and any fresh needs of the growing

---

[19] *Boro. Rec.* ii, 22, 206, 349. He is also supposed to have used his influence to secure army contracts for the Northampton shoe makers.

[20] The corporation subscribed £105. Assembly Bk., 5 June, 1812.

[21] In the British Museum custumal the town clerk's oath covers also the office of 'Prothonotary or clerk of the Recognizances of the Statute Merchant.' He had a seal in this capacity, reproduced *Boro. Rec.* ii, 142, fig. 4.

[22] Ibid. 69.

[23] Lee, Coll. pp. 130-1.

[24] *Boro. Rec.* i, 377. The steward's oath is given Add. MS. 34308, fo. 11 d, printed *Boro. Rec.* ii, 533; for 'the Mrs' read 'thy maystres.'

[25] *Boro. Rec.* ii, 116-8; *Parl. Papers*, 1835, vol. xxv, p. 1968.

[26] Ibid. p. 1968. For coroners' oath see *Boro. Rec.* i, 392.

[27] Ibid., 256.

[28] Ibid, ii, 58-65.

[29] Ibid. 66.

[30] *Parl. Papers*, 1835, vol. xxv, p. 1968.

[31] *Boro. Rec.* i, 244, 250.

[32] Add. MS. 34308, ff. 13, 15; *Boro. Rec.* ii, 74, 78.

[33] Ibid. 78.

[34] Ibid. 74-85.

[35] Ibid. i, 397, 393.

[36] Add. MS. 34308, fo. 12.

[37] *Boro. Rec.* ii, 139-142.

[38] *Parl. Papers*, 1833, vol. xiii, p. 50.

[39] *Boro. Rec.* ii, 85-92.

town were met out of the town rates, fixed by the magistrates at quarter sessions and kept distinct from the corporation accounts.[40] As early as 1692 a mayor is commended because 'he did not sell the town land for claret as others did.'[41] The corporation became, in fact, little more than a dining club with considerable powers of patronage.

One by-product of this stagnation was the difficulty found in filling municipal office and even in recruiting the corporation itself. A substantial sum was annually derived from the fines of those who refused office. We have seen that in 1694 eight mayors-designate refused to serve. This brought in £80. Similar difficulties occurred in 1711, 1713, 1723, and 1730.[42] The same reluctance to serve was shown by bailiffs-elect.[43] The records of the mayor and aldermen's court show the difficulty of filling up the vacancies in the Forty Eight created annually by the election of the two bailiffs. The first instance of refusal to act is recorded in 1696, and from that time complaints were constant.[44] On 7 August 1775, for instance, 13 persons who were elected to the Forty Eight were displaced because of their refusal to take the oath; ten of them, however, were immediately re-elected with six others. On 5 August 1776 twelve were similarly displaced and re-elected.[45] The assembly in its turn was endeavouring to compel persons to become freemen: on 23 May 1776, for instance, it was resolved that nine persons should be admitted freemen at £10 each, and prosecuted if they refused.[46] As a result, by 1791 the corporation consisted of a mayor, 18 aldermen, 22 bailiffs and 19 Forty Eight men, whilst 29 persons elected to the Forty Eight were refusing to act. Under the charter of 1663 the mayor and aldermen had power to fine, and if necessary imprison and distrain freemen who refused to serve.[47] Having taken legal opinion, in 1794 they had a mandamus served on several of the defaulters, and the case was brought before the court of King's Bench, with unforeseen consequences. It appeared that by the Act of 1489 the mayor must be elected by a majority of the Forty Eight, not being ex-bailiffs, and that for several years past the mayors had been elected by a minority, as no majority existed.[48] The corporation had thus no legal warrant for its existence, and the only remedy was to surrender the charter of 1663[49] and petition for a new one. The townsmen seized on the chance of asserting their rights and held a meeting on 1 June 1795 at the County Hall (not being allowed the use of the Town Hall) and a counter-petition organised by Edward Bouverie, the Whig member for the borough, was signed by five hundred persons, praying the King not to grant a charter without reference to the petitioners.[50] The attitude of the corporation is reflected in the resolution passed in the assembly of 8 June.[51]

'That it is the opinion of this Assembly that the peace and good government of this town and the interest of all its inhabitants whether free or not free of the corporation have been well secured under the Ancient Powers and Franchises heretofore and hitherto exercised by the Corporation.

'That it would not be wise to depart from a System which has been found upon such long experience to answer. And therefore it is the opinion of this Assembly that they should endeavour to procure such a Charter only as shall confirm and restore the ancient Rights and Franchises of the Corporation and leave the Government and the Election of its officers under the same regulations which have hitherto prevailed.'

Thanks were also voted to Mr. Charles Smith for his 'manly and steady conduct in resisting the unjust imputations aimed at the Corporation' at the late town meeting.

As was to be expected, the view of the assembly rather than that of the town meeting was accepted by the central government, and the charter of 2 April 1796[52] differed only in trifling respects from that of 1663. The right to fine freemen for refusal of office and to fine members of the corporation for non-attendance at assemblies was made definite, and the clause forbidding any but freemen to trade within the town was dropped. The fresh lease of life given to the old corporation led to no improvement either in zeal or in public spirit. Quorums were difficult to obtain,[53] and the worst instances of the expenditure of public funds on entertainment, of the exploitation of charity endowments for party purposes, and of political bias in judicial action belong to the period 1796-1835. A proposal from one of its own members in 1831 to reform the financial procedure of the corporation was quashed as 'unusual, improper and prejudicial,'[54] and the appointment of a special committee to audit the accounts in 1833, though it produced a valuable report, was in the nature of a deathbed repentance. The epitaph of the old régime was spoken by Cockburn in 1835: 'It seems impossible to justify a system which alienates from the municipal government the affections and respect of one half of the community and gives rise to complaints of so serious a character.'[55] In November 1835 the close corporation of the last three and a half centuries was replaced by an elective body of one mayor, 6 aldermen, and 18 councillors, representing the three wards into which the town was newly divided.

Under the Local Government Act of 1888 (51 and 52 Vict. c. 41) Northampton became a county borough in that year, but the form of its government was unchanged till 1898, when, owing to the victories of the Progressive party in the municipal elections of 1897,[56] a Boundaries Committee was appointed and a Provisional Order obtained from the Local Government Board, redividing the town into six wards. After further enquiry, the area of the town was enlarged by the act of 30 July 1900[57] so as to include nine wards,

---

[40] *Parl. Papers*, 1833, vol. xiii, p. 50.
[41] *Boro. Rec.* ii, 38 (Hall's MS.).
[42] Ibid. ii, 39.
[43] Ibid. 55.
[44] Ibid. 21-2.
[45] Northampt. Corp. Rec. Press N 4.
[46] Assembly Book, Press N, 10.
[47] *Boro. Rec.* i, 141.
[48] Ibid. ii, 24.
[49] The town was governed under this charter, and not that of 1683, as, the surrender of the former never having been enrolled, the latter (which had provided for a company of forty instead of forty-eight) was declared void by Sir Edward Northey, Attorney-General, 1701-1707, 1710-1718. Bridges, *Hist. of Northants.* i, 433.
[50] *Boro. Rec.* ii, 24.
[51] Assembly Book, Northampt. Corp. Rec. Press N, 10.
[52] *Boro. Rec.* i, 154-184.
[53] Ibid. ii, 25-6.
[54] Ibid. ii, 27.
[55] *Parl. Papers*, 1835, vol. xxv, p. 1981.
[56] *Northampt. Mercury*, 9 Nov. 1900.
[57] L.G.B. Provisional Orders Confirmation (no. 14) Act, 1900, 63 and 64 Vict. clxxxiii (Public Act of a local character). Northampton Workhouse serves Hardingstone Union.

BOROUGH OF NORTHAMPTON

each of which returned three councillors, who with nine aldermen, made up a council of 36 members. In 1911 the Northampton Corporation Act [58] was passed, under which the borough was divided into twelve wards, and from 1912 on the council has consisted of the time-honoured number of 48.

The first recorded representation of the borough in a parliament is in 11 Edward I,[59] and, except under the Commonwealth, there were two members up to 1918. The earliest writs are directed to the mayor and good men,[60] whilst the returns for Edward II's reign state that the members were elected by the bailiffs, by the mayor and bailiffs, or *per considerationem ville*.[61] From 1381 at least, the elections appear to have been made in the assembly at St. Giles'.[62] A comparison of the list of mayors and bailiffs with that of the members shows that the same group of burgesses performed both services.[63] In 1381 the assembly resolved that the borough should always be represented in Parliament by the ex-mayor, unless he had discharged the office of burgess before his mayoralty.[64] From 1489 onwards it appears that, as the parliamentary elections were still made in the assembly,[65] voting was restricted to members of the corporation. The act of 1489 did not mention elections to parliament, but the King's letter to Leicester in the same year definitely laid it down that only members of the common council should have votes for parliamentary elections,[66] and it is possible that the two acts, so nearly identical in form, were interpreted similarly. The members were chosen from among the corporation until the reign of Elizabeth, when the practice begins of choosing county gentlemen to represent the town. From 1553, the recorder was generally chosen as one member, and the Yelvertons of Easton Maudit established a strong family interest, whilst the Knightleys of Fawsley were another county family with influence in the borough. The notorious Peter Wentworth of Lillingston had sat for a Cornish borough before he represented Northampton in 1586, 1589 and 1592.[67] In 1601 the assembly books record that Mr. Henry Hickman, LL.D., and Francis Tate, Esq., made request to be chosen burgesses for the town and were accepted as being the first a resident and the second the son of a freeman, provided they paid their own expenses.[68] They were both made honorary freemen. Aldermen are still chosen as members after this date, but economy on the side of the corporation and solicitation from outside soon established the parliamentary representation of the borough as a prize to be competed for among the county gentry.[69] Henry Lee finds it noteworthy that in 1640 Zouch Tate of Delapré was elected burgess 'without his making any interest and without his knowledge till after the election.'[70]

Under the Commonwealth the representation of the borough was reduced to one. At the Restoration Northampton, like several other boroughs,[71] underwent a peaceful revolution; the parliamentary vote ceased to be the monopoly of the corporation. There must have been warning signs, for both at Leicester and Northampton the corporations prepared to resist an attack. The assembly at Northampton ordered on 19 June 1660 'That this town do unite with any other corporation of the neighbourhood for the maintenance and continuance of their constancy in the choice of Burgesses to serve in Parliament by the mayor, Bailiffs and Burgesses.'[72] In the elections for the convention two returns were made; the one of Francis Harvey and Richard Rainsford, the other of Sir John Norwich and Richard Rainsford. The Committee for Privileges reported that 'the commonalty as well as the bailiffs, aldermen and 48 common councilmen have the right to elect,' and that therefore Rainsford and Norwich were elected.[73] Harvey, the deputy-recorder, was the corporation candidate. In the elections of 1661 there was again a double return for Northampton: the sheriff brought an indenture with the names of Sir John Norwich and Sir James Langham; the mayor returned Langham and Harvey. The return of the mayor, the lawful returning officer, was filed, and Langham and Harvey were temporarily allowed to sit,[74] but after investigation the Committee for Privileges reported that the mayor had used menaces to such as would not give their votes to Mr. Harvey, had made infants free on the morning of the election that they might vote as he pleased, had caused persons to be put by who would not vote as he desired, had released Quakers from prison and put halberts in their hands to keep back such as would have voted contrary to his intentions, had adjourned the taking of the poll into the Church of All Saints and there behaved himself in a profane and indecent manner, and had declared beforehand that Mr. Rainsford should not be elected because he had given a charge for the Book of Common Prayer. On account of these irregularities the election was declared void by the Commons, by a vote of 185 to 127.[75] The mayor was brought into the House in the custody of the Serjeant at Arms, and making a humble submission on his knees, received a grave reprehension. Henry Lee, who appears to have confounded the elections of 1660 and 1661,[76] says that there were five candidates, and that the poll was held in the chancel of All Saints, by reason of the great rain that fell that day so that it could not be taken at the Market Cross. 'The election of burgesses,' he adds, 'was then ordered to be made in the town by the freemen and inhabitants of the town, and has continued a popular election ever since.'[77] Nevertheless more disputed returns followed, leading to a more precise definition of the franchise. The bye-election ordered on 13 June 1661 led to the return of Sir Charles Compton and Rainsford; but Compton died soon after and a fresh writ was issued on 5 Dec. 1661.[78] This time Sir J. Langham was elected, and the rival candidate, Sir W. Dudley, protested. The

---

[58] 1 and 2 George V, clxiv (Local Act).
[59] *Parl. Writs* (Rec. Com.), i, 16.
[60] Ibid.
[61] Ibid. I, lxxiii; II, 1, ccxxxiv.
[62] *Boro. Rec.* i, 248.
[63] *Parl. Writs*, II, 1, ccxxxii, ff; *Boro. Rec.* ii, 549 ff.
[64] *Boro. Rec.* i, 249.
[65] Ibid. ii, 494–6.
[66] Bateson, *Rec. Boro. of Leics.* ii, 325.
[67] See *Eng. Hist. Rev.* xxxix, 38, 46; and *Acts of Privy Council*, 1578–80, p. 218, for Wentworth's conventicles at Lillingston, attended by Northampton townsmen.
[68] *Boro. Rec.* ii, 495.
[69] Note Richard Spencer's account of his interview with the mayor and corporation in 1625. *Hist. MSS. Com. Rep.* vol. 82 (Buccleugh MSS.) i, 258–9.
[70] Lee, *Coll.* p. 93.
[71] Merewether and Stephens, *Hist. of Boro.* pp. 1763 ff.

[72] *Boro. Rec.* ii, 498.
[73] *Commons Journals*, viii, 70–71 (21 June 1660).
[74] Ibid. viii, 257 (22 May 1661).
[75] Ibid. viii, 269–70 (13 June 1661).
[76] He seems to have misled all later writers; the account given by Dr. Cox in the *Boro. Rec.* of the elections 1660–1664 is quite incorrect.
[77] Lee, *Coll.* p. 111–2.
[78] *Commons Journals*, viii, 326.

A HISTORY OF NORTHAMPTONSHIRE

Committee for Privileges reported on 26 April 1662 that lawful voters had been prevented from voting, but the matter was too intricate for them to determine; the House accepted their report and declared the election void.[79] The new bye-election was postponed for nearly a year by the rising of Parliament, but in February 1663 a fresh writ was issued[80] and the election took place on 7 March.[81] The mayor attempted to hold it in the assembly, but two of the members of the corporation protested and left the guildhall with many others, joining the 'popularity'[82] in the market square which was shouting 'A Hatton! a Hatton!' The rest of the corporation elected Sir W. Dudley; Mr. Hatton's party polled at the Market Cross, and the sheriff received two indentures. As in duty bound he returned the one sealed by the town clerk (Henry Lee himself), but Hatton appealed to the House of Commons, and the Committee for Privileges, after hearing much evidence, reaffirmed that 'the voices in election do not belong to the Mayor, Aldermen and Forty-Eight only, and that ... Mr. Hatton was duly elected.' The name of Dudley was erased from the indenture by the Clerk of the House and that of Hatton inserted.[83] In 1664 there was a fresh bye-election, necessitated by Rainsford's becoming a Baron of the Exchequer.[84] Again the return was disputed. On 26 April[85] the Committee of Elections reported that counsel on both sides agreed that whoever had the majority of voices of inhabitants being householders and not receiving alms ought to be elected; and that the Committee upheld this and were of opinion that the sharing of the charitable gift at Christmas was a taking of alms. On this interpretation, Sir Henry Yelverton was declared duly elected, and Sir John Bernard unseated. It would appear that the process of corrupting the popular electors had already begun.

From this time Northampton enjoyed what Tennant in 1782[86] calls the cruel privilege of a very popular franchise. It is not unlikely that the townsmen owed their enfranchisement to the fact that their political sympathies were more royalist than those of the corporation, even after the purging of 1662,[87] for in 1665 the mayor-elect was arrested by royal command.[88] Very soon, however, the corporation became more Tory than the town. In 1678 the Montagu interest, strong in the borough since the reign of James I,[89] was exerted on the Exclusionist side. 'There are four that stand,' young Perceval reports; 'Mr. Montagu is the only man who treateth ... the townsmen themselves say, both he and his father spend £100 per week, but to no purpose, for whomsoever the King will recommend they are resolved to choose, and there coming a letter in favour of Sir W. Temple, he, it is thought, will be the man.'[90] Owing to the Tory leanings of the returning officers, Temple was returned, but unseated by a vote of the House 'with so united a cry as made it very legible what inclination they bear to the patron of the first.'[91] From this time on the Montagu interest dominates the borough representation, and as the recordership had become a hereditary perquisite of the earls of Northampton, the Compton interest was equally strong and for a long series of parliaments the borough was represented by a Compton and a Montagu. In 1733 the assembly declared 'We think we have in some measure a right to be represented by a brother of the earl of Northampton.'[92] But on this occasion the corporation overreached itself. The parliamentary franchise was held to belong 'to every freeman, whether resident or not, and every householder, whether free or not,'[93] and the mayor, for the purposes of the election, admitted 396 gentlemen of the county to be freemen of the town, on payment of 3 guineas a man:[94] but the defeated candidate successfully petitioned against the return of Colonel Montagu, elected by these new votes. In 1740 legal opinion taken by the corporation upheld the ruling that only resident freemen had the parliamentary vote.[95] In 1768 a third great county interest entered the field. Earl Spencer put forward the Hon. Thomas Howe against the Montagu candidate, Sir G. Osborn, and the Compton candidate, Sir G. B. Rodney. It was popularly believed that £400,000 was spent on this election by the three patrons.[96] The campaign began at Michaelmas 1767 and lasted till April 1768, after fourteen days' polling. The mayor and corporation used all their influence against the Spencer candidate,[97] and by common agreement the oath as to bribery was not administered to any voter. A supporter of Halifax, rebutting the charge of bribery, wrote: 'I have never heard of any other expense on his part but that of eating and drinking.[98] ... How can it be avoided when an old family interest is to be defended against a sudden and unexpected invasion? In such a case one cannot blame what is done for self-defence.'[99] Another contemporary says: 'Each voter that would had twelve, fourteen or fifty guineas, some £100 to £500. The single article of ribbands cost £6,000.'[1] Osborn and Rodney were returned; but a scrutiny in the House of Commons in 1769 resulted in Howe's being declared elected, and Osborn and Rodney tossed for the other seat, which was retained by Rodney.[2] The expenses of the scrutiny, which took six weeks, during which Lord Spencer kept open house for members of Parliament, led to the Earl of Northampton's leaving the kingdom after cutting down the trees and selling the furniture at Compton Winyates, whilst Halifax and Spencer were also seriously crippled. The Compton and Spencer interests held the field after this for some years. From 1796–1812 Spencer Perceval, deputy recorder since 1787, represented the borough (at first as 'Lord Northampton's Man')[3] and there were a series of uncontested elections. In 1818

---

[79] *Commons Journals*, viii, 414.
[80] Ibid. viii, 436.
[81] *Boro. Rec.* ii, 498–9 (Hall's MS.).
[82] Lee, Coll. p. 113.
[83] *Commons Journals*, viii, 469.
[84] Ibid. viii, 535 (21 March 1663/4).
[85] Ibid. viii, 550.
[86] *Journey from Chester to London*, p. 310.
[87] See above, p. 12.
[88] *Boro. Rec.* ii, 35.
[89] Ibid. ii, 108.

[90] *Hist. MSS. Com. Rep.* (Egmont MS.), ii, 76.
[91] Ibid. Ormonde MSS. iv, 471.
[92] *Boro. Rec.* ii, 500.
[93] Bridges, *op. cit.* i, 434.
[94] *Boro. Rec.* ii, 500.
[95] Ibid. ii, 501.
[96] *Quarterly Review*, Jan. 1857, p. 32 (article by Rev. T. James).
[97] Among the corporation records is a list in the town clerk's handwriting of members of the Corporation in the interest of Osborn and Rodney, which includes the mayor, 9 aldermen, 18 bailiffs and 26 common council men. *Boro. Rec.* ii, 506.
[98] The voters having drunk up all Halifax's port at Horton, refused his claret, and went over in a body to Castle Ashby to sample Northampton's cellar.
[99] *Hist. MSS. Com. Rep.* 10, app. i, p. 409.
[1] *Boro. Rec.* ii, 506 (Hall's MS.).
[2] *Hist. MSS. Com. Rep.* 10, app. i, p. 412.
[3] *Boro. Rec.* ii, 508.

PLAN OF NORTHAMPTON IN 1746 BY NOBLE AND BUTLIN
(Reproduced by permission of Northamptonshire Libraries and Information Service)

BOROUGH OF NORTHAMPTON

the understanding that each party returned one candidate was terminated [4] and another fierce contest took place. The corporation supported the Tory interest energetically, and in 1826 went so far as to vote £1,000 out of the borough funds towards the expenses of a candidate in the ministerial interest : an action condemned by the commissioners of 1835, but falling far short of the party excesses of the Leicester corporation.[5] In 1768 the number of townsmen claiming votes was 1170, and some 900 were allowed to poll. In 1784 908 voted, in 1790 893,[6] and in 1818 1,287.[7] The number of electors under the Reform Act of 1832 was 2,497.[8] The last notable episode in the parliamentary history of Northampton was connected with Charles Bradlaugh. After two unsuccessful candidatures, he was elected M.P. for Northampton in 1880. He was unseated on his refusal to take the oath administered to members, and was re-elected by the borough four times—in 1881, 1882, 1884 and 1885. Finally, in 1886, he was allowed to sit, and he remained one of the burgesses until his death in 1891.[9] By the Representation of the People Act in 1918, the borough representation was reduced from two to one. The borough was represented by Miss Margaret Bondfield in the parliament of 1923–24.

In 1086 the sum payable to the sheriff by the burgesses was £30 10s. ; in 1130 the sheriff accounted for £100 at the Exchequer ; and in 1185 the *firma burgi* was fixed at £120. The burgesses had difficulty in paying this and they appear to have been badly in arrears at the beginning of the reign of Henry III, so that in 1227 the town was taken into the king's hand[10] and a *custos* appointed.[11] In 1334 the town applied in vain for a reduction of the farm,[12] but in 1462 Edward IV remitted £20 of it for the next twenty years, a period extended later.[13] In 1484 Richard III increased the relief to 50 marks,[14] but Henry VII reduced it again to £22.[15] Under a grant of 1514 the farm was permanently fixed at £98,[16] as it is to-day. It has been assigned from time to time to different persons, such as Robert de Crevequer in 1301,[17] and Roger de Beauchamp in 1338.[18] From 1351 £66 13s. 4d. of it has been payable to the Dean and Chapter of Windsor,[19] and the remaining £31 6s. 8d. is paid to Mr. George Finch, the representative of the earl of Winchilsea and Nottingham.[20]

By acquiring the *firma burgi*, the burgesses acquired the right of collecting the burgage-rents hitherto payable to the king. Early deeds frequently describe tenements held *de prepositura ville*. It is not always clear whether the rents are included in the farm, or whether in some cases the bailiffs are collecting them on the king's behalf and accounting for them separately at the Exchequer. Thus Hugh Gobion is said to hold his land in chief of the king by the service of 2s. payable yearly at the Exchequer by the hands of the *prepositura* of Northampton,[21] whilst Richard Gobion 'holds his land of the King in chief by burgage, paying 15s. 4d. to the *prepositura* of Northampton towards the farm of the said town.'[22] In a survey of 1291 of nine houses lately held by Jews in Northampton, three are said to be held *de prepositura*[23]—one in the Corn Row, one in the Market Place, and one not specified. The rents are 8d., 2s. and 8d., and in two of the three instances payments are due to other persons as well. In 1361 Hawise le Botiller (*née* Gobion) is said to have held 8 shops in Northampton, as burgage of the town, rendering to the king 12d. yearly towards the farm of the town.[24] The petition of 1334 refers to rents that go to make up the fee farm of the town,[25] and another petition in which Northampton joined with four other towns in 1376 shows that several burgesses who held burgages of the king had so wasted their land that the rents were not forthcoming for the payment of the borough farm.[26] In 1467 the rents due for the stalls in the market are described as the king's, and also as the property of the suitors to the town court, and they were collected by the bailiffs, 'fee farmers to the King within this town.'[27] When purprestures were presented, it was not uncommon for the encroacher to be allowed to keep the land usurped, paying for it a rent to the *prepositura* in aid of the *firma burgi*.[28] In 1391 the mayor and chamberlains are expressly given power to let to farm all waste places, for rents to be paid to them for the town.[29] Sixteen such holdings were let out by them in 1439.[30] Much property had come into the hands of the town by the close of the Middle Ages, and by the name of 'The Chamber lands' was confirmed to the town by the charter of 1599.[31]

The condition of the town of Northampton in 1504 is shown by a rental[31a] in which the town is divided into streets with the lanes running off on either side, into market rows and districts. Probably the most important area was ' Swinwel-strete,' now Derngate, which was apparently the residential quarter, and included the manor of Gobions and the Grange. The latter, which formerly belonged to Thomas Latimer, was late of Thomas Tresham, and then held by John Chauncy. It included land next the postern called Derngate and other adjoining land. Property here belonged to the chapel of Blessed Mary the Virgin in All Saints Church, and to the fraternity of Holy Trinity. There were inns called ' le Crown,' ' le Bell,' ' le Tabard,' and ' le Bulle,' and a house called ' le Blakhall.' St. Giles Street, which extended to the town wall, was mostly inhabited by tradesmen, bakers and fullers and Adam ' le Garlikemonger.' In Abingdon (Habyngdon) Street, leading to the East Gate, was a quarry. In St. Sepulchre's Lane, now probably Church Lane, was a house formerly of Thomas Tresham, then in the

---

[4] *Parl. Papers*, 1835, vol. xxv, p. 1976.
[5] Ibid. p. 1977 ; *Boro. Rec.* ii, 511.
[6] Poll Books, printed at Northampton in same years.
[7] *Boro. Rec.* ii, 509.
[8] *Parl. Papers*, 1835, vol. xxv, p. 1965.
[9] *Dict. Nat. Biog.*
[10] Mem. R. (K.R.) 8, m. 1 d.
[11] *Cal. Pat.* 1225–32, p. 171.
[12] *Parl. R.* ii, 85.
[13] *Cal. Pat.* 1461–7, p. 187 ; ibid. 1476–85, p. 99.
[14] Ibid. 1476–85, p. 434.
[15] *Boro. Rec.* i, 202.
[16] Ibid. i, 113.
[17] *Cal. Pat.* 1292–1301, p. 610.
[18] Ibid. 1338–40, p. 17.
[19] Ibid. 1350–4, p. 174.
[20] Information from the town clerk.
[21] *Cal. Inq.* ii, 78. The grant to his father merely says 2s. payable at the Exchequer, *Rot. Cart.* p. 93.
[22] Chan. Inq. post. Ed. I, ptf. 101, no. 2.
[23] Extents and Surveys, 143.
[24] *Cal. Fine*, 1356–68, p. 150.
[25] *Parl. R.* ii, 85.
[26] Ibid. ii, 348.
[27] *Boro. Rec.* i, 308.
[28] Assize R. 635, m 67 d.
[29] *Boro. Rec.* i, 251.
[30] Northampt. Corp. Deeds, Press C. 48.
[31] *Boro. Rec.* i, 123.
[31a] Recently discovered in the Andrew Collection of MSS. of Lt. Col. Packe, M.V.O., who has presented it (1929) to the Mayor and Corporation of Northampton to be placed with the Borough Records, of which it originally formed part.

A HISTORY OF NORTHAMPTONSHIRE

hands of the King. There were five tenements around the cross of Alnoth (*ad crucem Alnoth?*). In the Masters' Street (*in vico Magistrorum*) were various houses which had been acquired by the College of All Saints, and in the tenure of the College; near by were Fullers' Street and Weavers' Street. In the South Quarter (the south part of Bridge Street) and the parish of St. Gregory was 'Stokkwell Hall' and lands of the fraternities of Corpus Christi and St. Nicholas in the Wall, probably connected with the famous rood in the wall in St. Gregory's Church. Laundry Street was probably near the river. The district of Bridge Street (*in vico Pontis*) included the holme or island called Barmerholme (Baums holem) belonging to Sir John Longville, several tenements belonging to the chapel of the Blessed Mary and the fraternity of the Holy Trinity, and land at the South Gate belonging to the Hospital of St. Thomas the Martyr. Under Kingswell Street we have mention of a lane called 'Lewnyslane,' an inn in Bridge Street called 'the Angel,' 'Wolmongerstrete' and an ancient rent from a tenement in 'le Cowmede' where there was formerly a mill. We next come to the Market Place, where in the Glovers' Row there were 17 shops, in Mercers' Row 9 shops and 2 tenements, the Retailers' Row (*Rengum Regratorum Socorum (sic)*) 14 shops. In Butchers' Row there were on the north side 12 stalls and one shop and on the south side 14 stalls, many of which belonged to religious houses. In Fishers' Row there were shops and stalls. In Barbers' Row in the Old Drapery there were 22 shops. In Gold Street, the lands were largely in the hands of religious houses. In the parish of the Blessed Mary next the Castle there was a mill near the church and a tenement belonging to the fraternity of the Blessed Katherine in the church of St. Mary, and land outside the West Gate belonging to the fraternity of Corpus Christi. In the parish of St. Peter there was waste land about the town wall and there were tenements around the castle and the Friars Preachers. In the North Quarter into which 'Berwardstrete' ran was a house held by Peytmyn the Jew. St. Sepulchre's Street, now probably Sheep Street, extended to the North Gate. Newland in the parish of St. Michael seems to have extended to Bearward Street. There was a tenement called 'le Grenetree' near the Friars Minor. 'Le Fawkon' and an inn called 'le Hart' in the tenure of William Crawme, notary, were in Cornmongers' Row. There were also the Row where barley, oats and drage were sold, a Row opposite Bakers' Row, then called Potters' Hill, Shoemakers' Row, and the Tailory, where there was an inn called 'le Swan.'

NORTHAMPTON: THE BELL INN

A terrier of the town property in the year 1586 [32] shows that the borough then held houses and lands in all the five wards of the town, including a good number of stables, gardens and orchards, a house called St. George's Hall,[33] eight shops under the Town Hall, as well as arable and meadow lands in Milton, Heyford, Pitsford, and Cotton, and a house in Pitsford. A good many of these plots were sold by the town in 1621–2, probably in order to get together the purchase-money for Gobion's manor, which was acquired in 1622 at the cost of £1,520.[34]

The first mention of Gobions at Northampton seems to be in 1130, when Hugh Gobion paid 10 marks for a duel.[35] The Gobion family held a considerable amount of property throughout the Midland counties. Hugh Gobion witnessed a charter of Earl Simon II to St. Andrews,[36] and a Hugh Gobion was sheriff of Northants in 1161.[37] On the death of Hugh Gobion about 1166 the sheriff seized his land,[38] and accounted henceforth for 100s. a year from the land which was Hugh Gobion's[39] until it was recovered by his grandson in 1200.[40] Hugh's son Richard granted by deed to St. Andrew's Priory a shop, paying 5s. a year, 'which is set up at All Saints Fair before the house of Hugh my father, next the market place towards Northampton,'[41] This Richard had seven sons and six daughters and died before 1185.[42] Among the corporation records are deeds by which William de Vipont granted to Richard Gobion, second son of the last, lands in Cotes and beyond the South Bridge of Northampton.[43] This is the 'Earl Gobion' of Northampton tradition who gave goodly commons and liberties to the town.[44] His lands, including the recovered 'Grange,' were again seized into the king's hands later, as he joined the baronial faction against John, but in 1217 he was restored to favour.[45] He acted as royal Justice, and was the patron of the Franciscans on their first coming to Northampton, giving them shelter on his land outside the East Gate.[46] His son Hugh owed 16s. 4d. for relief, 'according to the custom of the town of Northampton,'

---

[32] Northampt. Corp. Rec. Press R. 22. An abstract is printed *Boro. Rec.* ii, 153-165.
[33] For account of St. George's Hall, see *Boro. Rec.* ii, 181-6.
[34] Northampt. Corp. Deeds, Press C. 101.
[35] Pipe R. 31 Hen. I.
[36] Farrer, *Honors and Knights' Fees*, ii, 298.
[37] Pipe R. 7 Hen. II.
[38] Ibid. 12 Hen. II. [39] Ibid. 13 Hen. II.
[40] Ricardus Gubiun r.c. de 40 M. pro habenda seisina de 100 solidatis terre infra burgum et extra quod dicitur terra de Grangia. Pipe R. no. 45, m. 2 d; cf. *Rot. Cart.* p. 93.
[41] Cott. MS. Vesp. E xvii, fo. 92.
[42] W. Farrer, *Honors and Knights' Fees*, i, 84.
[43] Northampt. Corp. Deeds, C 11.
[44] Lee, Coll. p. 94.
[45] Close R. 17 John, mm. 11, 12; ibid. 1 Hen. III, m 12.
[46] Eccleston, *De Adventu fratrum* (ed. A. G. Little), p. 29-30.

20

BOROUGH OF NORTHAMPTON

in 1230.[47] This Hugh joined the barons against Henry III, was taken prisoner in the siege of Northampton in 1264, and was disinherited after Evesham.[48] He recovered his lands from Robert de Turbervil, lord of Crickhowel, for a payment of 95 marks,[49] in 1267–70. A deed of his at Northampton locates Gobion's grange as being near St. Giles' churchyard.[50] In 1275 his son Richard succeeded,[51] and the *inquisitio post mortem* of the latter in 1301 gives a list of 49 houses and shops held of him in Northampton, with the names of the tenants.[52] Richard left two daughters, of whom the younger, Elizabeth, wife of Sir Thomas Paynell, inherited Gobion's manor in Northampton, together with Knaptoft. Her son took the name of Gobion,[53] but his successors were known as Paynells. The manor descended to Margaret Paynell, wife of Thomas Kennisman, whose daughter Elizabeth married John Turpin, who died in 1493, when 13s. 4d. was still payable as burgage rent to the mayor and corporation of Northampton.[54] From her the manor descended to George Turpin, who in 1558 sold the manor to Robert Harrison for £420,[55] who in turn sold it to the mayor and corporation of Northampton on 20 April 1622.

Among the town muniments, besides the title-deeds of Gobion's manor, are deeds recording the acquisition of Marvell's Mill, Millholme and Foot meadow in 1656,[56] and records of various sales of town property, notably of lands near the castle to Sir R. Haselrige in 1680.[57] In the 17th and 18th centuries a great deal of the town property was let at a low rent on long leases, the lessee having, however, to pay a heavy fine for renewal.[58] In the 16th century the borough held on lease lands to the west of the town formerly held by St. James' Abbey, known as Duston lordship, where the burgesses exercised common rights as in the town fields. The borough failed, however, to obtain the freehold of the lordship by purchase.[59]

In 1835 the property of the borough, including property whose origin was unknown, Gobion's manor, the bailiff lands, land acquired more recently, the profits of the butchers' stalls and the fees on the old commons brought in £1,448 12s. 3d. per annum.[60] In addition to this the tolls were let at £200 a year, and the trust estates and charity endowments brought in £3,304 odd.[61] With the administration of these charities went certain rights of patronage: the corporation appointed the warden of St. Thomas' Hospital,[62] the headmaster of the Free Grammar School[63] and the corporation schools and the Vicar of All Saints'. The Assembly Books record various resolutions with regard to the management of St. Thomas' Hospital,[64] which appears to have been well administered. It was moved in 1834 from the old building at the bottom of Bridge Street (destroyed in 1874)[65] and the charity, in a house in St. Giles' Street, still supports both inmates and out pensioners.[66] The advowson of All Saints was sold to the mayor and corporation by Sir Thomas Littleton and his wife in 1619 for £200,[67] and remained in their hands till 1835 when, under the Municipal Corporations Act, they had to sell it. Appointments to the living were made by trustees, being such of the corporation as lived in All Saints' parish.[68]

In 1275 it was alleged that the appointment of the master of the hospital of St. John belonged to the borough,[69] and an attempt was made by the mayor and corporation to get control of the nomination in the 17th century in vain.[70] The bishop of Lincoln was and is patron of the hospital,[71] which was intended for the poor of the county, as that of St. Thomas was for the townspeople.[72] The mayor and burgesses also had the right, probably from its foundation, of presentation to the chapel of St. Leonard attached to the Hospital of St. Leonard without Northampton.[73] In 1282 they asserted that the wardenship belonged to them of the right and in the name of the lord king. Down to 1294 the prior of St. Andrew's and the Vicar of Hardingstone had to sanction the chaplain's appointment; after that the mayor and burgesses were the sole patrons and the mayor was *ex officio* master of the hospital. In 1473 he and the Twenty Four calmly reduced the number of beneficiaries to one, and leased the hospital with all its lands and appurtenances to John Peck of Kingsthorpe for life, on the condition that he should provide the chaplain's board and lodging, keep the buildings in repair, and maintain one man or woman leper in place of the brothers and sisters of former times.[74] When the lessee died in 1505 the assembly resolved to keep the management of the hospital in their own hands, and each mayor had to take an oath to govern the hospital truly.[75] Two of the aldermen were to act as wardens, with a bailiff under them to levy the rents, and they were to render accounts annually. In 1546 St. Leonard's Hospital was said to have lands worth £10 15s. 9d. a year, and to be held by the mayor and Twenty Four in free alms, for the keeping of one leper;[76] and in 1547 it was taken into the king's hands, and granted out again to F. Samwell, together with the chapel of St. Katharine, in 1549.[77] The mayor and corporation protested vigorously, asserting in a petition to the Chancellor of the Court of Augmentations[78] that for four hundred years and more they had been lawfully seised of the hospital and chapel of St. Leonard's. In response to this an inquiry was held which vindicated the claims of the corporation,[79]

---

[47] Fine R. 15 Hen. III, m. 7.
[48] *Annal. Mon.* (Rolls Ser.), iii, 229–30.
[49] Northampt. Corp. Deeds, C. 15; cf. Cal. Misc. Inq. I, 122.
[50] Ibid. C 17.
[51] *Cal. Inq.* ii, 78.
[52] Chan. Inq. Ed. I, ptf. 101, no. 2.
[53] Northampt. (Rolls Sec.) Corp. Deeds, C. 15; cf. Cal. Misc. Inq. I, 122.
[54] Inq. p.m., Hen. VII, Ser. ii, vol. 9, no. 42.
[55] Northampt. Corp. Deeds, C 61, 63, 64. The manor then included 3 messuages with orchards, etc., 600 acres of arable, 200 of meadow, 30 of pasture, 200 of heath or moor and 10 acres of woodland.
[56] Northampt. Corp. Deeds, C 106.
[57] Ibid. C 109.
[58] *Boro. Rec.* ii, 166.
[59] Ibid. ii, 229.
[60] *Parl. Papers*, 1835, vol. xxv. p. 1971.
[61] Ibid. pp. 1971–5.
[62] See *V.C.H. Northants.* ii, 161.
[63] Ibid. ii, 235–241.
[64] *Boro. Rec.* ii, 341.
[65] *Assoc. Arch. Soc. Reps.* xii, 226.
[66] R. M. Serjeantson, *The Hospital of St. Thomas*, p. 7.
[67] Feet of F. Trin. 17 Jas. I; R. M. Serjeantson, *Hist. of Ch. of All Saints, Northampt.* p. 185.
[68] Lee, Coll. p. 129.
[69] *Rot. Hund.* ii, 3.
[70] *Northants. Nat. Hist. Soc. and Field Club*, xvi, 229.
[71] Ibid. xvii, 12–18.
[72] Lee, Coll. p. 96.
[73] R. M. Serjeantson, *The Leper Hospitals of Northampt.* reprinted from *Northants. Nat. Hist. Soc.* xviii, March 1915, supplements the account in *V.C.H. Northants.* ii, 159–161.
[74] *Boro. Rec.* i, 402–5.
[75] Add. MS. 34308, fo. 21; *V.C.H. Northants.* ii, 160.
[76] Chantry Certificates for Northants. 1546, R. 36, no. 37.
[77] Pat. 2 Ed. VI, Pt. 2, m. 25.
[78] Aug. Off. Proc. bdle. 27, no. 4.
[79] Ibid. Misc. Bks. 132, fo. 136.

A HISTORY OF NORTHAMPTONSHIRE

and they were allowed, on payment of £41 to Samwell, to keep the hospital as well as the chapel of St. Katharine, to serve as a chapel of ease for the sick. After this the rights of the corporation were unchallenged. As leprosy died out, one poor man or woman was maintained up to 1840, when the last beneficiary died, and the considerable endowments of the hospital were applied to the reduction of the rates. An investigation by the Charity Commissioners was hampered by a refusal of the corporation to produce the records, and in 1857 the Attorney-General filed an information in Chancery and the facts were made public. After long discussion, the property of St. Leonard's was assigned to the support of the grammar school in July 1864. The lands of the charity are described in detail in the town terrier of 1586.[80]

The town property was administered by the mayor and chamberlains, who had power from the 14th century to let out lands under their common seal.[81] The existence of a common seal seems to be implied in the reference to the letters patent of the town in the charter of 1227—an addition to the charter of 1200 which it mostly repeats. In 1282 it is definitely stated that the common seal has been attached to certain letters patent,[82] and there is at the Record Office one such letter patent to which a seal was formerly attached.[83] The oldest known common seal of Northampton appears to have belonged to the early 13th century. It was circular, 1⅝ in. in diameter and bore an embattled tower with closed portal, the walls and battlements charged with fourteen irregular quatrefoils. Over the battlements appears the head of a knight, to the left, holding a crossbow and a bannerflag; in the field a sprig and leaves of foliage. The inscription was SIGILLUM : COMMUNE : NORHAMPTONE.[84] The mayor's official seal, of less rude design, appears to have been made early in the 14th century,[85] and is perhaps to be associated with the charter of 1299. It was used for sealing letters accrediting freemen in other towns and returns of writs by the bailiffs,[86] authenticating exemplifications of deeds enrolled on the Town Memoranda Rolls[87] and adding authority to private deeds when the seals of the parties were not well known.[88] It was circular, 1⅝ in. in diameter, and bore a triple-towered castle, walls masoned and embattled, doors open, supported by two lions passant guardant of England; in the field above, a reticulated pattern. The inscription ran : ✱ S' MAIORITATIS VILLE NORHAMTONIE.[89] These two seals were in use down to the last quarter of the 17th century[90] and were probably destroyed when superseded. The common seals of 1667 and 1796 are in the keeping of the corporation. That of 1667 is oval, and 1¹⁵⁄₁₆ in. long, and bears a circular triple-towered castle, flanked by two lions, with the inscription NORTHAMPTONIÆ 19 CAROLI 2 R. ANGLIÆ. The common seal of 1796 is also oval and is 1¼ in. long, bearing on a shield the town arms of a castle and two lions. The inscription runs : NORTHAMPTON CHARTER RENEWED XXXVI GEO. III. The common seal now in use, made in 1879, is circular, 2¼ in. in diameter, and bears on a shield the borough arms, with the inscription, CASTELLO FORTIOR CONCORDIA.

Impressions are extant of three other town seals. There were two seals for use under the Statute of Merchants for sealing recognizances; the mayor's seal and the clerk's counterseal. A letter from the burgesses in 1319 to the Chancellor reports that they have elected their mayor to keep the great seal and a clerk, their comburgess, to keep the small one.[91] In 1351 Edward III appointed one of his yeomen to keep the smaller seal, but as he could not execute the office in person, it fell back into the hands of the Northampton clerk.[92] In 1408 the clerk lost the smaller seal, and the mayor sent him up to the Exchequer to get it renewed.[93] The inscription on the mayor's seal (circular, 1⅝ in.) is s' REGIS EDWARDI AD RECOGN' DEBITORUM. The design is like that for London. The inscription on the clerk's counterseal is

S : cl'ici : de : stat : m'cat : norhton,

and it bears a representation of St. Andrew on his cross.[94] The cloth seal, of which a cast is preserved at Northampton,[95] was used for stamping Northampton cloth which had paid the subsidy. Only three other instances of a cloth seal are mentioned in the British Museum Catalogue of Seals, whilst there are seventeen distinct examples of town seals under the Statute Merchant.[96] The Northampton cloth seal is an inch in diameter, and bears a king's head in the centre and round it the inscription, s' : PANORUM : NORHAMTON :[97]

The open fields lay to the north and east of the town, the meadows to the south being used for pasture after haytime. There is a good map of the lands formerly belonging to St. Andrew's Priory in the year 1632; it shows a North Field, a Middle Field, and a South Field, as well as Monkspark, Rushmill Meadows and the Priory Leaze, and the town lands, including the recently acquired Gobion's manor, are indicated scattered among the other holdings.[98] Among the borough records is a deed of 1373 which mentions lands lying in the North Field (Whetehul, Nether Whetehul, and Bartholomew furlong), in the East Field (Monkespark furlong) and the South Field (Brerewong and Mede furlong) as well as the Portmede.[99] There are constant references to the town meadows and pastures. In 1391 it was ordered that no freeman should graze more than two beasts in the common pastures without payment.[1] In 1553 the assembly ordered 'That no man shall keep moor for his franchis than iij bestes upon the commons in alle, and that they be his owne ... upon payne of xld ... Item that the Cowe medowe, the horse medowe next ytt and Rawlines holme shal be kept

---

[80] Printed in full by Serjeantson, *ut supra*, pp. 42–4.
[81] *Boro. Rec.* i, 251.
[82] Serjeantson, *Leper Hospitals of Northampt.* p.10.
[83] Exch. K. R. Bills 7/2.
[84] *Cat. of Seals, Brit. Mus.* ii, p. 141. For reproduction see *Boro. Rec.* ii, 142.
[85] It is affixed to a deed of 1337. (Add. Ch. 729).
[86] *Boro. Rec.* i, 380, 384.
[87] e.g. Add. Ch. 732, 735, 22371.
[88] e.g. Add. Ch. 729, 730, 731, 22368.
[89] *Cat. of Seals, Brit. Mus.* ii, p. 141.
[90] Add. Ch. 6132 (1684) bears the common seal. For an example of the personal seal of a mayor of Northampt. see that of Robert Fitz Henry, mayor 1279 and 4 times afterwards, reproduced in Serjeantson, *Leper Hospitals of Northampt.* p. 49, from Northampt. Corp. Deeds, C 23.
[91] Anct. Corresp. xxxv, 198.
[92] *Cal. Pat.* 1350–54, p. 99.
[93] Anct. Corresp. lvii, 29.
[94] See *Boro. Rec.* ii, 142; *Cat. of Seals Brit. Mus.* i, p. 145.
[95] It is in the collection of the Northants. Arch. Soc. in their rooms at the Ladies' Club, Northampt.
[96] *Cat. of Seals Brit. Mus.* i, p. 141.
[97] See *Boro. Rec.* ii, 142.
[98] A copy is in the public library, Northampt., the original, made by Marcus Pierce, being in Messrs. Markham's office, Guildhall Road.
[99] Northampt. Corp. Deeds, Press C, 42.
[1] *Boro. Rec.* i, 253–4.

BOROUGH OF NORTHAMPTON

severall from the purification of Saynt Mary the Virgin untyll the invention of the holy crosse in May and likewise from the assumption of our lady unto saynt luke day the evangeliste upon payne of xld. every beast.'[2] In 1556 the right of common was restricted to freemen 'downlying and uprising and dwelling within the liberties' and further regulations enforcing this restriction were passed in 1599. Rules were laid down in 1582 for the times for throwing open The Cow Meadow, St. George's Leys, Balms Holme and the Foot Meadow, and there were regulations from time to time as to the branding of the cattle, the turning out of diseased beasts and the nuisances caused by curriers or fullers, whilst from time to time the rates payable for depasturing beasts and the numbers allowed gratis to each freeman were altered. The freemen enjoyed rights of common during 'the open tide' not only in the lands owned by the corporation but in those of other proprietors, and Henry Lee describes a dispute between the freemen and Mr. Bryan, the owner of Marvells Mills and Millholm, in 1648, about the date on which Millholm and Footmeadow were thrown open. The freemen declared it should be Midsummer day; Bryan claimed as right the nine days' grace which custom had sanctioned.[3] The Chamberlain's accounts frequently mention the town bull.[4] They show that 280 horses and 103 cows were depastured by freemen on the town commons in 1692 and 233 horses and 221 cows in 1698. The annual branding of the freemen's cattle by the town chamberlain became the occasion of a public holiday and a town feast.[5]

In 1778, in spite of the opposition of the corporation,[6] an act was passed for enclosing the open fields.[7] That the scheme was in contemplation as far back as 1752 appears from a lease in that year of a farm in Northampton Fields for fifteen years 'if the open fields remain so long unenclosed.'[8] The fields of Hardingstone, Kingsthorpe, Moulton and Duston had been enclosed between 1765 and 1776. The commissioners' award under the act of 1778, dated 24 June 1779, is at the County Hall. It assigns to the corporation 133 acres of land in five allotments, and to the freemen, at the special request of the corporation,[9] 87 a. 1 r. 29 p. on the raceground, to be subject to a horserace to be held between 20 July and 20 October every year. Trustees were appointed for the management of the new commons created by the award.[10] In 1870 the town held 189 a. 0 r. 39 p. of commons, including the Freemen's common on the racecourse (formerly part of Northampton Heath), where every freeman could pasture 6 head of cattle at fixed rates; the Old Commons, vested in the corporation, comprising Midsummer Meadow, Cow Meadow, Calves Holme, Baulms Holm and Foot Meadow; and the New Commons, also vested in the corporation.[11] Under the Northampton Corporation Markets and Fairs Act of 1870,[12] the freemen were given certain rights in the New Commons in return for giving up their rights in a portion of the Cow Meadow for the building of the present Cattle Market (1870-73). In 1882, under the Northampton Corporation Act of that year,[13] the freemen's rights of common of pasture and all other rights in the freemen's commons were sold to the corporation for a perpetual annuity of £800, to be paid yearly to the Freemen's trustees.[14] This marks the end of the common pastures of the town as such; the racecourse is now preserved as an open recreation ground for the growing population of the northern part of the town, whilst Cow Meadow, Calvesholme and Midsummer Meadow serve that purpose in the south. The laying out of pleasure walks in Cow Meadow began as far back as 1703, when the assembly authorised the expenditure of £30 in planting trees, making walks and 'other occasions and conveniences to be ornamentall and useful.' The discovery of a chalybeate spring, called Vigo Well from the victory of 1702, had roused the hope of making Northampton a fashionable watering place.[15] In 1784 a new walk was laid out from St. Thomas of Canterbury's well to Vigo well, planted with trees 'to form an agreeable shelter' and fenced to preserve them from the cattle.[16] Since 1884 further park lands and pleasure grounds have been acquired by the town, which owned, by 1921, 409 a. 3 r. 26 p. for these purposes. Of these Abington Park was acquired in 1895 and 1903, 20 acres being presented to the corporation, with Abington Hall by Baroness Wantage in 1893, and the rest being purchased by the town; Victoria Park in St. James' End was acquired partly by purchase, partly by the gift of Earl Spencer in 1898 and 1910; Far Cotton Recreation Ground and Kingsthorpe Recreation Ground by purchase in 1912 and 1920, and Dallington Park (22 a. 3 r. 28 p.) by the gift of Messrs. C. E. and T. D. Lewis, in 1921.[17]

The first reference to a fair at Northampton is found in the charter of Simon II granting to the monks of St. Andrew's priory a tenth of the profits of the fair held on All Saints' Day in the church and churchyard of All Saints[18] which is described (1180-1183) as *ecclesia de foro in Northampton*.[19] The fair may have grown out of the church wake, and be older than the Conquest. On 9 November 1235 Henry III by letters close forbade the holding of either market or fair in the church or churchyard of All Saints, and ordered them to be held henceforth in a waste and empty place to the north of the church—the present market square.[20] The inspiration of the reforms undoubtedly came from Robert Grosseteste, Archdeacon of Northampton from 1221.[21] The date of this and many other letters of Henry III which concern the fair makes it clear that it went on well into the second half of November in the 13th century, and the parliamentary petition of 1334[22] states that at that time it lasted from All Saints' Day (November 1) to St. Andrew's (November 30). It came to be associated especially with the feast of St. Hugh (November 17),

---

[2] *Boro. Rec.* ii, 215; see following pages for detailed references to regulations here quoted.
[3] Lee, Coll. p. 106.
[4] *Boro. Rec.* ii, 222-3.
[5] Ibid. ii, 223.
[6] See Assembly Books for 7 Feb. 1770; 20 Sept. and 14 Nov. 1776.
[7] 18 George III, c. 77 (Private Act).
[8] *Northants. N. and Q.* i, 3 (1886).
[9] See Assembly Book, 18 Sept. 1778.
[10] Ibid. 2 March 1778.
[11] *Parl. Papers*, 1870, vol. 55. *Return of all Boroughs possessing common lands*, p. 22.
[12] 33 and 34 Vict. c. 45. (Local Act).
[13] 45 and 46 Vict. c. 212. (Local Act).
[14] Information from Mr. A. E. Chick.
[15] Morton, *Natural Hist. of Northants.* (1712), p. 279, says the waters are good for the stone.
[16] *Boro. Rec.* ii, 262-3.
[17] Information from *Corporation Year Book*, p. 43.
[18] Cott. MS. Vesp. E xvii, fo. 6.
[19] Serjeantson, *Hist. of Ch. of All Saints, Northampt.* p. 14.
[20] *Cal. Close*, 1234-1237, pp. 206-7.
[21] *V.C.H. Northants.* ii, 10-11.
[22] *Parl. R.* ii, 85.

A HISTORY OF NORTHAMPTONSHIRE

that Bishop of Lincoln who, in 1190, had braved the fury of the burgesses of Northampton by suppressing the cult of a pseudo victim of the Jews in All Saints' Church,[23] and had been canonised in 1220.

The fair of Northampton was one of the four or five great fairs from which purchases were systematically made for the royal household in the reigns of John and Henry III.[24] In 1208, 1212, 1213 and 1214, for instance, John ordered purchases of robes and horses to be made there.[25] In 1218 two royal bailiffs were appointed to 'keep the fair,' and look out for the royal interests there.[26] Whatever other duties these terms may cover, the two men were empowered to make prises of wool, cloth and hides for the king's use, payment being promised later. A subsequent order directed that the wool seized at the fair should be sold at rates fixed by the mayor and reeves of Northampton.[27] In 1231 William de Haverhill and William the king's tailor were ordered to buy at Northampton fair 150 robes for the knights of the king's household, 100 robes for his clerks and serjeants, fur robes for grooms (garciones), and 300 tunics for alms.[28] Other orders for the purchase of cloth at the fair of Northampton occur later.[29] In 1240 the King and Council arranged that all the King's prises from merchants should be paid for at four terms; the Northampton purchases being paid for at the fair of St. Ives, the St. Ives purchases at Boston, the Boston purchases at Winchester, and the Winchester purchases at Northampton.[30] In spite of the provision, the jurors of 1274-5 complained that Henry III owed the commonalty of Northampton £4,000 and £100 for cloth bought at the fairs of Northampton and other places.[31] Both the king and burgesses of Northampton were also in debt to Douai merchants for cloth sold at Northampton,[32] and there is an account of an uproar raised by merchants of Ypres and Douai at Northampton Fair in 1254 when the King's officials enforced the Assize of cloth.[33] The charter of 1257 provided that no foreign merchants should lodge in Northampton during the fairs without the licence of the bailiffs.[34] A deed of 1280 records the grant by Robert of Pitsford of a house in Abington Street to a burgess of Northampton on condition that during the fairs he should provide a kitchen and stabling for nine horses for the Burellers of London.[35]

In 1268 the king granted a yearly fair on St. James' day (July 25) to the abbot and monks of St. James' without Northampton,[36] and this fair, held outside the town at St. James' End beyond the west bridge, was a frequent source of dispute between the town and the abbey till the dissolution of the monasteries, when the expenses and the profits of it cancelled out.[37] After that date it became a town fair, but it continued to be held in 'le fayre yard,'[38] or elsewhere in the Abbey ground[39] till about 1700. Dr. Cox found references to a fair on St. George's day as early as the reign of Edward I.[40] In 1334, the town petitioned for a fair to last from Whitsuntide to the Gules of August, and the council recommended the grant of an eight days' fair.[41] The charter of 1337, however, granted a fair to last for four weeks from the second Monday after Trinity.[42] This fair is not mentioned in the charter of 1495, which clearly reflects the decline in Northampton trade by limiting the duration of the spring and autumn fairs to eight days each.[43] In 1566 there were still only two fairs—St. George's and St. Hugh's.[44] The charter of 1599 sanctions the holding of seven fairs, each to last three days, on St. George's Day (23 April), St. Hugh's (17 November), the Nativity of Our Lady (8 September), the Annunciation (25 March), the Conception of the Virgin (8 December), the Assumption (15 August), and St. James' (25 July).[45] When Bridges wrote (before 1724), an eighth fair had been added on 9 February.[46] The charter of 1796 retained these eight fairs, but as the old calendar was followed, the date of each was put forward eleven days. A new fair was sanctioned for 19 June (new style.)[47] By 1815 a tenth fair had been added, on the first Thursday in November, which was toll-free.[48] In 1849 there were thirteen fairs. In addition to those just mentioned there were fairs on the second Tuesday in January and the third Monday in March, whilst a new fair called the Wool Fair, on 1 July, had been recently established.[49] The fair on 19 September was known as the Cheese Fair, an innovation of Mr. Slowick Carr, Mayor of Northampton 1750-51.[50] An Act of 1870 empowered the corporation of Northampton to establish markets and fairs,[51] and at present there are twelve fairs, the wool fair having been dropped.[52]

The charter of 1599 sanctioned the holding of a free market every Wednesday, Friday and Saturday by the burgesses 'as heretofore accustomed.'[53] In 1683 they were also granted a cattle market for the first Thursday in every month.[54] In 1740 the market day was Saturday;[55] in 1849, as now, Wednesday and Saturday were the market days.[56] Wednesday is the day for fat stock, Saturday for store cattle. The cattle market, opened in 1873, is on part of the Cow Meadow, and extends over six acres, with accommodation for 5,000 sheep, 5,000 beasts, and 500 pigs. The regulation of the markets was in the hands of the mayor as clerk of the markets from 1385 by charter, and probably before that date by custom. The standard weights and measures belonging to the corporation, including a bushel and gallon dated 1601, are preserved in the Town Museum.[57]

---

[23] *V.C.H. Northants.* ii, 12.
[24] The others were Boston, Stamford, Winchester, St. Ives, Bury St Edmund's. *Rot. Hund.* ii, 5.
[25] *Rot. Litt. Claus.* i, 100, 127, 154, 177.
[26] *Cal. Pat.* 1216-25, 178.
[27] *Rot. Litt. Claus.* i, 383.
[28] *Cal. Close,* 1231-34, p. 1. See also *Cal. Liberate R.* i, 3.
[29] *Rot. Litt. Claus.* i, 580b; *Cal. Pat.* 1232-47, p. 239; ibid. 1247-58, p. 371; ibid. 1266-72, pp. 393, 718.
[30] *Cal. Pat.* 1232-47, p. 239.
[31] *Rot. Hund.* ii, 5.

[32] *Cal. Pat.* 1232-47, p. 393; ibid. 1266-72, pp. 393, 717.
[33] Ibid. 1247-58, p. 430.
[34] *Boro. Rec.* i, 47.
[35] Anct. D. (P.R.O.), B.2465.
[36] *Cal. Chart.* ii, 100.
[37] *Valor. Eccl.* iv, 319.
[38] Chan. inq. p.m., Charles I, ccccxviii, 68.
[39] Bridges, op. cit. i, 501.
[40] *Boro. Rec.* i, 187.
[41] *Parl. R.* ii. 85.
[42] Chart. R. 11, Ed. III, m. 32, no. 67.
[43] *Boro. Rec.* i, 107.
[44] Ibid. ii, 297.

[45] Ibid. i, 124.
[46] Bridges, op. cit. i, 433.
[47] *Boro. Rec.* i, 177.
[48] *Hist. of Northampt.* 1815, p. 20.
[49] G. N. Wetton, *Guide-book to Northampt.* p. 86. The fair is now held in the Cattle Market.
[50] *Boro. Rec.* ii, 40.
[51] 33 and 34 Vict. c. 45. (Local Act).
[52] Kelly, *County Directory* (1924).
[53] *Boro. Rec.* i, 134.
[54] Ibid. i, 146.
[55] Bridges, op. cit. i, 433.
[56] Wetton, op. cit., p. 86.
[57] *Boro. Rec.* ii, 194-5.

BOROUGH OF NORTHAMPTON

The street names of Northampton are a fairly clear indication of the marketing centres of the medieval town. Sheep Street, The Horse Market, and the Hog Market lie in the north-western quarter; Corn Hill,[58] Malt Hill and Wood Hill north and east of the Market Square; Mercers Row to the south and the Drapery to the west of it, whilst Woolmonger Street runs to the south west, and Gold Street (once Goldsmiths' Street) runs west from the centre of the town. Henry Lee believed that the original market square was in the open space known as the Mayorhold or Marehold where the first Town Hall stood;[59] but the early description of All Saints' as *de foro*[60] suggests that in the 12th century the market was already held where it is to-day. The market square itself, known as the Chequer from the 14th century, has long been held one of the chief distinctions of Northampton. Morton in 1712 says 'The Market Hill is lookt upon as the finest in Europe; a fair, spacious, open place.'[61] Pennant calls it 'an ornament to the town; few can boast the like,'[62] and the Chartist Gammage calls it 'one of the prettiest in England.'[63] The butchers' stalls or shambles to which a number of early deeds refer[64] were probably placed here, and it is supposed that the rows mentioned in early deeds, such as wimplers' row, mercers' row, cobblers' row, cooks' row and malt row[65] ran along the west side of the square, where to-day a line of shops separates the Drapery from the market place. A market cross is mentioned in 14th and 15th century deeds, and the new one, erected in 1535, a fine piece of Renaissance work, as described by Henry Lee,[66] was destroyed in the fire of 1675. The market place also contained the great conduit, erected about 1481, a building of two or three stories, with a hall above the conduit which was used for meetings of companies that had constitutions for regulating trade,[67] and with arches below containing shops in the 17th and a bridewell in the 18th century. These, with all the buildings round the market square, except the Town Hall and Dr. Danvers' House in its north-east corner, were destroyed in the fire of 1675.[68] From an early date the market square has been the centre of the civic no less than the mercantile life of the borough, and has witnessed a series of notable public meetings such as the holding of the forest eyre of 1637,[69] the disputed election 'by the popularity' in 1663,[70] the great debate between Fergus O'Connor and Richard Cobden in 1844,[71] down to the public reception of the present King and Queen on 23 September 1913.[72]

The fair and market days were the only occasions on which foreigners were allowed to sell their wares in Northampton, and the fair and market tolls made an important part of the borough revenues. They were levied by the town bailiffs or their deputies at a fixed scale of rates, revised from time to time in the assembly.[73] Besides the market tolls, smaller tolls on the sale of corn and wood in the town were leviable, and the corn toll was collected in kind down to 1775.[74] The position of Northampton as the county market town is well illustrated by the corn riots of 1693-4. In November 1693 the 'mobile' cut sacks of corn and threw the wagons into the river on several market days in succession, whilst many came to the market with knives in their girdles to force the sale of corn at their own prices.[75] In June 1694 again loads of corn were seized and the mayor and his brethren defied and knocked about; and a free fight took place in which two were killed and some sixty wounded.[76] The occasion of the riots was the dearth noted by Lee, together with the sight of corn being sold in large quantities out of the town—presumably for the troops over sea.[77] The market for beasts and sheep, of little or no importance in the 18th century, was revived in 1802 by the mayor of that time and developed steadily thenceforward.[78]

Besides the tolls on sales, traverse tolls were collected, from the 12th century if not earlier, from beasts and burdens passing through the town. In the oldest borough custumal (*c.* 1190) it is said that these tolls are collected at certain fixed places.[79] According to the presentment of the jurors in the eyre of 1329,[80] they had been collected since 1264, when the town was in the king's hand, at points along the roads leading to Northampton, distant, in some cases, as much as fifteen miles from the town, so as to prevent strangers evading the toll by going round the town instead of through it. At this date the toll places were at Slipton on the Kettering road, at Billing Bridge on the Wellingborough road, and at Syresham Cross on the Brackley Road.[81] In the reign of Elizabeth the tolls were collected at the entrance to the town, and it had become customary for the bailiffs to lease the right of collecting them to private persons.[82] In 1765 the market tolls and traverse tolls together were let at a rent of £87 a year. The system was continued to 1829, the rents falling to 70 guineas in 1801 and rising to £219 in 1829, owing probably to stricter exaction. This increased stringency led to resistance, and finally to the great Toll Cause of *Lancum v. Lovell* in 1831, when the corporation incurred expenses of over £2,000 in defending its rights to levy the tolls.[83] The test case was fought on a claim for 11d. toll upon oxen bought in

---

[58] The *Corn Chepinge* is mentioned in 1265 (*Cal. Chart.* ii, 53) and the *Strauschepinge* in 1301 (*Hist. MSS. Com. Rep.* 15, App. x, p. 73).
[59] Lee, Coll. p. 91.   [60] See above.
[61] Morton, *Nat. Hist. of Northants.* p. 23.
[62] *Journey from Chester to London* (1780), p. 306.
[63] R. G. Gammage, *Hist. of the Chartist Movement*, 1894, p. 117. The iron lamp in the middle of the market square was given in 1863 by Capt. Samuel Isaacs of the Northants Rifle Volunteers.
[64] Anct. D. (P.R.O.), B. 2466, 2467, 2484, e.g. 'quoddam schamellum in rengo schamellorum carnificum,' cf. 'Butchers Row,' in Anct. D. B. 3232; 'Kytstalles,' *Boro. Rec.* ii, 283.

[65] Northampt. Corp. Deeds, Press C. 1, C. 6; Anct. D. (P.R.O.), 6444, 2549, 2764; Add Ch. 6117.
[66] Lee, Coll. pp. 94-5.   [67] Ibid. p. 132.
[68] Hartshorne, *Hist. Mem. of Northampt.* p. 234. The Riding, a small street in this neighbourhood, is named after the Riding School, where Methodism was first preached in Northampton in 1766.
[69] Bridges, op. cit. i, 431.
[70] Lee, Coll. p. 113
[71] Gammage, *Hist. of Chartist Movement*, p. 254-5.
[72] *Northampt. Independent*, 2.
[73] *Boro. Rec.* ii, 188-90.   [74] Ibid. 191.
[75] *Cal. S. P. Dom.* 1693, p. 397.
[76] Ibid. Add. 1689-1695, p. 262.
[77] Ibid. p. 263; 1694-5, p. 228.

[78] *Report of the Trial for the Northampt. Toll Cause* (Northampt. 1833), pp. 241-2. The receipts for tolls and rents at the Cattle Market were in 1914 £2,923, and in 1927 £4,462 and for the General Market in 1914 £2,100 and in 1927 £7,035.
[79] Douce MS. (Bodl. Lib.), 98, fo. 159 vo.
[80] Assize R. 635, m. 51, m. 70.
[81] So in the Liber Custumarum of *c.* 1460, *Boro. Rec.* i, 222. See also *Rot. Hund.* ii, 2, and Assize R. 619, m. 75, for private persons who were trying in 1274 and 1285 to usurp the town's right of collecting these tolls.
[82] *Boro. Rec.* ii, 201-206.
[83] *Parl. Papers* 1835, vol. xxv, pp. 1971, 1973.

A HISTORY OF NORTHAMPTONSHIRE

Northampton market, and 10d. traverse toll upon laden waggons going through the town, and a great body of legal precedents was cited—and misinterpreted—by counsel for and against the corporation.[84] Judgment was given for Lancum, the lessee of the corporation, in February 1832, but an application for a new trial was granted, on the ground of the rejection of legal evidence, in January 1833.[85] However, the defendant, an old countryman, died in July 1833 before the fresh trial could be held.[86] The case revealed a good deal of ill feeling between the corporation and the agriculturists of the surrounding district, though a declaration signed by 244 farmers and graziers of the neighbourhood expressed their appreciation of the value of the Northampton fairs.[87] One of the first acts of the reformed corporation was to discontinue the traverse tolls, as contrary to the spirit of the time and the freedom of trade, in 1836.[88]

TRADES The fact that leather clippings were found with a coin of Edward the Confessor at the bottom of a well covered by the Norman earthworks of the castle[89] has been adduced in proof of the existence of a pre-Conquest leather trade. There is, however, no early evidence of any outside market for Northampton leather goods and all the medieval sources suggest that textile industries took the first place in the days of the town's early prosperity. The earliest custumal (c. 1190) mentions no craft but that of the weaver, who is classed with the nurse as a domestic servant not to be enticed away by a rival employer.[90] It also refers to the sale of wool, thread, fresh hides, honey, tallow, cheese and flesh by the burgesses at the fair. In 1202 Northampton was one of eleven towns which purchased the right to buy and sell dyed cloth as they were wont to do under King Henry, that is, without keeping the assize of 1197.[91] We have seen that the Northampton fairs were noteworthy for the sale of cloth and of furs in the reigns of John and Henry III, and the petition of the burgesses to Parliament in 1334 indicates that some of this cloth at least was home made. ' In the time of King Henry . . . when the staple of wool was at divers places in England . . . there were at Northampton 300 workers of cloths, who paid on every cloth a fixed sum towards the farm of the town, as well as a fixed rent from their houses where they used to dwell in the said town, which are now fallen to the ground.'[92] The 13th century custumal contains regulations as to dyeing, and regulations as to the weaving of cloth, dated 1251, which bear out the other evidence as to the importance of the trade.

Clause 23. Consideratum est quod nullus operarius pannorum ponat in panno suo, sc. imperiali, brasil nec tinctum de verme, nec in albo stragulato scorthe neque aliam falsam tincturam. . . .

24. Si pannus inueniatur terra tinctus, et proprius pannus fuerit tinctoris, amittatur, et si alienus et ex consensu ipsius fecerit, similiter amittatur. Et sinon de consensu ipsius tinctor abjuret officium suum per annum et diem. . . .

25. Nullus tinctor menstruet aliquem pannum calce. . . .

26. Nullus operatur pannos nisi pannus sit de rationabili sequela sc. peior ulna in panno tincto non valeat minus unum denarium ad plus et imperiale unum obolum.

34. Consideratur quod si aliquis textor alicuius pannum male texerit et super hoc convictus fuerit amittat laborem suum (et) duos denarios ad commodum ville.

35. Operatores pannorum qui textores sunt non sedeant super utensilia[93] ad pannos suos proprios nec alienos texandos.[94] . . .

36. Provisum est quod quilibet pannus albus sit de triginta et triginta porteriis et imperiale de viginti et sex et viginti septem. Albus stragulatus eius latitudinis.[95]

These regulations indicate advanced development both in technique and in organisation; both dyers and weavers are represented as working with other men's material. Other regulations provide that woaders from outside the town may only bring in woad and sell it by licence of inspectors,[96] and forbid dyers to throw their waste products into the streets.[97] Scarlet Well is mentioned as early as 1239,[98] and local tradition, according to Morton, asserted that London cloth had formerly been sent to Northampton to be dyed,[99] and that cloth miscoloured at Nottingham was brought to a good scarlet here.[1] The eyre roll of 1247 records the death of a dyer, scalded by falling into a vat of his own dye.[2] The Fullers' Street is mentioned in a deed of 1250-60,[3] the Drapery 1202-1220,[4] the Wimplers' Row as early as 1189-94.[5] Northampton burgesses were employed as experts by Henry III to buy cloth for him at Lynn and Stamford.[6] In 1274 the jurors giving a list of the craftsmen (*menestralli*) who have left the town to escape the heavy tallages, mention fullers, weavers, dyers, drapers, glovers and skinners,[7] and mention burgesses with the surnames Waydour (or woader) Mercer, Comber, Tinctor, as well as a *linarius*. The estreats of the town court, c. 1290, mention a taverner, a carpenter, a baker, a fisher, a maltmongere, a miller, a knyfsmith, a carter, a peyntour, a skynnere, a woman maker of cords, a catour, a laver, a latoner, a tailor, and a plomer.[8] Pentecost de Kershalton, mayor of Northampton in 1297, 1301, 1302, 1304, 1307 and probably some other years also, was a ' deyster.'[9]

The petition of 1334 testifies to a decline in cloth

---

[84] *Report of the Trial of the Northampt. Toll Cause, Lancum v. Lovell.* Northampt. 1833.
[85] Ibid. pp. 313-455. [86] Ibid. p. 461.
[87] *Boro. Rec.* ii, 207. [88] Ibid. ii, 208.
[89] *Assoc. Arch. Soc. Rept.* xv, pt. ii, p. 205.
[90] Bateson, *Boro. Customs* (S.S.) i, 215.
[91] Pipe R. 48, m. 11 d.
[92] *Parl. R.* ii, 85.
[93] This would appear to forbid the use of a loom in which the warp was kept tight by means of a bar on which the weaver sat, instead of his usual separate seat. This would produce an uneven strain, and so bad cloth. (Information from Mr. L. F. Salzman.)
[94] The last two clauses are dated 25 March, 35 Henry III.
[95] Douce MS. (Bodl. Lib.), 98, ff. 161 v, 162.
[96] Ibid. fo. 162 v.; c.f. Bateson, *Rec. of Boro. of Leices.* i, 250.
[97] Douce MS. (Bodl. Lib.), 98, fo. 161 v.
[98] *Boro. Rec.* ii, 256.
[99] Morton, *Nat. Hist. of Northants.* (1712), p. 270. *Not* as stated in *V.C.H. Northants.* ii, 336, in Morton's own time.

[1] *Boro. Rec.* ii, 256.
[2] Assize R. 614 B. m. 48 d. This seems to be the meaning of ' cecidit in uno plumbo bullienti de jaleis ' (weld ?).
[3] *Anct. D.* (P.R.O.) A. 9876.
[4] Cott. MS. Tib. E. 5, fo. 181 b.
[5] Northampt. Corp. Deeds, Press C 1.
[6] *Cal. Pat.* 1232-47, pp. 300, 449.
[7] *Rot. Hund.* ii, 3.
[8] *Northants. Notes and Queries* (New Ser.), v, 203-211.
[9] *Boro. Rec.* ii, 549; Memoranda Rolls; Northampt. Corp. Deeds, Press C. 43.

BOROUGH OF NORTHAMPTON

working in the 14th century, shared by Northampton with Leicester, Oxford, Stamford and Nottingham.[10] Nevertheless, Northampton, as we have seen, had its own seal for the cloth subsidy. James Hart, writing in 1633, speaks of the ruins of great buildings once employed in the clothing trade,[11] but the only building recorded is the Wool Hall, and 14th century notices of Northampton refer rather to the wool trade than to the cloth industry. In 1274 six burgesses had been presented for exporting wool to foreign parts, contrary to the king's prohibition, one being responsible for 68 and another for 80 sacks.[12] Northampton sent four of its merchants to the merchants' assembly of 1337 which formed the syndicate that cornered the wool of England for the benefit of Edward III,[13] and there are other indications of a wool trade of some importance.[14] But in its wool trade no less than its cloth trade it was completely outdistanced by other towns and counties of England.[15]

The frequent presence of the king and court must have stimulated various other crafts besides the textile. In 1224, when besieging Bedford, Henry was able to call on the smiths of Northampton for 4,000 quarrels, well headed and feathered, and for 150 good pickaxes.[16] Two cartloads of Gloucester iron were also to be sent from Northampton to Bedford for the king's works there. Hides, both white and tanned, were demanded, and with them two saddlers with their craftsmen for making targes.[17] The trades mentioned in 1274 not concerned with the clothing or leather industries were mostly victualling; vintners, spicers, mustarders, fishmongers.[18] A goldsmith is mentioned in 1233;[19] a tanner and a parchment maker in 1247.[20] In 1325 37 pairs of shoes and two of boots were stolen from one shop;[21] and there were a Tanner's Street, a Glovery, a Saddlery and a "Cordwauria" near All Saints' in 1332.[22] In the eyre roll of 1329 there is mention of weavers, skinners, barbers, dyers, tailors, shearmen, brewers, taverners, garlic-mongers (or aillours), masons, cordwainers, cobblers, curriers, and a *romongeour*.[23]

Amongst the economic ingredients of medieval Northampton, the Jews ought not to be overlooked. Jews of Northampton occur on the Pipe Rolls from 1170,[24] and there was an anti-Semitic riot here in 1190 which St. Hugh intervened to check.[25] In 1194 Northampton with 39 Jews comes fifth on the list of English towns with Jewries, after London (112), Lincoln (82), Norwich (42), and Gloucester (40).[26]

In that year a chest was set up at Northampton, as elsewhere, for the deposit of Jewish bonds and deeds, and two Jews and two Christians appointed as custodians. Henry III commanded in 1237, not for the first time, that no Jew should live in Northamptonshire outside the king's town of Northampton,[27] and showed his sense of responsibility for them by his command to the leading burgesses in June 1264 to protect the Jews who had taken refuge in the castle during the disorders of the spring.[28] Some of the Jews who had deposited their chattels with Christians for safe-keeping in the emergency found it difficult to recover them later.[29] The Plea Rolls of the Jewish Exchequer shew us the Jews of Northampton acting as bankers for both town and county. Burgesses like Robert son of Henry or Robert of Leicester borrowed money from them at the illegal rate of 10d. a week in the pound;[30] knights of the shire, like Robert de Pavely of Paulers Pury or Hugh de Chanceaux of Upton, pledged their manors to them.[31]

In the 13th century the Jewish community in Northampton must have been shrinking steadily. A number of houses once possessed by Jews in Northampton are mentioned as being granted by the king to other persons, such as to the Master of the Temple in 1215,[32] the earl of Winchester in 1218,[33] Philip Marc in 1219,[34] Stephen de Segrave in 1229,[35] and Robert de Mara in 1248.[36] In 1277 the Northampton Jews were charged with a ritual murder,[37] and in 1278 a general attack on them for clipping and forging coin led to the execution and forfeiture of many Northampton Jews.[38] A series of grants of houses once belonging to Jews are enrolled on the Charter Roll 1280-1286.[39] When the Jews were finally expelled in 1290 the inquest into their houses, rents and tenements showed that 5 houses were held in Northampton by five separate Jews, and the community of the Jews held a synagogue, two houses near its entry, two houses outside the north gate and a burial ground.[40] A later document suggests that the synagogue of the Jews, granted to the Abbot of St. James in 1291,[41] lay in Silver Street.[42] Other Jews' houses are described as lying in the Corn Row,[43] in the market place,[44] in Larttwychene,[45] in Berewardstrete,[46] in the Cornechepyng,[47] whilst Henry Lee describes as Jewish three houses standing before the fire of 1675, one near the Red Lion in the Horsemarket, one near the Ram in the Sheepmarket, and one in Silver Street.[48] The Jewish community then were not confined to one

---

[10] *Eng. Hist. Rev.* xxxix, 22.
[11] Hart, *Diet of the Diseased*, p. 149.
[12] *Rot. Hund.* ii, 4.
[13] Unwin, *Finance and Trade under Edward III*, p. 189.
[14] Woolmonger Street is mentioned 1329 (Assize R. 635, m. 67 d.) A bond of 1319 is extant for the delivery of a half-sack of good ewes' wool by a Northampton merchant to a man of Ashby St. Ledgers. Anct. D. (P.R.O.) A. 9616.
[15] *Eng. Hist. Rev.* xxxix, p. 34; *Parl. R.* v, 275.
[16] *Rot. Litt. Claus.* i, 612, 613, 615.
[17] Ibid. i, 606.
[18] *Rot. Hund.* ii, 1–5.
[19] Anct. D. (P.R.O.) C. 2280.
[20] Assize R. 614 B. m. 48.
[21] Ibid. 635, m. 64.
[22] Add. Ch. 6117.
[23] Assize R. 635, mm. 61–70.
[24] Jacobs, *Jews of Angevin England*, p. 73
[25] *V.C.H. Northants.* ii, 11.
[26] Jacobs, op. cit. pp. 378, 381. In 1255 the relative position of Northampton was a good deal lower; the share of the Northampton Jewry in the tallage of that year was equal to that of Bedford and Bristol, and below those of Oxford, Worcester, Winchester, York and Canterbury. *Cal. Pat.* 1247–58, p. 443.
[27] *Cal. Close*, 1234–7, p. 425.
[28] *Cal. Pat.* 1258–66, p. 320–1. The baronial party was responsible for massacres of Jews at London and Canterbury in April 1264. *Annal. Mon.* (Rolls Ser.), iii, 230; *Liber de Ant. Leg.* p. 62.
[29] Rigg, *Cal. Plea R. of Exc. of Jews*, p. 191.
[30] Ibid. pp. 34, 39.
[31] Ibid. pp. 114, 287; *Cal. Pat.* 1266–72, p. 534.
[32] *Rot. Litt. Claus.* i, 196.
[33] Ibid. i, 366.
[34] Ibid. i, 386.
[35] *Cal. Close*, 1227–31, p. 276.
[36] Ibid. 1247–51, p. 130.
[37] *V.C.H. Northants.* ii, 13.
[38] *Annal. Mon.* (Rolls Ser.), iii, 279; *Cal. Pat* 1272–81, p. 362.
[39] Chart. R. 73, mm. 2, 3, 4; 74 m. 4; 75 m. 2.
[40] Extents and Surveys, 143, 1-2, no. 40. See *Cal. Pat.* 1281–92, p. 381, for safe conduct oversea to a Northampton Jew mentioned in the Extent.
[41] *Cal. Pat.* 1313–17, p. 199.
[42] Cox and Serjeantson, *Hist. of Ch. of Holy Sepulchre, Northampt.*, p. 126.
[43] Extents and Surveys, 143, 1-2, no. 40.
[44] Ibid.
[45] Ibid.
[46] Chart. R. 74, m. 4.
[47] *Cal. Pat.* 1358–61, p. 211.
[48] Lee, Coll. p. 95.

Jewry, though they seem to have preferred the northern and western parts of the town.

There is no clear reference to any craft organisation till the 15th century, though the 13th century custumal refers to master butchers,[49] and the expression *bachelerie de Northampton* has been interpreted to mean associations of journeymen,[50] the economic equivalent of the political *bacheleria*. The economic regulations of the 13th century custumal show the *prepositura* as the authority regulating primarily conditions of buying and selling,[51] but also, in the case of weavers, dyers and butchers, the quality of the goods offered for sale. The butcher pays a fee to the town, ' as he used to do to his peers,' for the right to become a master.[52] And when in the 15th century the town records begin, it is noteworthy that the town government takes the initiative, in one instance at least, in forming a craft gild, and keeps throughout a controlling hand on the regulations of the crafts, both assisting in drafting the rules, swearing in the wardens and demanding reports from them, and enrolling the constitutions in the town records. In these craft ordinances the textile industries are still prominent. In 1427 the shearmen are commanded to organise themselves under two wardens, who are to inspect the quality of the work and report to the mayor.[53] The existence of turbulent organisations of journeymen is indicated in the regulations for the weavers' craft in 1432,[54] which are designed to put an end to ' many and dyverse unfittyng contestes and debates . . . which have long tyme regned in the Crafte of Englisshe wevers of Norhampton bitwene the Maistirs and the jorneymen of the seide crafte.' The ordinances of 1432 refer to old-established customs such as the Easter procession to St. Mary de la Pré outside the town, and the ' customable drinking' that followed the offering of wax tapers there, and further illustrate the cleavage within the craft by the prohibition of ' confederacyes, conventicles and gederyngs.' Supplementary regulations of the weavers' craft were passed in 1439, 1441, 1448[55] and 1462, when a six years' apprenticeship was provided for, and a supervision of the licensing of new weavers by the warden of the craft, acting with two of the Twenty Four comburgesses.[56] In 1511 the inspection of cloths by the ' searchers ' was further regulated.[57] The formation of the Tailors' Craft Gild in 1444-5 is of great interest : the industry was so important to the town as a whole that the town government took the initiative and compelled the tailors to accept a constitution. ' Full many gentilmen and other people of oure lorde the Kynge for the shapyng of theire clothyng and of their servauntes and of theire lyvereys dayly comen to the same town. Nevertheles noo Rule ne order put ne is in the said Crafte betwene thartificers and mynystres of the seide Crafte. . . . Wherefore the seide gentilmen . . . oft tymes for unhable shapyng . . . aren . . . disseived to her prejudice and also sclaunder and detriment to the saide toun. And therefore the saide Maire and his Comburgeis by the comyn Assent of the seide toun wyllen in the saide Crafte ordynaunce and good Rule be putt.'[58] By this constitution overseers were set up, with power to correct and to call meetings of the craft. The town assembly confirmed the regulations for tailors and woollen drapers jointly in 1588.[59] In 1452 the fullers' craft was organised on similar lines,[60] further regulations being added in 1464, 1511 and 1585.[61] In like manner, constitutions or regulations were made for the corvisers and cordwainers in 1401 and 1452,[62] the shoemakers in 1552,[63] the glovers in 1594;[64] the whittawyers and tanners in 1566 and 1582;[65] the bakers in 1467, 1518, 1545 and 1553;[66] the butchers in 1505, 1558, and 1568;[67] the fishmongers in 1467 and 1574;[68] the innkeepers in 1383, 1568 and 1570;[69] the brewers in 1545,[70] the carpenters in 1430;[71] the slaters in 1509;[72] whilst in 1562 the ironmongers' constitution was cancelled.[73] All these regulations are duly enrolled in the *Liber Custumarum* or, after 1553, the Assembly Books. In 1574 a number of unorganised trades—mercers, haberdashers, linendrapers, grocers, apothecaries, upholsterers, salters and tryers of honey and wax—were ordered to meet at St. Katharine's Hall in the last week of October and choose themselves wardens, with various other regulations to bring them into line with the other tradesmen.[74] In all these constitutions, drafted by the mayor and the craftsmen jointly, the craftsmen elect their own wardens or searchers, who are sworn in before the mayor at the guildhall on the court day.[75] Regular fees are payable to the town chamber and fines for breaches of the regulations are divided between the craft and the town. Many of the crafts with constitutions used to meet, as we have seen, in the hall over the great Conduit in the market place. The fullers and slaters used to meet at the Black Friars' House,[76] the shearmen and the shoemakers at the White Friars.[77] After the Dissolution the shoemakers used to meet in St. George's Hall.[78]

Some indication of the comparative importance of different trades in the town is given by the lists of town bailiffs between 1386 and 1461,[79] in which in many instances, their crafts are named. Nineteen bailiffs were mercers, eleven drapers, eight dyers, six fullers, six hosiers, two weavers, and two woolmen. There were eight bakers and six fishmongers ; five glovers and five ironmongers. Other evidence suggests that Northampton continued to be of some importance as a clothing centre. There are frequent references to the fullers and their tenters in the Assembly Books from 1550 to 1630.[80] The Privy Council notes in 1577 that merchants of Norwich, London and Northampton are in the habit of buying and selling wool at Northampton, driving up the price, to the

---

[49] Douce MS. (Bodl. Lib.), 98, fo. 162 (cl. 27).
[50] *History Teachers' Miscellany*, v, 31.
[51] E.g. : purchase of a stall (cl. 3, 11), freeman's share in bargains (cl. 4), forestalling and regrating (cl. 5, 7, 9, 16, 21), weights and measures (cl. 6, 13), sale of woad (cl. 31, 39).
[52] Custumal cl. 27.
[53] *Boro. Rec.* i, 356–8.
[54] Ibid. 268–72.
[55] Ibid. 272–4. [56] Ibid. 298–9.
[57] Ibid. 331.
[58] Ibid. 265 ; cf. 278–82.
[59] Ibid. ii, 295. [60] Ibid. i, 290–4.
[61] Ibid. 302, 332 ; ii, 288.
[62] Ibid. 245, 294.
[63] Ibid. ii, 293.
[64] Ibid. 289. [65] Ibid. 295–7.
[66] Ibid. i, 309, 333, 380 ; ii, 278.
[67] Ibid. 334 ; ii, 280.
[68] Ibid. 307 ; ii, 286.
[69] Ibid. 249 ; ii, 295–7.
[70] Ibid. 352.
[71] Ibid. 237.
[72] Ibid. 329. [73] Ibid. ii, 290.
[74] Ibid. 276–8.
[75] The oaths of the wardens and searchers of the crafts are enrolled in the Liber Custumarum, *Boro. Rec.* i, 394–397, including one for the chandlers, whose constitution is not enrolled.
[76] *Boro. Rec.* i, 291, 330.
[77] Ibid. i, 356 ; ii, 183.
[78] Ibid. ii, 181–5.
[79] Ibid. 556–8. [80] Ibid. 217–8.

BOROUGH OF NORTHAMPTON

great decay of clothing in the shire.[81] The enrolments of apprentices on the town records show the tailors as the most popular industry in the 16th and early 17th centuries, and the clothing trades running the leather trades close for the first place in the town. There is a marked revival in weaving in the second half of the 18th century, and though the shoemaking trade is by now well ahead, the poll books of the elections of 1768, 1784 and 1790 show a large number of woolcombers and weavers. 'A century ago,' says James, writing in 1857, 'the woolstaplers of Northampton were the local magnates, the weavers of serges, tammies and shallons more numerous than the shoemakers of the present day.'[82] In 1768 the weavers seem to have congregated about the Mayorhold and St. Giles', and the woolcombers in Bridge Street and the south quarter in general, where it may be presumed the fullers would also be found, from the proximity of the Cow Meadow, where their tenters stood in the 16th and 17th centuries.[83]

The apprenticeship statistics cannot be regarded as exhaustive, but they give some indication of the proportion in which the different industries were pursued in Northampton in the 17th and 18th centuries, and of the extent to which the town population was recruited from the country.[84] Of the great advance of the shoemaking industry in this period an account has been given in the previous volume.[85] In 1619 the complaint of the nuisances caused by tanners, glovers, whittawyers and parchment makers washing their hides in the river and the watercourses of the Cow Meadow[86] suggests that the leather trade was active, but the glovers were still, apparently, as important as the shoemakers. By 1662, however, Fuller could say 'This town stands on other men's legs,'[87] and in 1689 the shoemakers of Northampton, petitioning against a bill for the free transport of unwrought leather overseas, asserted, 'A very considerable part of the trade of this town has consisted, *time out of mind*, in the manufacture of boots and shoes, great quantities of which have been sent abroad.'[88] The colonial and military demand for Northampton boots and shoes is thus of old standing, and war, from 1642 onwards, has been a marked stimulant to the industry. In 1794 the town was producing from 10,000 to 12,000 pairs a week, as against 7,000 to 8,000 in time of peace,[89] and its achievements in the war of 1914-18 were in accordance with previous traditions. During the four years of the war Northampton supplied the Allied forces with 23 million pairs, Northamptonshire contributing another 24 million, as against 23 million from the rest of the country.[90] These included infantry boots for the French, Serbian, Italian, Roumanian and American forces, Russian Cossack boots, Canadian knee boots, ski boots, rope-soled boots for the Tank corps, submarine deck boots, Flying corps boots, highland shoes, mosquito boots, seamen's shoes, and hospital slippers, as well as the standard B.5. British infantry boot.[91] When the period of Army requisitioning ended, however, the *Northants Journal of Commerce* observed that the army boot was a far heavier product than Northampton manufacturers and Northampton operatives cared to handle, as they preferred a higher grade boot.[92]

In the 17th and 18th centuries Northampton was noted as a centre for the purchase of horses. Baskervill refers to the horse fairs in 1673,[93] and Morton in 1712 says that Northampton is famed for the best horses in England.[94] The Earl of Moray writes of a friend in 1683: 'He is busy getting horses: he is resolved to have them good or not at all, and if he get them not here (in London) he will go down to Northampton, where the best are.'[95] The horse fairs were still well attended in 1815. They are now held in the cattle market on the Saturday nearest to June 24.

The mills of Northampton, though not mentioned in Domesday Book, have a long history. Conches melne or the mill of Conge[97] is mentioned before 1135, and its tithe was granted to St. Andrew's Priory by Grimbold.[98] In 1274 there were two mills of that name;[1] in 1539, if we may identify the Quengions mills of the Court of Augmentations with the Congenes mill of 1329,[2] there were five, two being used for grinding 'meselyn corn,' one a 'colyn' mill for grinding wheat, and the other two being fulling mills.[3] Marvells mill is apparently identical with the Merewyns mill of 1253,[4] the Merthensmylne of the Hundred Rolls[5] and the Mervyns mylne of the Valor Ecclesiasticus.[6] It also was held by St. Andrew's,[7] like St. Andrew's mill north-west of the town and Rushmill[8] to the south-east. A postern in the town wall and a causeway seven feet wide led to it.[9] After the Dissolution it was acquired by the town, and a windmill was erected alongside of the water mills.[10] The mills having been leased to a succession of tenants,[11] were employed about 1740 for a new venture in cotton-spinning, financed by Edward Cave, the founder and editor of the *Gentleman's Magazine* and one of the original patrons of the Northampton infirmary. The carding and roller-spinning machinery invented by Lewis Paul,[12] which anticipated Cartwright's inventions, was set up in

---

[81] *Acts of the Privy Council* 1577-8, pp. 24-5.
[82] *Quarterly Review*, Jan. 1857, p. 30.
[83] *Boro. Rec.* ii, 217-8; Speed's Map of 1610.
[84] Compare evidence of registers of St. Giles, in R. M. Serjeantson, *Hist. of Ch. of St. Giles, Northampt.* p. 210-11.
[85] *V.C.H. Northants.* ii, 317 ff.
[86] *Boro. Rec.* ii, 217.
[87] Morton in 1712 (p. 23) and Lysons in 1724 (iii, 513), confirm Fuller's account of the importance of the hosiery trade, which is not reflected in the apprenticeship statistics.
[88] *Hist. MSS. Com. Rep.* xii, app. 6, p. 115. The petition is signed by fourteen shoemakers.

[89] J. Donaldson, *A View of the State of Agriculture of the County of Northampt.*
[90] W. H. Holloway, *Northampt. and the Great War*, p. 205.
[91] Ibid. pp. 207-8.
[92] *Northants. Journal of Commerce*, May 1919, p. 8.
[93] *Hist. MSS. Com. Rep.* vol. 51, p. 290.
[94] *Nat. Hist. of Northants.* p. 23.
[95] *Hist. MSS. Com. Rep.* vol. 100, p. 164, cf. vol. 117, p. 550.
[96] *History of Northampt.* (by John Cole), publ. by Birdsall, Northampt. 1815, p. 49.
[97] Northampt. Corp. Deeds, C. 14.
[98] MS. Vesp. E. xvii, fo. 18.
[1] *Rot. Hund.* ii, 1.
[2] Assize R. 635, m. 63 d.
[3] *L. and P. Hen. VIII*, vol xv, p. 563. Of the two Quengions Mills one was a fulling mill and the other a gygg mill. (Inf. from Mr. Beeby Thompson.)
[4] Assize R. 615, m. 14. A Mervin was grandfather of a donor to St. Leonard's Hospital, whose gift is dated 1190-4 by R. M. Serjeantson. *Leper Hospitals of Northampton*, p. 4.
[5] *Rot. Hund.* ii, 3.
[6] Dugdale, *Mon.* v, 193.
[7] Rot. Fin. 15 Edw. III, m. 23.
[8] Ibid.; also Assize R. 1187, m. 14 d.
[9] *Rot. Hund.* ii, 3; Assize R. 615, m. 14. This causeway was uncovered in 1889, in course of excavations at the gas works.
[10] *Boro. Rec.* ii, 291. [11] Ibid. 292.
[12] See appendix to G. J. French, *Life of Crompton*, which shows that Wyatt was not, as stated in the previous volume, the inventor.

them under the management of T. Wyatt, as described in the previous volume,[13] and for a while Marvell's Mills were known as the Cotton Mills. The venture failed, for lack of capital as much as of good management. The Nuns' mills to the south-east of the town were held by Delapré Abbey.[14] After the shoemaking and leather currying industry, the town is to-day noted for its flour mills, as well as its maltings and breweries. There are also iron-foundries of some importance.

The Northampton Chamber of Commerce was founded in 1917, and its organ, *The Northants Journal of Commerce*, began to appear in January 1919, announcing as its aim 'to extend the fame of our members' productions in every market throughout the world.'[15]

DESCRIPTION The parts of the town that have been longest inhabited are round the castle site and the churches of St. Peter and the Holy Sepulchre. The convergence of streets on the Mayorhold,[16] together with the name Newland and the reference to the waste open space by All Saints' Church in 1235 suggest that the oldest town lay entirely to the west of the road from London to Leicester. Dr. Cox believed that the wall built by Simon de Senlis I (1090–1111) ran south of St. Andrew's Priory and west of St. Giles' Church, and that the tower which was still standing not far from the Derngate in Lee's time was a survival from the Norman wall, whilst the line of wall shown on Speed's map in 1610 is assigned by him to about 1301.[17] Grants of murage were made to the town in 1224,[18] 1251,[19] and 1301,[20] the last on so large a scale as to suggest rebuilding rather than repairing. On the other hand, the action of the prior of St. Andrew's in 1264[21] seems to prove that the priory was then inside the town wall. Further repairs of the wall were authorised in 1378,[22] 1400,[23] and 1549.[24] The wall ran north and east of the town; to the west and south the river and the castle fortifications formed adequate defences. The line of the later wall and ditch is still clearly traceable from its north-west corner on the river, along the south side of St. George's Street (North Gate), Campbell Street, the Upper and Lower Mounts (East Gate), York Road, Cheyne Walk (Dern Gate), Cattle Market Road (South Gate), Weston Street, across the gas works (Marvell's mill postern)[25] and so up to the West Gate near the castle, on Black Lion Hill. There was also a postern between the East Gate and the Dern Gate, near St. Giles' Churchyard,[26] and another called the Cow Gate,[27] leading from Cow Lane (now Swan Street) into Cow Meadow. The four main gates stood where the Market Harborough, Kettering, London and Daventry roads entered the town.

The gates,[28] and the East Gate in particular,[29] are mentioned in John's reign. Those mentioned by Lee in the 17th century appear from his description to have been built in the 14th century, the East Gate being very handsome and adorned with coats of arms; the other three main gates being then used as tenements for the poor.[30] Sir Thomas Tresham describes the guard kept at the South Gate, with partisans and halberds, on the morning of Lady Day 1603, when he came to the town with the news of Queen Elizabeth's death.[31] The wall, or a part of it, between the East and North Gates, is described in an inquisition *ad quod damnum* of 1278. It was then crenellated and much used for walking purposes, by sick burgesses when they wished to take the air, by all who wanted to take short cuts to avoid the muddy lane below in winter, and by the night watchmen who spied through the battlements upon malefactors as they came in and out of the town.[32] The sheriff notes that the opposition to blocking up the battlements and the wall-walk was so strong in the town that he chose the jury from outside the borough, from Billing, Boughton, Moulton, Weston and Overstone, but their verdict was as emphatic as the townsmen could wish, and nothing was done. The walls, which had been allowed to fall into a bad condition in the 16th century, were repaired by the strenuous labours of the townsmen in 1642–3;[33] and they were destroyed by royal order in 1662.[34] A drawing in the British Museum by a foreign artist shows them as they were in 1650, when there was, apparently, no wall between the East Gate and Marvell's Mill postern.[35] The town ditch, mentioned in the inquests of 1274–5[36] and the town terrier of 1586,[37] survived the walls for a good while; part of it, near St. Andrew's Mills, was still visible in 1849,[38] whilst the section north of the Cow Meadow had only recently been filled in.[39]

If the earliest centre of the town was indeed, as the evidence indicates, the Mayorhold, it was probably the building of the castle[40] which caused the centre of gravity to shift eastwards. From the 13th century the modern market square is the commercial and civic heart of the town; and a series of deeds dealing with the transfer of house property, shops and stalls suggest the growth of a thriving eastern quarter. Early in the 14th century, however, complaints are heard of the 'decay' of the town. The petition of 1334 speaks of houses fallen to the ground, and rents thus lost;[41] an ordinance of about 1390–1400 provides for the letting out by the mayor and chamberlains of certain waste places from which no returns or profits have accrued for some time past.[42] In 1484 Richard III, in remitting fifty marks of the fee farm, accepts the mayor's account of the town as in great

---

[13] *V.C.H. Northants*. ii, 334–5.
[14] Another mill was later known as the Clack Mill, and later still as Mulliner's Mill. *Northants. Nat. Hist. Soc.* xv, 247–9.
[15] *Northants. Journal of Commerce*, no. 1.
[16] Kingswell Street led directly from the South bridge to the Mayorhold.
[17] *Boro. Rec.* ii, 515, and see map at end, which, however, represents the wall as continued along the river between St. Andrew's and the castle.
[18] *Pat. R.* 9 Hen. III, pt. 2, m. 8.
[19] Ibid. 36 Hen. III, m. 12.
[20] Ibid. 29 Edw. I, m. 6.
[21] See above, p. 3.
[22] *Pat. R.* 2 Ric. II, pt. i. m. 31.
[23] Ibid. 2 Hen. IV, pt. 1, m. 40.
[24] *Acts of Privy Council*, 1547–50, p. 391. For later repairs ordered by the town assembly, see *Boro. Rec.* ii, 428 ff.
[25] *Rot. Hund.* ii, 3.
[26] Possibly the '*posterna de Lurteborn*' of *Rot. Hund.* ii, 3.
[27] *Rot. Hund.* ii, 3.
[28] *Mem. Walt. de Coventria* (Rolls Ser.), ii, 219.
[29] *Chart. R.* 2 John, m. 4.
[30] Lee, Coll. p. 91.
[31] *Hist. MSS. Com. Rep.* vol. 103, pp. 117-123.
[32] Inq. a.q.d. 6 Edw. I, file iv, no. 21.
[33] See above, p. 12.
[34] Lee, Coll. p. 112.
[35] Add. MS. 11564 fo. 49. It is possible that this part of the town defences never had more than a ditch; but the existence of the west gate and the south-west postern seems to imply a wall here.
[36] *Rot. Hund.* ii, 3.
[37] Northampt. Corp. Deeds, Press C. 107; *Boro. Rec.* ii, 155.
[38] G. N. Wetton, *Guidebook to Northampt. and its Vicinity* (1849), p. 29.
[39] Ibid. p. 62.
[40] R. M. Serjeantson, *Hist. of the Ch. of St. Giles, Northampt.* p. 15.
[41] *Parl. R.* ii, 85.
[42] *Boro. Rec.* i, 251.

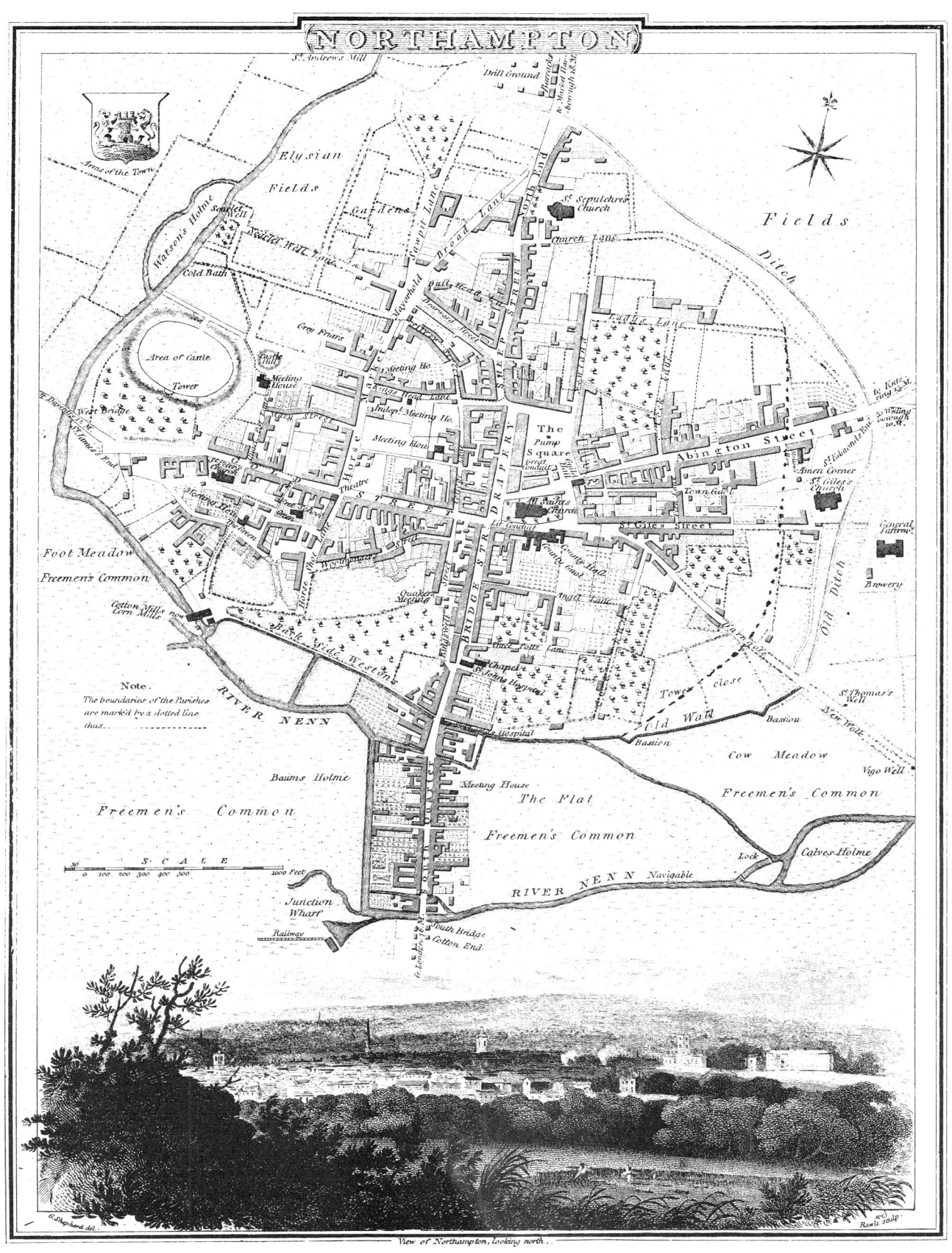

PLAN OF NORTHAMPTON IN 1810, FROM JOHN BRITTON, *BEAUTIES OF ENGLAND AND WALES*
(Reproduced by permission of Northamptonshire Libraries and Information Service)

BOROUGH OF NORTHAMPTON

desolation and ruin, half of it almost desolate and destroyed.[43] Conditions were presumably made worse by the fire of 1516, which, according to Henry Lee, consumed the greatest part of the town.[44] In 1533, Leland noted that all the old houses in Northampton were built of stone, but the new houses of wood. In 1535 an Act of Parliament empowered the mayor and burgesses, in view of the great ruin and decay of the town, to take into their hands any houses which the tenants and landlords both failed to repair, and rebuild them themselves. If the mayor and burgesses failed to do so, anyone who pleased might rebuild the houses and so acquire possession of them and the land on which they stood.[45] Again, in 1622, the mayor, in sending up to the Privy Council the corporation's contribution to the fund in aid of the palatinate, explained that the decay of the town prevented the general contribution from being good.[46] Some of these complaints may be common form; but the maps of Northampton before the fire of 1675 show large vacant spaces within the walls, especially in the S.E. quarter of the town.[47] There seems no reason to doubt that houses fell into ruin and were not rebuilt, and that the open spaces shown in Noble and Butlin's map of 1746 represent some of the 'ruin and desolation' described in 1484. The terrier of 1586 describes a large number of closes and orchards within the walls, and Northampton was long after that date noted for its cherries.

The returns of 1274–5 suggest that one cause of this 'decay' may have been the exodus of burghers who settled outside the borough boundaries to escape the burden of tallages and the like. From an early date there are references to houses in the suburbs, outside the walls,[48] though the Portsoken of the 1189 charter is probably a clerical error. To the north and east, where the town fields extended to the parishes of Kingsthorpe, Abington and Weston, there were houses outside the North Gate along the Market Harborough road round the churches of St. Bartholomew and St. Lawrence;[49] whilst outside the east gate St. Edmund's End grew up round St. Edmund's church,[50] and Gobion's homestead is described as lying in the suburb in John's reign,[51] though it rendered an annual rent to the *preposituram ville*.[52] South of the town, between the walls and the river, grew up the south quarter, still containing many waste places in 1430 which the mayor and chamberlain leased to sixteen different tenants in that year.[53] Here later was the important house of the Fermors or Farmers. Besides these suburbs, within the liberties but outside the wall, there were from a very early date important suburbs outside the liberties. Round the abbey of St. James,[54] founded about 1100 on the west side of the river, grew up St. James' End, in the parishes of Duston and Dallington. The earliest reference to the name that has been traced is in 1358,[55] but a 13th century cartulary of the abbey which mentions various streets by name shows that it was then of considerable extent.[56] South of the river, in Hardingstone parish, Cotton End[57] or St. Leonard's End, grew up along the London road round St. Leonard's Hospital and chapel.[58] In 1618, by the charter of James I to the town, St. James' End, Cotton End and West Cotton were included within the liberties, but this extension seems only to have lasted a few years, and these suburbs passed back to the county until 1901.[59]

On 20 September, 1675, a fire broke out in St. Mary's Street, near the castle, which, driven by a strong west wind across to St. Giles' Street and Derngate, destroyed more than half the town in 24 hours. Corn ricks and maltings in the Horsemarket, thatched roofs and wooden houses everywhere, oil and tallow in College Lane and timber stacked in the market place for building the new County Sessions House, all fed the blaze. The 15th century market cross, the great part of All Saints' Church with the town records stored in it, and some 600 houses were destroyed. The town hall escaped, though the staircase in front of it was burnt, but most of the buildings round the market square perished. Only one house in the Drapery survived, and Dr. Danvers' house on Market Hill, which, like the Hesilrige Mansion in Marefair, now the Ladies' Club, is still standing.[60] The tradesmen of the town had just restocked their shops at Stourbridge Fair, and the general loss of property was estimated at £150,000. In this emergency both town and county acted with promptitude. The town Recorder, the Earl of Northampton, sent in supplies at once; a meeting at the town hall 'principally managed by him,' led to the opening of a subscription list and the setting up of a committee; and by his help an Act was got through Parliament before the close of the session for the rebuilding of the town. By this Act[61] a special court of record was constituted to sit at the guildhall and determine all disputes between neighbours, landlords, tenants and occupiers as to boundaries and titles, with power to alter the lay-out of the town if it should seem necessary, and

---

[43] *Boro. Rec.* i, 98.
[44] Lee, Coll. p. 93.
[45] Stat. 27 Henry VIII, cap. i.
[46] *Cal. S. P. Dom.* 1619–23, p. 397.
[47] See especially the map of 1633 showing the property once St. Andrew's, a copy of which is in the Public Library, Northampt.
[48] Feet of F. Hen. III. 172/17, 19, 22, 25.
[49] Anct. D. (P.R.O.) C. 5147.
[50] Ibid. B. 2473.
[51] Feet of F. 1 John, no. 2.
[52] *Cal. Inq.* ii, 78.
[53] Northampt. Corp. Deeds, Press C. 48.
[54] *V.C.H. Northants.* ii, 127–30.
[55] *Cal. Pat.* 1358–61, p. 36. (*In suburbio de Northamptona vocato le Seint James-end.*)
[56] Cott. MS. Brit. Mus. Tib. E v, fo. 16 (e.g. Harper Street, St. James' Street).

[57] Northampt. Corp. Deeds, C. 19, 28, show burgesses holding land in Cotes and Coten Without.
[58] *V.C.H. Northants.* ii, 159–60.
[59] For charter (original at Northampton) see *Boro. Rec.* i, 126–7. Borough constables were appointed for Cotton End and St. James' End in 1618 and 1619, and no later. (Ibid. ii, 140). The county magistrates had jurisdiction in Cotton End in 1630. *Quarter Sessions Records of Co. of Northampt.* i, 9, 60. For St. James' End (1657) see p. 214. No explanation of this cancellation of the grant has been found. Possibly it is to be associated with the disgrace (1620–21) of Sir Henry Yelverton, Attorney-General and Recorder of the town, at whose instance James says the charter was granted. The chief charge against Yelverton was that he had inserted clauses in the charter to the city of London which the King had not authorised. The record of his trial before the Star Chamber throws no light on the Northampton charter (Star Chamber Proc. J. I. Bdle. 30, File 5). I owe this reference to the kindness of Miss W. Taffs. It should also be noted that the Privy Council memorandum of new clauses in the charter granted to the town of Northampton (Letters and Papers Domestic, James I, vol. civ, no. 83) contains no reference to St. James' End or Cotton. It is possible that the fate of London's attempt to increase her liberties surreptitiously caused Northampton to drop her acquisitions quietly.
[60] There are also groined arches remaining in the cellars of some houses in College Street.
[61] 27 Chas. II.

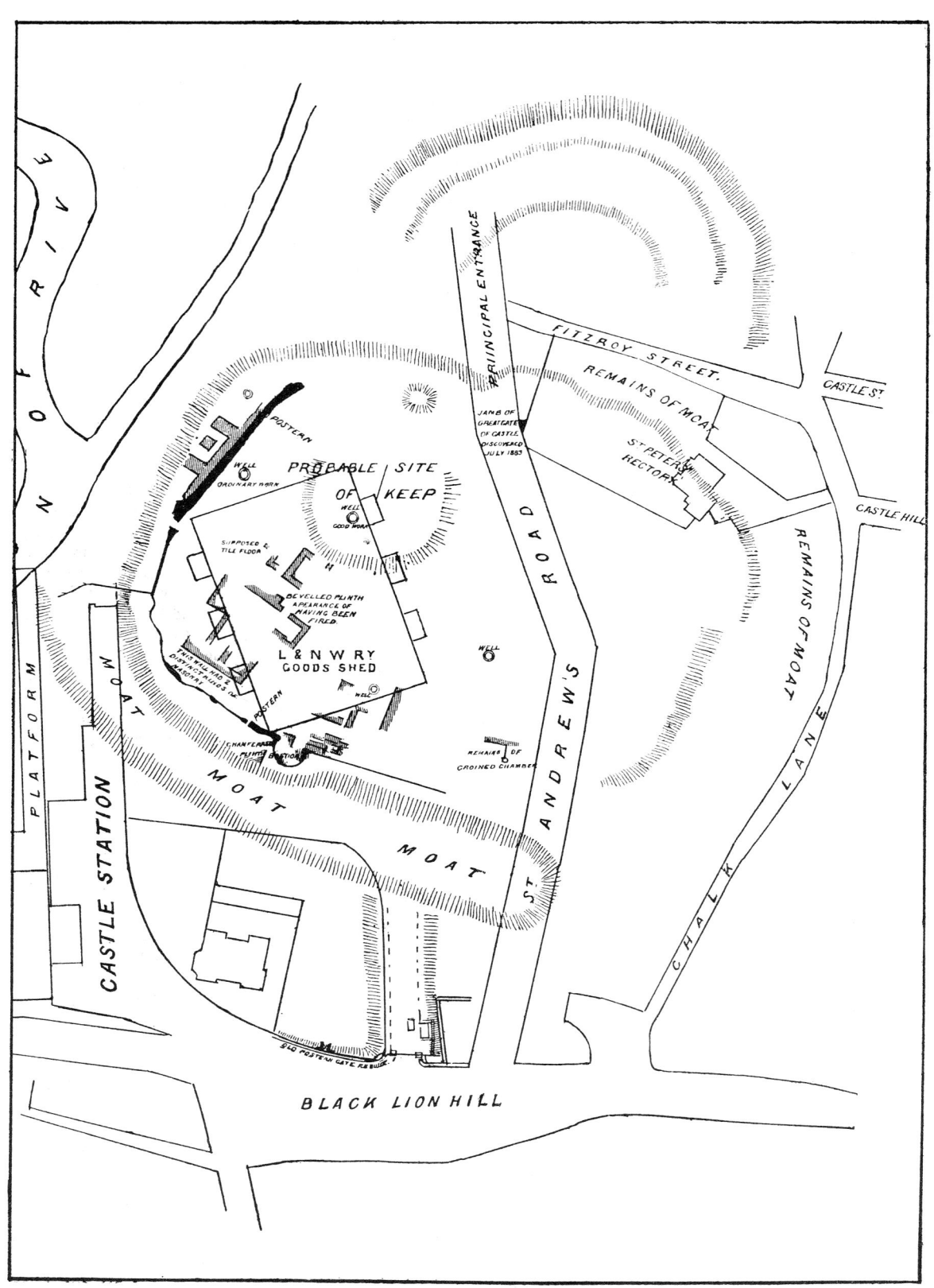

PLAN OF NORTHAMPTON CASTLE
(*Reproduced by permission of the executors of the late Rev. R. M. Serjeantson*)

BOROUGH OF NORTHAMPTON

to prescribe rules for rebuilding and enforce obedience to them. The records of this court are preserved at Northampton and form a substantial volume. They extend from April 1676 to October 1685, and deal with 79 cases.[62] Briefs and pamphlets[63] brought in generous contributions from all over England, from individuals, beginning with the King, from towns and from the two universities, amounting in all to £25,000, and the subscription list drawn up by Henry Lee the town clerk is still to be seen in All Saints' Church.[64] No great alterations were made in the town plan; the definite recommendations of the Act for widening the approaches to the market square, the narrowness of which had much increased the loss of property, were for the most part not followed, though All Saints' Church was shortened by the length of its nave and more space was thus secured in the south-west corner. Eighteenth century taste entirely approved the style of the rebuilding: Northampton, 'nobly re-edified after the fire, is now universally owned to be one of the neatest towns in the kingdom,'[65] but it was admitted that the town arose 'though much more beautiful, less spacious.'[66] The great increase in the size of the town began in the second half of the 18th century. The population rose from 5,136 in 1746[67] to 7,020 in 1801, 15,351 in 1831, 32,813 in 1861, 87,021 in 1901 and 90,923 in 1921. The increase between 1801 and 1831, which is well above the average increase over all England, is attributable to the stimulus given to the boot trade by the Napoleonic wars. The number of houses increased from 2,086 in 1821 to 3,239 in 1831.[68] The main growth of the town in the 19th and 20th centuries has been to the north-east, in the direction of Kingsthorpe, Kingsley and Abington. There has also been a considerable extension to the west and south, and a recent survey of the town[69] with a view to its future development advocates the formation of a garden city suburb on the rising ground south of the river, round the site of Delapré Abbey. The second Reform Act added parts of Dallington, Duston, Hardingstone and Kingsthorpe to the Parliamentary borough, but the municipal boundaries remained unchanged till 1901, when they were extended so as to include half Kingsthorpe, the whole of St. James' End and Far Cotton, with the exception of some small agricultural areas, and a large part of Abington, the area of the borough being thus enlarged from 1311 to 3,392 acres.[70]

In the early middle ages the borough was, like Leicester, divided into four quarters, named after the four points of the compass. These are mentioned in the rolls of the eyre of 1253.[71] To these a fifth, the Chequer Ward, round the market place, was added, Dr. Cox thought about 1300.[72] These five wards, supplemented for a few years by those of St. James and Cotton End[73] in 1618, lasted down to 1835. Under the Municipal Corporations Act of that year the town was divided into three wards; the South Ward, south of Gold Street, St. Giles' Street and Billing Road; the East Ward, east of the Drapery, Sheep Street and the Kingsthorpe Road, and the West Ward, west of the same line.[74] Each ward was represented by six councillors on the borough council. With the increase in the population, the East and West Wards outstripped the South Ward, originally the most populous, and in 1897 the East Ward contained 6,898 voters, the West 2,325, and the South 1,380. In 1898, by an order of the Local Government Board, the town was divided into six nearly equal wards: the Castle Ward, the North Ward, St. Crispin's, St. Edmund's, St. Michael's and the South Ward. Further, after a two days' inquiry at Northampton Town Hall at the beginning of 1900, the Local Government Board approved a scheme for the enlargement of the municipal borough which was embodied in an Act passed on 30 July, 1900.[75] This Act[76] added to the six wards formed in 1898 the three new wards of Far Cotton, Kingsthorpe and St. James, each, like the six old wards, returning three councillors and one alderman. In 1912, under the Northampton Corporation Act,[77] the borough was divided into twelve wards, of which Castle and St. James' Wards were unchanged from those of 1901. The name of Far Cotton Ward was changed to Delapré Ward. Part of St. Edmund's Ward was added to South Ward. Three new wards were added: Kingsley, carved partly out of the old Kingsthorpe and St. Edmund's Wards; Abington, out of the old St. Edmund's and St. Michael's Wards; St. Lawrence's, out of the old Kingsthorpe, North and St. Crispin's Wards. These twelve wards each return three councillors and one alderman.[78]

Corresponding changes took place in the civil parishes of the town in 1902 as a result of the enlargement of the borough. In 1909 the four civil parishes of All Saints, St. Giles, St. Peter and St. Sepulchre were consolidated and formed into the civil parish of Northampton.[79] In 1914 the civil parishes of Kingsthorpe, Duston St. James and the parts of Dallington and Abington within the municipal boundary were added to the civil parish of Northampton.[80]

The *CASTLE OF NORTHAMPTON*, like most royal castles, was outside the borough liberties. Originally built by earl Simon I, from the time that it

---

[62] Northampt. Corp. Books, Press N, 2a. Inrolments of decrees of Court of Judicature appointed 1675.

[63] *The State of Northampton from the beginning of the Fire . . . to November 5 . . . now recommended to all well-disposed persons in order to Christian charity and speedy relief for the said distressed people, by a Country minister.* London, 1675, Nov. 22. Reprinted in Hartshorne, *Mem. of Northampt.* pp. 224-257. *Sad and Lamentable news from Northampton,* 1675. The account given above is based upon these and Henry Lee's narratives.

[64] Printed *Boro. Rec.* ii, 250-1.

[65] Morton, *Natural History of Northants.* (1712), p. 23. See also Pennant, *Journey from Chester to London* (1782), p. 307: 'Much of the beauty of the town is due to the fire of 1675'; and Baskerville: 'Phœnix like risen out of her ashes in a far more noble and beauteous form.' *Hist. MSS. Com. Rep.* xiii, app. 2, p. 289.

[66] Notes to Noble and Butlin's map of 1746.

[67] *Parl. Papers,* 1826-27, vol. iii, p. 63.

[68] *Parl. Papers,* 1835, vol. xxv, p. 1965.

[69] *County Borough of Northampt. Proposals for Development and Reconstruction.* Published by authority of the County Borough of Northampt. 1925.

[70] 63 and 64 Vict. c. clxxxiii.

[71] Assize R. 615, m. 14.

[72] *Boro. Rec.* ii, 517.

[73] Ibid. II, 140.

[74] Northamp. Corp. Rec. Misc Docts. 45/1.

[75] *Northampt. Mercury,* 9 November 1900.

[76] L. G. B. Provisional Orders Confirmation (No. 14) Act, 63 and 64 Vict. c. clxxxiii. (Public Act of a local character.)

[77] 1 and 2 Georgii V, c. lxiv (Local Act).

[78] Information from Mr. H. Hankinson, Town Clerk.

[79] L. G. B. Order, No. 53404.

[80] Ibid. No. P. 1623.

A HISTORY OF NORTHAMPTONSHIRE

became the king's[81] it served the purposes of royal residence and stronghold and county government office and prison. The jurors of 1274–5 said that it 'belonged to the county,'[82] and an inquest of 1329 found that its constableship was by old custom appurtenant to the county and jurisdiction of the sheriff.[83] The uses to which the castle was put are illustrated by the fact that this inquest was held in the castle hall which the sheriff had been commanded to be prepared for the sessions of the justices in eyre, who sat from November 1329 to May 1330,[84] the mayor having been ordered to oversee these preparations.[85] In the same eyre the mayor protested on behalf of the town against the burgesses being forced to plead outside the liberties, but was unable to obtain a special sessions for the borough like that of 1285.[86] The castle was still outside the jurisdiction of the borough in 1655. A Duston litigant in that year writes, 'I delivered writs to the undersheriff to arrest G. and the rest. . . . He said Northampton was a privileged place and he durst not serve them. They durst not come down to the castle at Easter sessions last, for they had been out of their liberty and had been arrested.'[87] When the castle was dismantled in 1662, Charles II directed that as much should remain as was necessary for the shelter of the justices of the Bench,[88] and Henry Lee could remember the judge of Nisi Prius sitting at the castle with his back against the west wall of the Chapel of St. George.[89] The county magistrates sat there for quarter sessions down to the Epiphany term, 1671,[90] after which they sat in the town, presumably in the temporary building erected for the use of the Judges on Assize.[91] From 1670 to 1675 the town and county authorities were wrangling as to whether the new sessions house should be built in the town or on the castle site.[92] After the fire, however, it was mutually agreed that the county sessions house should be built in the town 'as an encouragement to rebuilding,'[93] and the castle ruins ceased to have any connection with the government of the county.

The greater part of the site of the castle was levelled in 1880 for the erection of the London and North-Western Railway Company's station and goods shed, and the records of what formerly existed are so fragmentary that it is difficult to reconstruct the original form of the castle. It seems to have been of the 'motte' and bailey type, common to the more important castles of the time.[94] The 'motte,' upon which stood the keep, surrounded by a moat, was apparently on the north-east side of the bailey where a flat-topped conical mound called Castle Hill was still a playground for children in the middle of the 19th century. This mound, under which a skeleton was found in 1827,[95] was approximately bounded by Chalk Lane, Castle Street, Phœnix Street and Castle Hill. The bailey, which was fortified by a rampart and ditch, was roughly circular in shape and covered about 3½ acres. It is now traversed by St. Andrew's Road, and a little to the east of the point where this road would cross the southern part of the moat was the southern entrance to the bailey, and at the spot where it would cross the northern part of the moat was the northern or principal entrance. The jamb of the gateway here was discovered in 1883. Outside this entrance were some earthworks, which it is thought covered the approach to the gate; they may, however, have been thrown up for siege purposes. The position of the curtain wall of the bailey is known on the south and west sides, and photographs exist of the wall and of a bastion on the south side. On the west side of St. Andrew's Road remains of buildings have been from time to time discovered together with four wells, and remains of the moat still exist at the north-east of the bailey in the garden of St Peter's Rectory, off Fitzroy Street.[96] Building accounts of the 12th century refer to repairs to the tower or keep (*turris*) as well as to houses in the castle (*castellum*).[97] The survey of 1323, moreover, refers to 'an old tower called Fawkestour,' which seems to have been at that date outside the curtain wall.[98] It does not appear to have formed part of the later fortifications, being ignored in Speed's map, and in the military drawing of 1650,[99] but it is shown in the plan in the *Gentleman's Magazine* for 1800,[1] which is of value as giving a cross-section from north to south of the bailey and the triple rampart guarding the northern entrance. It was finally levelled between 1827 and 1832, the earth from it being used to fill in the moat.[2]

The first Norman buildings may well have been of wood, since it would take time for the earthworks to become settled. Excavations in 1863 revealed, amongst later remains, a Norman chamber with a groined roof and a central column, which may have belonged to the castle of the time of Henry II.[3] The accounts of Becket's interviews with the King in 1164 mention a castle gateway, through which the archbishop rode; a hall; an inner chamber; an upper chamber where the King received the bishops who tried to mediate between Becket and himself; and a chapel.[4] From the time of Henry II onwards there are constant references on the Pipe Rolls, Close Rolls and Liberate Rolls to constructions and repairs at Northampton Castle.[5] The masonry uncovered in 1863 belonged mainly to the 13th and 14th centuries, and the records indicate the greatest building activity under Henry III, with extensive repairs under Edward II and Edward III. There is specific reference to the King's

---

[81] Before 1130; see Pipe R. 31 Hen. I.
[82] *Rot. Hund.* ii, 1 : *pertinet comitatui.*
[83] Fine R. 3 Ed. III, m. 4.
[84] Close R. 3 Ed. III, m. 9; 4 Ed. III, m. 32 d.
[85] *Cal. Pat.* 1327–30, p. 441.
[86] See above, p. 10, and below, p. 36.
[87] *Hist. MSS. Com.* Rep. xii, app. 3, p. 344.
[88] S. P. Dom. Charles II, Entry Book I, fo. 62.   [89] Lee, Coll. p. 98.
[90] See Records of Quarter Sessions, at County Hall, Northampt. I owe this information to the kindness of Miss Joan Wake.

[91] *Boro. Rec.* ii, 148. Note also Henry Lee's statement, that in 1670 the sessions house was removed from the castle to the Market Cross (Lee, Coll. p. 118).
[92] R. M. Serjeantson, *The Castle of Northampt.* reprinted from *Northants. Nat. Hist. Soc. and Field Club,* xiv, pp. 49–52.
[93] Ibid. p. 53.
[94] This account is based on *Assoc. Arch. Soc. Repts.* xv, ii, 198–209; xvi, 63–70, 243–251, and notes by Dr. Cyril Fox, National Museum of Wales.
[95] *Assoc. Arch. Soc. Repts.* xv, 208.
[96] Ibid. xv, 205; xvi, 247.
[97] Pipe R. 20, 23, 28, 29 Hen. II. These have been interpreted as referring to the tower in Latimer's Croft, near Derngate. If this tower was a part of the town wall there seems no reason for its appearance in the sheriff's accounts, and nothing in its later history supports this identification.
[98] Chan. Misc. Inq. 16 Edw. II, 80/15.
[99] Add. MS. 11564; reproduced in Serjeantson, *Castle of Northampt.* p. 23.
[1] *Gent. Mag.* lxx, 929.
[2] *Assoc. Arch. Soc. Repts.* xv, 208.
[3] Serjeantson, op. cit. p. 55.
[4] *Gent. Mag.* 1860, part i, 385–8.
[5] Serjeantson, op. cit. pp. 9, 11, 12, 21.

NORTHAMPTON CASTLE WALL (NOW DEMOLISHED)

NORTHAMPTON: THE OLD TOWN HALL
(*From an Old Drawing*)

BOROUGH OF NORTHAMPTON

great chamber in the castle in 1235,[6] the King's chapel in 1244,[7] the building of the Queen's chapel in 1247,[8] fitted with glass windows in 1248,[9] the King's wardrobe, the great hall and the chaplain's room in 1249,[10] the wall of the castle and the bailey next the river in 1251,[11] further alterations to the chapel in the tower, and stained glass windows in the hall in 1252 and 1253.[12] A survey of 1253 refers to repairs already carried out on the great wall, but says that it needs further repairs.[13] In 1318 the great hall, the lower chapel and two other larger chambers were destroyed by fire. The survey of the castle in 1323, which reports this, mentions the 'new tower,' six small towers in the circuit of the castle wall, two stables, a new gate, two old gates, an old barbican, the *mantellum* of the castle, the hall court, the castle court and the garden. The repairs said to be necessary are estimated at £1,097 6s. 8d.[14] It does not seem probable that they were ever carried out; but the great hall, as we have seen, was made fit for the holding of the eyre of 1329–30, and the castle continued to be used both for royal and shrieval purposes. During the parliament of 1380, however, the king stayed at Moulton, and not at the castle,[15] and St. Andrew's Priory was used for the sessions.[16] Repairs mentioned in 1347[17] and 1387[18] suggest that the castle was being used mainly as a county gaol and sheriff's office—a checker house and a checker board are named. When Leland saw the castle it still had a large gate,[19] but in 1593 Norden described it as ruinous. It was probably repaired for the use of the Parliamentary garrison, and the drawing of 1650 shows a wall round both the inner and the outer bailey, and four turrets in the wall of the inner bailey. Soon after the castle ceased, about 1671, to be used as gaol and sessions house, the site which had been originally sold by the crown in 1629[20] was resold to Robert Hesilrige, who acquired the adjoining strips of land from the borough in 1680.[21] A survey of the property in 1743 shows that the outer bailey was then known as the old orchard, and the inner bailey as the young orchard, both being well planted with fruit trees; the moat was called the upper and nether roundabout; the northern rampart, called the Fort in 1680, was known as the Castle Ground, and the whole, including the Castle holme, came to 18 acres. No traces existed, apparently of the wall of the outer bailey. The castle ground was built over between 1863 and 1880; in 1859 a small railway station was built on part of the old orchard, and in 1876, for the purpose of building the present Castle Station and goods yard, the rest of the site was bought by the London and North-Western Railway Company, and the remains of the masonry, including a circular bastion on the south, and a solid fragment of the wall on the river side, Norman at the core, reinforced with Edwardian facing and buttresses, were destroyed. The course of the Nene was diverted, the greater part of the earthworks levelled, and a new road cut across the levelled castle site joining Black Lion Hill to St. Andrew's Road. A postern from the wall above the river was re-erected in the southern boundary wall of the goods station, and this is all that now remains of the castle buildings.[22]

Whilst prisoners were still kept at the castle in 1655,[23] as early as 1630[24] a house of correction for the county had been set up in the town, under the control of the county justices. This was in or near the old Bell Inn,[25] across the road from the south-east corner of All Saints' Churchyard, and it served as a county gaol, supplementary to that in the castle. Here probably the Quakers were confined, between 1655 and 1664[26], who issued various tracts from their prison, and died, several of them, of their hard usage.[27] It was formally conveyed to the use of the county in 1670, as a gaol and bridewell.[28] The buildings were destroyed by the fire of 1675, and on the same site, as it seems, the present County Hall was erected between 1676 and 1678 from the designs of Sir Roger Norwich, by H. G. Jones, who rebuilt All Saints' Church.[29] The County House of Correction was at the same time rebuilt behind the Sessions House, and a house built by Sir William Haselwood on a piece of land to the west was used as a gaol and bought by the county in 1691.[30] Then, and for many years later, the county gaol looked south across Angel Street to the open country with no houses intervening. In 1777, when Howard visited it, some new cells had been built, but there was still an underground dungeon like that in which the Quakers had suffered.[31] In 1792–4 a new gaol and bridewell were erected to the south of the County Hall, and the old gaol was made into the turnkey's house. The new gaol was built so as to conform with Howard's recommendations and held 120 prisoners. This in its turn was found inadequate by rising standards, and an addition to the gaol was built to the east and south of the old site in 1846 by J. Milne.[32] This latest gaol, built for 140 prisoners, served the county till 1889, when, all prisons having been vested in the Secretary of State by the Act of 1877,[33] it ceased to be used, and the former borough gaol became the only prison in the town. The old county gaol was sold to Mr. J. Watkins in 1880, who sold the portion now used as the museum and art gallery to the Town Council. The remainder of the property was bought by the Salvation Army in 1889 and purchased from them by the County Council in 1914. The Salvation Army remained in occupation as tenants till early in 1928. The building is now being reconstructed to serve as

---

[6] *Cal. Close* 1234-7, p. 138.
[7] Ibid. 1242-7, p. 195.
[8] Ibid. p. 522.
[9] Liberate R. 33 Hen. III, m. 11.
[10] Liberate R. 33 Hen. III, m. 3.
[11] *Cal. Close*, 1247-51, p. 510.
[12] Liberate R. 36 Hen. III, m. 15; 37 Hen. III, m. 11.
[13] Printed in full, Hartshorne, *Mem. of Northampt.*, pp. 136-7.
[14] Chan. Misc. Inq. 16 Edw. II, 89/15.
[15] Hartshorne, *Mem. of Northampt*, 164.
[16] *Parl. R.* iii, 89-90.
[17] *Cal. Close*, 1346-9, p. 196.
[18] Enrolled Accounts (Foreign), 13 Ric. II, Roll E, m. 38 d.
[19] *Itinerary*, i, 9.
[20] Serjeantson, *Castle of Northampt.* p. 45.
[21] Northampt. Corp. Deeds, Press C. 109.
[22] Photographs of the remains before demolition are preserved in Northampt. Public Library, and several are reproduced in Serjeantson, *Castle of Northampt.*
[23] *Quarter Sessions Records* (*Northants. Rec. Soc.*), vol. i, 194.
[24] Ibid. p. 55.
[25] C. A. Markham, *Hist. of the County Buildings of Northampt.* (1885), pp. 5-8.
[26] Ibid. pp. 3-4.
[27] Ibid. pp. 53-5. List of Tracts written in Northampton gaol. See also *Quarter Sessions Records*, i, 191; *Brief Account of the Sufferings of the People called Quakers.*
[28] See Quarter Sessions Files—Acts of Court; Epiphany, 21 Charles II.
[29] Markham, op. cit. p. 42.
[30] Ibid. p. 11.
[31] Howard, *State of the Prisons in England and Wales*, 1777.
[32] Markham, op. cit. pp. 10-24.
[33] 40 and 41 Vict. c. 21.

A HISTORY OF NORTHAMPTONSHIRE

additional offices for the County Council and a record room and students' room for the Northamptonshire Record Society.[33a]

The prison of the vill of Northampton, as distinct from the prison in the castle, is mentioned in 1253[34] when the keeper of the prison is named. From an incident narrated by the jurors of 1274–5 [35] it appears that the bailiffs kept the key of the prison, and that any person who had a thief to imprison could apply to them for it. There is no means of locating the town gaol till the 16th century; then it is mentioned as adjoining the town hall, in Abington Street, and from 1584 some of the rooms under the town hall were used as prisons for some 200 years.[36] In 1777, owing, it may be, to Howard's visit, complaint was made that the town gaols were close and unfit for the reception of prisoners,[37] and a levy upon the town was ordered for the necessary repairs.[38] About 1800 the use of these rooms was abandoned, and a gaol was built by the town on a site in Fish Lane given by the corporation, and subsequently altered in 1823 and 1840.[39] This gaol was superseded in 1845 by the new town gaol on the Mounts, built by Hull on the Pentonville model and capable of holding 80 prisoners.[40] The gaol in Fish Lane became a police station. The gaol on the Mounts, the only prison in Northampton after the closing of the county gaol in 1889, was also closed in 1922, and Bedford prison now serves Northampton for male prisoners and Birmingham for female.

The earliest mention of the Town Hall is found in 1285, when the justices in eyre held their session for the borough 'in the common hall' (*in communi aula*).[41] The Guildhall or 'Gihalda,' is mentioned in the charter of Richard II of 1385,[42] as the place where the mayor and bailiffs hold their pleas, and in 1387[43] as the place where the court of husting sat. Henry Lee says that the old Town Hall was in a little close, adjoining the last house on the right hand in the lane going from the Mayorhold to the Scarlet well, and he had seen a circular mark of stonework on the west end of the adjoining houses.[43a] The second Town Hall, which stood at the south-east of the Market Square, between Abington Street and Dickers Lane, was apparently of 14th century origin.[44] The third story may have been added in the 15th century: possibly when the assembly began to be held here after 1489. The basement was used for shops in the Tudor period, and in the 17th and 18th centuries for a town gaol. The assembly books and the accounts report various repairs to the Town Hall in the 17th and 18th centuries.[45] The building was of three

NORTHAMPTON: THE COUNTY HALL

[33a] Inf. from Clerk to the Co. Council.
[34] Assize R. 615, m. 14d.
[35] Rot. Hund. ii, 5.
[36] Boro. Rec. ii, 175.
[37] Assembly Book, 3 Feb. 1777.
[38] Ibid. 9 Feb. 1778.
[39] Boro. Rec. ii, 176; Parl. Papers, 1833, vol. xiii, p. 52.
[40] G. N. Wetton, Guidebook to Northampton and its Vicinity (1849), p. 47.
[41] Assize R. 619. m. 74.
[42] Boro. Rec. i, 367 (gilda aula).
[43] Ibid. i, 260. Gyldeballe 1432, ibid., i, 269.
[43a] Lee, Coll. 91.
[44] Boro. Rec. ii, 172.
[45] Ibid. 172-3.

36

BOROUGH OF NORTHAMPTON

stories with battlemented parapet, the hall being on the first floor, and the ground story originally open. Several pointed two-light windows on the first floor long survived, though latterly in a more or less mutilated state, but the upper windows were square-headed. The door and the outside staircase were burnt in 1675, but the rest remained until 1864, when, on the building of the new Town Hall in St. Giles Street, the old hall and its site were sold by auction for £1,200, and the old hall destroyed.[46] Some oak wainscot from the council chamber and an Elizabethan table with bulbous legs are in the Abington Museum.

The east wing of the present Town Hall, designed by E. W. Godwin, was built in 1861–4; the west wing, added in 1889–92, was designed by A. W. Jeffrey and M. H. Holding, the restorers of Castle Ashby. The public library was housed here with the museum, until 1883; the borough records are now preserved here.

Of the few surviving houses which escaped the fire of 1675 the most notable is No. 33 Marefair, known as the Hazlerigg Mansion, since 1914 a ladies' club.[47] It is a stone-fronted building of two main stories, and attics with three rounded dormer gables corbelled out from the wall, and appears to date from the end of the 16th or early years of the 17th century. It was purchased by Robert Hesilrige in 1678,[48] and continued in the family till about 1835,[49] when it was bought by George Baker,[50] the historian of the county, who with his sister resided in it and died there. The building formerly extended farther to the east, with five gables to the street, and a frontage of about 97 ft., now reduced to 51 ft. 3 in. It has a square-headed moulded doorway, and mullioned windows of two or three lights, all without transoms or hood moulds. There seems originally to have been a porch.[51] The interior has been much altered and the plan modified. None of the old fireplaces remains, but there is a good contemporary staircase with twisted balusters and moulded handrail. In one of the bedrooms are three large and two smaller pieces of tapestry.[52] The garden extended from St. Peter's Church to the present Freeschool Lane, and contained a summer house. The building was recently restored.

The so-called 'Welsh House' or 'Dr. Danvers' House' from Dr. Daniel Danvers who lived in it at the end of the 17th century (No. 2 Newland) at the north-east corner of the Market Place,[53] was until recently a building of some architectural interest, but the ground floor was first converted into shops and in 1924 the three lofty dormers of the attic story, with three-light windows and curved gables, were taken down. Little old work therefore remains except the walling and mullioned windows of the first floor, between which on the upper part of the wall are three shields with the arms of Wake of Courteenhall and Parker, and another shield which has been attributed to Danvers.[54] There is also a shaped device with tall finial, formerly surmounting one of the lower

NORTHAMPTON: THE TOWN HALL

windows, on which are the initials and date 'W.E.P., 1595,' and the motto ' HEB . DYW . HEB . DYM . DYW . A DIGON ' (Without God, without everything, with God enough). Below the motto is a large shield with the arms of Parker with crescent for difference, flanked by two smaller unidentified shields.[55] The history of the building is not known, but judging from the initials and two of the shields, it may have been the residence of John Parker, serjeant at law, of Northampton, and built by one of the family.[56] It has a frontage facing west of 60 ft. and a depth of

---

[46] Boro. Rec. ii, 175.

[47] It is also the headquarters of the Northampton and Oakham Arch. and Archæol. Soc. It is on the south side of the street, and is also known as Cromwell House from a local tradition that Cromwell slept there the night before the battle of Naseby.

[48] Serjeantson, Hist. of Ch. of St. Peter, Northampt. 138.

[49] Northampt. N. and Q. i, 57.

[50] Ibid. Before purchase by Mr. Baker the house had remained so long empty and shut up that the title was rumoured lost. It was stripped of much of its wainscot and ornament at this time.

[51] A square projection is shown on a plan of 1723; ibid. 58.

[52] Northampt. N. and Q., i, 59, where they are described.

[53] It was the only house on the Market Place spared by the fire of 1675.

[54] Arch. Journ. xxxv, 436. The third shield 'three bars ermine' is not that usually attributed to Danvers.

[55] A chevron between three roses, and a chevron between three birds.

[56] Sir Henry Dryden in Northampt. N. and Q. i, 185.

37 ft., and is built of red sandstone, but the front was stuccoed and painted. Before the removal of the ground floor wall there was a pedimented doorway, two low mullioned windows, and a modern bay-window at one end. The roof was covered with stone slates, and there were three gables at the back corresponding with those in front, but plainer. The interior has been so altered that the original arrangements are lost.

A building on the east side of Sheep Street, the ground floor of which has been converted into six shops,[57] was originally the property of Lord Halifax and probably his town house, but it is best known as the residence of Dr. Doddridge and the seat of his

NORTHAMPTON: THE HAZLERIGG MANSION, NOW THE LADIES' CLUB

Northampton Academy from 1740 to 1752. It is a long stone-fronted early 18th century building of three stories, the upper part of which remains unchanged, with sash windows and unbroken eaved roof. The middle story is divided by Ionic pilasters into a series of bays, as was also the ground floor, but the top story, which was added in Doddridge's time,[58] is quite plain. There was originally a wide central gateway, two arched recesses over which still remain.

The County Hall, erected at the close of the 17th century in the Classic Renaissance style of the day, is a simple but dignified building of a single story, with high-pitched hipped roof, in which the entablature is supported by pilasters and coupled columns of the Composite order standing on a high base. The main front, facing north to George Row, is a well-balanced composition with a balustrade and curved pediment at each end containing the Royal Arms. The great hall has a richly ornamented plaster ceiling, completed in 1688.[59] The County Council Chamber, erected in 1890, and a Record Room built early in the 18th century stand behind the Hall.

The Judges' Lodging, a plain 18th century stone-fronted house adjoining the County Hall on the east, was formerly a private residence, but was acquired for its present purpose in 1819.

The nucleus of the Public Library was the Northampton Mechanics' Institute, set up in 1832 in George Row. Though in 1849 it was described as 'more flourishing than most in the kingdom'[60] and possessed a library of 7,500 volumes, by 1876 it was in financial difficulties, and its books were handed over to form the beginnings of the Public Library. It was at first housed in the Town Hall; transferred in 1884, with the museum, to the old county gaol in Guildhall Road, which had been purchased by the town and reconstructed for the purpose; augmented in 1885 by the library of the Religious and Useful Knowledge Society (founded in 1839, consisting of some 5,000 volumes) and by a collection of Northamptonshire books, purchased by public subscription. A new wing was added in 1889. In 1901 the open access system was introduced; and in June 1910 the present buildings in Abington Street were opened. A juvenile library and reading room were added in 1912, and in 1921 a special local room, containing some 16,000 items dealing with the town and county, including books, pamphlets, prints, drawings, maps, plans, posters, playbills, photographs, manuscripts and transcripts. The Photographic Survey of the district is kept here. The library possesses a complete file of the *Northampton Mercury*, going back to May 1720.[61]

The Museum, in Guildhall Road, on the site of the county gaol, contains the remains from Northampton Castle, from Hunsbury, from Duston, from Towcester and Irchester, various Anglo-Saxon antiquities, and a collection of boots and shoes and other leather articles. There is also a small art gallery.

Another museum is at Abington Hall, which was presented to the town by Lady Wantage in 1894; most of the Natural History specimens are preserved here, and there are also local engravings and portraits of local worthies.

The first proposal for a county infirmary[62] was put forward by Dr. John Rushworth, son of a vicar of St. Sepulchre's, who practised as a surgeon in Northampton for many years. In a pamphlet addressed to the Surgeons' Company in 1731 he urged the desirability of Parliament's assisting in the erection of an infirmary in the centre of every county. He followed this up by an advertisement in the *London Gazette*, offering to give £50 towards the building of such an infirmary in his own county, and suggesting the calling of a meeting to discuss it, at Quarter Sessions or some other time.[63] Nothing, however, came of his suggestion till after his death.[64] In 1743 Dr. James Stonhouse, then aged 27, came to the town to practise, and within two months had circulated papers entitled 'Considerations offered to the Nobility, Gentry,

---

[57] Numbered 18 to 24.

[58] Arnold and Cooper, *Hist. of Ch. o, Doddridge*, 83.

[59] The ceiling, which was the work of Edward Goudge, 1684-88, was cut in two in 1812 when the Criminal Court was taken out of the hall.

[60] Wetton, *Guide to Northampt. and the Vicinity*, p. 65.

[61] *Illustrated Guide to Northampt. Public Library*, issued by Northampt. Public Library Committee (1926).

[62] The following account is based on that by C. A. Markham in *Northampt. N. and Q.* New Series. Vol. II.

[63] *Northampt. Mercury*, 20 December 1731.

[64] He died in 1736; in 1747 his son Daniel writes from the County Hospital to solicit Lord Townshend's support for the scheme. *Hist. MSS. Com. Rep.* xi, app. iv, p. 368.

BOROUGH OF NORTHAMPTON

Clergy and all who have any property in the County, with regard to the establishment of a County Hospital in Northampton.' The subject was brought up before the Grand Jury at the Assizes on 21 July, and the design being approved, a subscription was started on the spot. The project was warmly supported both by the county, the corporation, and the influential minister of Castle Hill Chapel, Dr. Doddridge, who preached a sermon on 4 September 1743, ' In favour of a design to erect a County Infirmary,' in which his detailed account of the eleven existing provincial and London infirmaries suggests that he must share with Rushworth and Stonhouse the honour of originating the scheme. A large edition of this sermon was printed. At a meeting of the subscribers on 20 September 1743, a committee was elected, and on 17 November 1743 the statutes and rules for the government of the hospital, modelled upon those of the Winchester Infirmary, were confirmed; and a house in George Row, to the west of the County Gaol, was obtained and fitted up by December. ' Thus has the project of a County Hospital at Northampton, of which some persons there wholly despaired, been brought to maturity in less than two months from the first meeting on this occasion.'[65] Three physicians, including Dr. Stonhouse, two surgeons and an apothecary, were appointed to the staff. All those who subscribed £2 a year or more were governors, the Grand Visitor was the Duke of Montagu, and the Perpetual President the Earl of Northampton. The formal opening took place on 27 March 1744.[66] The hospital contained thirty beds at its opening, and issued its first report in October 1744, when 103 in-patients and 79 out-patients had been treated. Up to 1829 the subscribers used to assemble on Anniversary Day to hear the annual report, and proceed to All Saints' Church to hear a special sermon and contribute to collections when the bag was taken round by the Countess of Northampton and other ladies of title. In 1753 the building was enlarged and the number of beds increased to 60, the financial strain being met by fresh appeals to the public, and in spite of setbacks the work of the hospital developed steadily and a further enlargement was made in 1782. In 1790 it was resolved to erect a new hospital, in view of the unfavourable report of Dr. Kerr, one of the governors, on the site, the offices and the water supply.[67] The new hospital was to accommodate 90–100 patients; and amongst other conditions it was laid down that each patient should be allowed 90 square feet, that no ward should contain more than 10 beds, and that the lavatories should be out of the wards. The new site was near St. Giles' Church, and had formerly been part of the possessions of St. Andrew's Priory. The new building was completed and opened for use in October 1793, patients from other counties besides Northamptonshire being admitted for treatment. In January 1804 the practice of free vaccination of out-patients was begun, and 1,882 persons were inoculated in the next five years. It is interesting to note that the building of the London and Birmingham railway, 1835–37, produced so many casualties that the Hospital Committee resolved ' that the managers of the railroad within reach of Northampton be informed that it is impossible that any more cases of simple fracture can be received into the House; compound

NORTHAMPTON : DR. DANVERS' HOUSE BEFORE 1924

fractures or such cases only as are attended with danger can be admitted.' The use of anæsthetics for surgical operations began in January 1847. In 1872, 1879 and 1889 further additions were made to the hospital, the last to commemorate Queen Victoria's jubilee; in 1896 a new operating theatre was added. The name of General Infirmary was changed in 1903 to ' The Northampton General Hospital.' In 1901 two new wings were erected, and the old building became a home for the staff, with a library and laboratories: the new buildings were opened on 2 June 1904. The constitution of the hospital was drastically revised in 1904 and a new board of management set up. The hospital has now 231 beds, with an average yearly number of 2,891 in-patients and 12,449 out-patients.

Other hospitals now existing in Northampton are : St. Andrew's Hospital (for Mental Diseases), the scheme for which originated at a meeting of the governors of the General Infirmary in 1814, but which owes its beginning to a gift from the second Earl Spencer in 1828. It was opened in 1836–7. The Northamptonshire poet, John Clare, died here in 1864. It will hold 500 patients, many of whose payments are assisted from the charity.

The Royal Victoria Dispensary, opened in 1845, served a useful purpose till the 20th century in providing medical service, on an assisted contributory basis. It was dissolved in February 1923, the

---

[65] *Gent. Mag.* xiii, 610. The editor of this periodical, Edward Cave, the proprietor of the Cotton Mills then recently started in Northampt., was one of the original subscribers to the hospital.

[66] The sermon preached by Dr. R. Grey on the opening day was printed by W. Dicey of Northampt., together with the statutes of the infirmary, and an engraving, after a drawing by K. Gravelot, of a ward in the infirmary.

[67] *Northampt. Mercury*, 9 Jan. 1790. Dr. Kerr was surgeon at the Infirmary, 1765–1815.

A HISTORY OF NORTHAMPTONSHIRE

building sold, and the assets handed over to the General Hospital.

The Northampton Queen Victoria Nursing Institution, opened in 1901, has two maternity homes dependent upon it, opened in 1918 and 1919, in Colwyn Road and Kingsthorpe Road. There are at the present time eight Infant Welfare Centres in the town, with an attendance of 700 mothers, and a staff of one lady doctor, and 4 health visitors assisted by 70 voluntary workers.

Of other important buildings, the Barracks in St. George's Square were built in 1796 on the petition of the townsmen; the Working Men's Club in St. Giles' Street was founded in 1865 by the late Major Whyte-Melville; the Opera House in Guildhall Road was erected in 1884, the Temperance Hall in Newland in 1887 and the Masonic Hall in Princess Street in 1889-90. A statue in terra-cotta of Charles Bradlaugh, for many years member of Parliament for the city, was unveiled by Sir Philip Manfield, M.P., on 25 June 1894 in Abington Square. There is also in the Market Square a monument with a bronze bust of Lieut.-Col. Edgar R. Mobbs, D.S.O., 'a great and gallant sportsman,' who raised a company of the Northamptonshire Regiment in 1914 and was killed in action 31 July 1917. The monument was unveiled by Lord Lilford on 17 July 1921. There is a bust of King Edward VII in the north-west angle of the wall in front of the General Hospital in the Billing Road.

A large proportion of the names associated with Northampton are those of divines of varying denominations. The famous schoolman, Duns Scotus, was ordained a priest in St. Andrew's Priory Church by Bishop Oliver Sutton on 17 March 1291.[67a] Among the friars of the Northampton houses were the famous 13th-century Franciscan, Thomas Bungay, lecturer at both Oxford and Cambridge, who died and was buried here; the Dominican, Robert Holcot, the reputed author of *Philobiblon* and 26 other treatises, who died here in 1349; the Augustinian friar, Geoffrey Grandfelt (d. 1340); the Carmelites, John Avon, a distinguished mathematician, who died in 1349; William Beaufeu, a noted theologian (d. 1390), and Thomas Ashburne, the author (in 1384) of *De Contemptu Mundi*. Among the Anglican divines, besides a number of distinguished rectors of All Saints' and St. Peter's Churches, are T. Cartwright (1634-89), born at Northampton and educated at Chipsey's Grammar School, Bishop of Chester, 1685, and a wholehearted supporter of James II, like his fellow-townsmen, Samuel Parker (1640-88), Bishop of Oxford, 1686-88, and intruded by James II into the presidency of Magdalen College, Oxford. Among the famous Nonconformists, besides Doddridge and the Rylands, should be mentioned John Penry (1559-93), the reputed author of many of the Marprelate Tracts, whose wife was a native of Northampton, and who lived here 1587-1590; Robert Browne[68] (1550-1633), founder of the Brownists, who died in Northampton Gaol and was buried in St. Giles'

Churchyard; and Samuel Blower (d. 1701), the founder of Castle Hill meeting house. Of literary worthies, Anne Bradstreet, the New England poetess (1612-1672), should be noted as a native of Northampton; also Thomas Woolston, the freethinker (1660-1733), the son of a Northampton currier, deprived of his fellowship at Sidney Sussex College for his iconoclastic criticism of the Old Testament; Simon Wastell (d. 1632), headmaster of Chipsey's school and author of *Microbiblion*; and William Shipley (1714-1803), drawing master in Northampton, originator of the Royal Society of Arts; the two antiquaries, George Baker (1781-1851), author of an unfinished *History of Northants*, and his sister, Ann Baker (1786-1861), who helped to save St. Peter's Church from neglect and ruin, and compiled a glossary of Northamptonshire words and phrases; John Cole (1792-1848), bookseller and antiquary, the friend of Baker, the author of a short account of Northampton (1815), who published many antiquarian works, and made a collection of books on the town and county, now in the Public Library. E. A. Freeman, the historian, was a schoolboy in Northampton from 1829-37, and James Rice, collaborator with Sir Walter Besant in novel writing, was born here in 1843. Of the medical profession, besides Rushworth (1669-1736), Sir James Stonhouse (1716-98) should be mentioned, the founder, with Doddridge, of the County Infirmary, converted by Doddridge, and ordained as a deacon of the Church of England in 1749, practising medicine in Northampton 1743-64, and ending his life as a parish clergyman. Sir Charles Locock (1799-1875), accoucheur to Queen Victoria, was a native of Northampton. In connection with political life, Sir Richard Lane (1584-1650), deputy recorder of Northampton, a native of Courteenhall, defended Strafford on his trial, and was made Lord Keeper in 1645. Spencer Perceval and Bradlaugh have been mentioned in connection with the parliamentary history of the borough. R. G. Gammage (d. 1888), a native of Northampton, was an active organiser of Chartism in Northampton and the neighbourhood, and author of a History of the Chartist Movement (1854). W. L. Maberley (1798-1885), member for Northampton from 1820 to 1830, was secretary of the General Post Office and a diehard opponent of Rowland Hill's postal reforms from 1846 to 1854, 'wasting millions of public money.'[69]

CHURCHES.

The church of *ST. PETER* stands on the south side of Marefair, near the west end of the town, close to the site of the castle. The building is chiefly of late 12th century date, but two fragments of pre-Conquest cross-shafts[70] found in 1850 point to an earlier church having occupied the site. No part of the present building, however, is older than c. 1150-75, to which period the chancel and nave arcades, the tower arch and part of the clearstory walls belong; the arcades are very perfect examples of the highly decorated work of the time, and have frequently been noticed and illustrated.[71]

[67a] *Arch. Francis Hist.* ann. xxii, Fasc. I, II, 1929.

[68] A. Jessopp's life of R. Browne in the *Dict. Nat. Biog.* should be supplemented by R. M. Serjeantson's account in *Hist. of Ch. of St. Giles, Northampt.* (pp. 188-202). A monument to his memory was erected in the churchyard in 1923.

[69] *Dict. Nat. Biog.* for all preceding.

[70] *V.C.H. Northants.* ii, 189. They were found under the west responds of the nave arcades, and are now in the Public Museum. They are figured in R. M. Serjeantson's *Hist. of Ch. of St. Peter, Northampt.* 12. Mr. Serjeantson's work has been used in the following description.

[71] See references in Serjeantson, op. cit. 40.

BOROUGH OF NORTHAMPTON

The church consists of a continuous clearstoried chancel and nave under one roof about 93 ft. long[72] by 18 ft. wide, continuous north and south aisles 6 ft. 6 in. wide, north porch, and west tower 12 ft. 4 in. by 12 ft. 8 in., all these measurements being internal. The width across nave and aisles is 35 ft., and the total internal length of the church is 108 ft. 6 in.

Except at the west end the plan is substantially the same as when first set out, though the walls of both aisles and the east end of the chancel have been rebuilt at different times. Originally the nave extended about 10 ft. further west, with tower beyond, but was shortened and the tower rebuilt in its present position probably in the early years of the 17th century.[73] The aisle walls were rebuilt in the

The walling is generally of ironstone rubble and the main roof is covered with stone slates with slightly projecting eaves; the aisle roofs are leaded, behind plain parapets. Internally the walls are plastered.

The chancel is structurally an eastward extension of the nave, the dividing piers of the arcades being common to both. There is no chancel arch, and the design of the arcades precludes there having been one. The nave originally consisted of three double bays, with arches arranged in pairs, supported alternately by slender cylindrical pillars and by more massive compound piers, but the western double bay was cut in halves at the time of the alterations recorded above, and only its eastern portion remains. The rebuilt tower thus encroaches on the

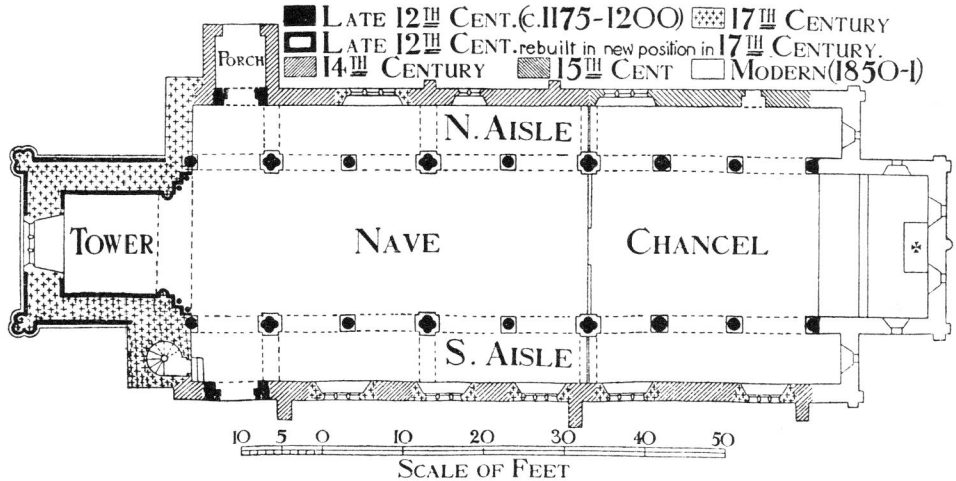

PLAN OF ST. PETER'S CHURCH, NORTHAMPTON

14th century, the old doorways being retained, and some alterations were afterwards made at the east end of the north aisle, where a 15th century window still remains.[74] Square-headed windows were inserted in the aisles in the 17th century, and the east end of the building seems to have been reconstructed about the same time,[75] the projecting square end of the chancel being removed and the aisles shortened.

After long years of neglect, the building was restored in 1850-51 by Sir Gilbert Scott,[76] when the east end was rebuilt in its present form,[77] the clearstory (which had been mutilated and modernised)[78] restored to its original character, and the nave and chancel new roofed. The aisle roofs were renewed in 1882. The tower was further restored externally in 1901, and 1912-13.

clearstory and arcades, the present west responds of which are in reality whole pillars partly built into the wall.[79] The chancel arcades consist of three single bays, with cylindrical pillars on each side.

The arches throughout are semicircular, and of about 7 ft. span, of a single order, with bold chevron ornament on each side and plain soffits, but without hood moulds. The compound piers are of quatrefoil section, consisting of four clustered shafts, those facing east and west forming responds to the intermediate pillars. The shafts on the side towards the nave are continued up to the top of the clearstory as supports for the roof principals, and have scalloped capitals, while those towards the aisles formed springers for transverse arches now destroyed. The diameter of the compound piers is considerably greater than

---

[72] Of this the chancel is 42 ft. 6 in.

[73] Sir Gilbert Scott reported that he had been informed by the clerk that there were foundations extending from the tower westward which prevented the digging of graves: Serjeantson, op. cit. 262. Prof. Hamilton Thompson suggests that it is possible that the rebuilding of the tower and of the east end and the insertion of the numerous square-headed windows all took place early in the reign of Charles I while Dr. Samuel Clerk was rector. Clerk was one of the commissioners appointed by the Bishop to see that the churches were decently kept, and he would feel bound to set his own house in order to begin with. *Arch. Jour.* lxix, 437.

[74] A crypt at the east end of the aisle is probably not older than the 15th century alteration. It was examined in 1850 and found to be 16 ft. by 9 ft., with two windows in the north wall, and the roof supported by five segmental stone ribs: ibid. 61.

[75] During its demolition in 1850 a coin of Charles I was found in the then existing east wall. The reconstruction of the east and west ends of the church may have been contemporaneous.

[76] His first report is dated May 1849. The restoration was begun in June 1850, and the church reopened in April 1852.

[77] The original foundations of the chancel were found some 12 ft. eastward of the then existing east wall, and new walls were built upon them. Many 12th century fragments were found in the wall during demolition. The aisles, which had apparently been shortened about 5 ft., were extended to their former length: Serjeantson, op. cit. 61.

[78] On the south side the clearstory arcade had been cut away to admit two late windows, presumably of 17th century date: Serjeantson, op. cit. 60.

[79] Ibid. 59.

the thickness of the wall above them, while that of the intermediate pillars, which are banded at rather more than half their height, is something less. In the ornamentation of the bands the cable moulding predominates, and it occurs also in great variety in the necks of the capitals throughout. The moulded bases stand on square plinths and some of them have acutely pointed foot ornaments. The whole of the capitals and their square abaci in both nave and chancel are most elaborately sculptured, the deep, intricate chiselling on the former contrasting strongly with the

St. Peter's Church, Northampton : Capital

comparatively rough axe work on the arches.[80] The capitals are all different, and their beautiful and delicate sculpture, which includes interlacing foliage and some animal and figure subjects, is of its kind unsurpassed in the kingdom.[81]

In the chancel the two pairs of pillars differ in size and design; the eastern pair is similar to those in the nave, while the western pillars are of greater diameter, without bands, and built of ironstone. The eastern responds correspond with the western pillars, the idea of alternation being thus in some measure carried out.[82] Elsewhere in the interior free-stone is used.

The modern east end of the chancel is in the style of the 12th century, with round-headed windows disposed in a somewhat unusual manner.[83] No ancient ritual arrangements remain either in the chancel or aisles, having no doubt perished at the time of the destruction of the original east end.

The clearstory consists externally of a shallow arcading of semicircular unmoulded arches on detached shafts with scalloped capitals and moulded bases running the whole length of chancel and nave. Every seventh space is pierced for a window, and above the arcades is a contemporary corbel table of heads and grotesques. Internally the windows are perfectly plain and widely splayed, but do not correspond with the arches below, the clearstory having been designed with a single window immediately over the pillars in the eastern and western double bays of the nave, and with two windows in the middle double bay. Of the two western windows, one was pushed out of shape and the other actually cut in halves when the tower was re-erected further east.

The east end of both aisles was rebuilt at the same time as the chancel, but the outer walls elsewhere appear to be of the 14th century. In the north wall a re-used 12th century stringcourse is continued round the westernmost buttress, and the original round-headed doorway is of two square orders and plain hoodmould, the outer order resting on mutilated scalloped capitals.[84] The contemporary south doorway is also of two plain orders, the outer on shafts with divided capitals and moulded bases. One 14th century square-headed window of two trefoiled lights remains on the north side, and in the south aisle, near the east end of the nave portion, is a moulded segmental tomb recess of the same period, the arch supported by small attached shafts with capitals and bases. The 15th century window in the north aisle is of three cinquefoiled lights with Perpendicular tracery, but all the other windows are late, square-headed, and of three unfoliated lights.

The tower is of three unequal and irregular stages, and offers many evidences of reconstruction. The lowest stage, which has a boldly moulded plinth,[85] is faced with alternate courses of ironstone and freestone forming broad bands of contrasting colour, and inserted in the west wall is a remarkable and beautiful arch of three delicately carved orders all flush with the wall plane, with hoodmould and imposts similarly carved, but no jambs. Set within this arch, above the plinth, is a much restored square-headed window of three trefoiled lights, but there can be little doubt that the arch belonged originally to a 12th century west doorway of three or more[86] recessed orders the jambs of which were removed when the tower was rebuilt. On the north and south sides of the lowest

---

[80] Serjeantson, op. cit. 42. The capitals were probably carved after the completion of the building.

[81] The capitals were for long covered by plaster and whitewash, but about 1839 were carefully scraped by Miss Baker and their original beauty revealed: Serjeantson, op. cit. 66.

[82] Ibid. 47.

[83] In the east wall there are nine openings, two in the lowest stage, four in a quintuple arcading of the middle stage (the centre arch being left blind),
and three in the gable—a central round-headed light like the others, and on each side of it a small quatrefoiled circle: ibid. 47. A semicircular central buttress, which survived the 17th century alterations and has been retained, was apparently the determining factor in Scott's design: ibid. 60.

[84] The jambshafts were originally cylindrical and detached: ibid. 51.

[85] Sir Gilbert Scott in his report referred to 'the extremely un-Norman appearance
of the basecourse round the tower': ibid. 261.

[86] Sir Gilbert Scott made incisions in the west wall and found that there had existed one or more additional orders, but that they had been taken out; there were, however, no traces of jambs: Serjeantson, op. cit. 59, 261. 'A capital which was dug up on relaying the floor may have belonged to a jambshaft of this doorway, which in its original state must have been one of exceptional splendour': ibid. 59.

NORTHAMPTON : ST. PETER'S CHURCH FROM THE NORTH-WEST

NORTHAMPTON : ST. PETER'S CHURCH : THE INTERIOR, LOOKING EAST

BOROUGH OF NORTHAMPTON

stage, above the plain masonry, are two courses of fine carving, and over these an arcade of blind arches ranging with those of the clearstory. The middle stage is separated from the lower by a string course of trowel point ornament supported by a corbel table of heads and grotesques, and has an arcade of round arches on each of its three sides, the arches being moulded and supported by octagonal detached shafts with scalloped capitals and moulded bases. Above these is another corbel table and stringcourse with double roll-moulding.

The two western angles are covered, to the top of the middle stage, by large buttresses of unusual design, consisting of triple clustered freestone shafts, perhaps fashioned from 12th century columns or jambshafts,[87] and at the north-east angle is a massive four-stage buttress, of alternate courses of ironstone and freestone, projecting in its lower stages beyond the width of the aisle. At the south-east angle a large square staircase turret serves as a corresponding buttress.

To the top of the middle stage, after the cessation of the alternate bands, the tower is mainly of freestone, but above the arcades ironstone is used. The upper stage is later in character, with battlemented parapet, pyramidal stone slated roof, and transomed bell-chamber windows of two trefoiled lights with separate hoodmoulds. The triple-shafted buttresses are continued as single shafts, in two stages to the underside of the parapet. The walls of the upper part of the tower are said to be largely built of moulded and wrought stones of 13th century date,[88] which may have been brought from one or other of the destroyed monastic buildings in the neighbourhood,[89] and there is reason to believe that the whole of this work in its existing form dates only from the early 17th century rebuilding.

The reconstructed late 12th century tower arch occupies the whole width of the west end of the nave, and consists of three orders all richly decorated with cheveron moulding,[90] and a bold square-edged hoodmould ornamented with fine chiselled work. The orders spring from half-round responds and detached jamb-shafts with elaborately carved capitals[91] and moulded bases. Three of the shafts are enriched, one on the north side with a spiral pattern, while two on the south are ornamented respectively with interlaced work and with studded cheverons.[92]

The unmounted octagonal font is of late 14th century date, the sides panelled with cusped tracery under straight-sided crocketed canopies which spring from dwarf buttresses at the angles and terminate in floriated finials. In the upper part, between the canopies, the angles are ornamented with crocketed attached pinnacles.

The stone pulpit, low chancel wall, and all the roofs and fittings are modern. The carved oak reredos, first erected in 1878, was completed in 1914, as a memorial to Edward Nichols Tom, rector 1873–1905. There are modern screens north and south of the chancel.[93]

In addition to the high altar, mention is made in the 15th and 16th centuries of the high rood loft, the chapel of the Blessed Virgin Mary, and the altars of St. Nicholas, St. John Baptist and St. Katharine, and to St. Eregaiar's altar (1535).[94]

There are monuments to John Smith of London (d. 1742), 'the most eminent Engraver in Mezzo-Tinto in his time'; William Smith LL.D. (d. 1839),

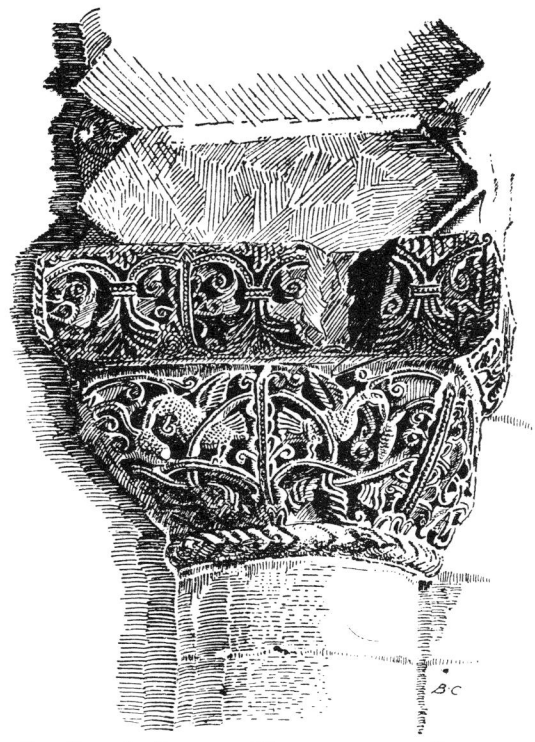

St. Peter's Church, Northampton: Capital

the 'father of British geology,' with white marble bust; George Baker[95] (d. 1851), historian of the county, and his sister, Ann Eliza (d. 1861); Edward Lockwood (d. 1802), rector for 52 years; John Stoddart (d. 1827), headmaster of Northampton Grammar School; and a brass plate in the chancel in memory of Robert Meyricke Serjeantson, rector and historian of the Northampton churches (d. 1916). In the churchyard is a memorial cross to the men of the parish who fell in the Great War (1914–18).

There is a ring of eight bells by Abraham Rudhall, 1734.[96]

The plate consists of a paten of 1709, a cup and paten of 1711, a flagon of 1715, and a breadholder of 1713.[97]

---

[87] *Arch. Jour.* xxxv, 417. The moulded plinth is continued round these buttresses.
[88] Serjeantson, op. cit. 56, ex. inf. Matthew Holding, architect.
[89] Either from St. Andrew's Priory or from St. James's Abbey: ibid. 56.
[90] In the middle order the cheveron and ball ornament is used. The arch is quite plain on the west side.
[91] 'The capitals of the jambshafts are not properly fitted to the orders of the archivolt above them, nor to the jambs below them, and some of the stones composing the shafts seem upside down': Serjeantson, op. cit. 59.
[92] Sir Gilbert Scott was of opinion that the enriched shafts had been brought from elsewhere, probably from the original western doorway: ibid. 262.
[93] The organ occupies the north aisle of the chancel and vestries the south aisle.
[94] Serjeantson, op. cit. 62–64.
[95] Buried, with his sister, at King Street chapel.
[96] North, *Ch. Bells of Northants*, 348, where the inscriptions are given. The tenor was the gift of Sir Arthur Hasilerige. The bells were rehung in 1893, and again, with new fittings, in 1928.
[97] Markham, *Ch. Plate of Northants*, 211. The flagon was the gift of Sir Robert Hesilrige, but not purchased till two years after his death in 1713; the bread-holder was given by Sir Arthur Hasilerige in 1728.

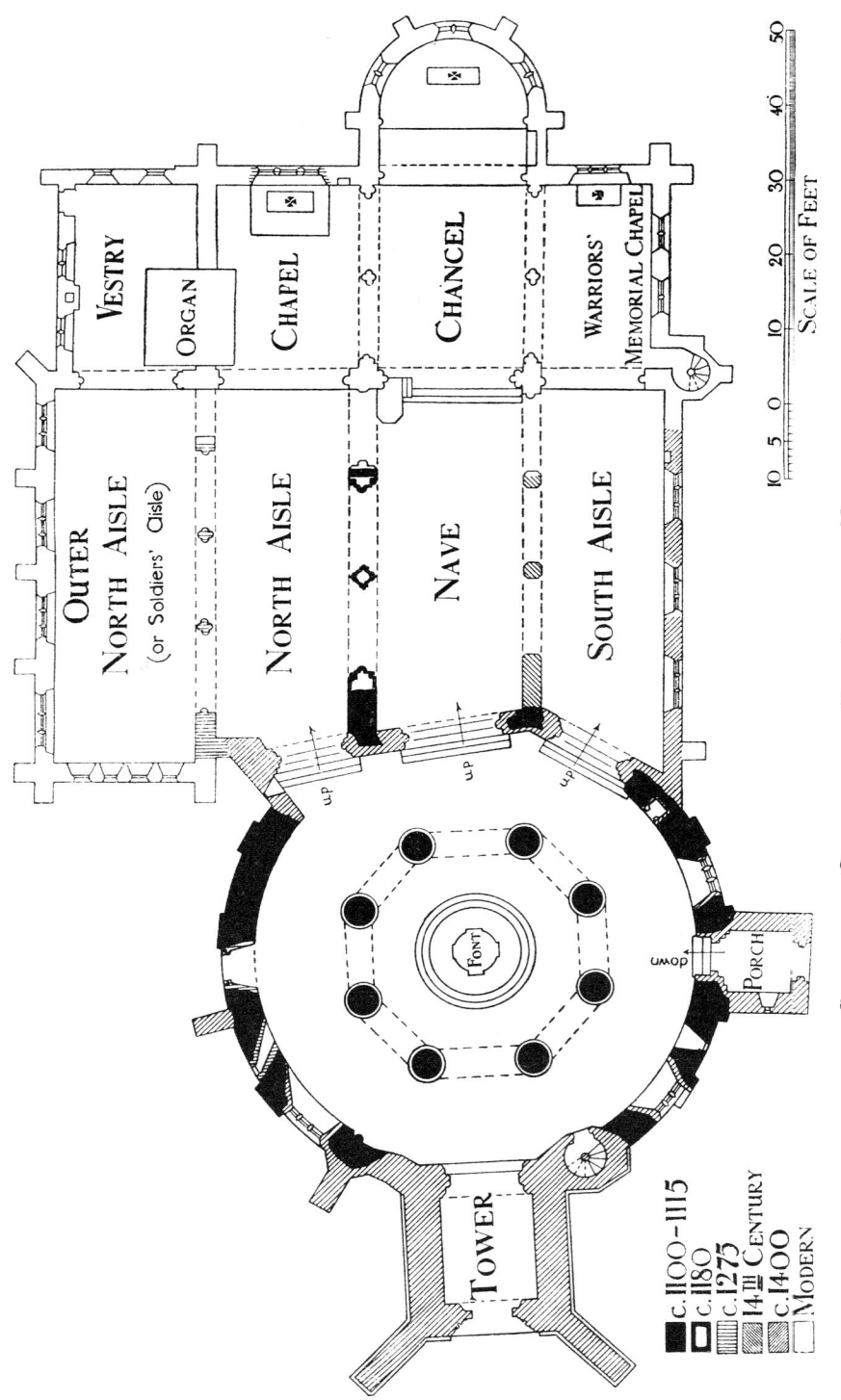

Plan of the Church of the Holy Sepulchre, Northampton

BOROUGH OF NORTHAMPTON

The registers before 1812 are as follows: (1) baptisms, marriages, and burials, 1578-1737; (2) baptisms and burials, 1737-1797, marriages, 1737-1754; (3) marriages, 1756-1794; (4) baptisms and burials, 1797-1812. The earliest vestry book begins in April 1736.

The church of *THE HOLY SEPULCHRE*,[98] one of the four[99] remaining round churches in England, dates from the early 12th century, and probably owed its origin to Simon de Senlis earl of Northampton, by whom it was granted *c*. 1111 to the monastery of St. Andrew.[1] Like other churches of this type, it was built in imitation of the church of the Holy Sepulchre in Jerusalem, and consisted originally of a circular nave and small oblong chancel, which probably ended in an apse. About 1180 the north wall of the chancel was pierced by arches to form a chapel, and towards the close of the 13th century a second aisle was thrown out on the same side. The present south aisle dates from the first half of the 14th century, and about 1400 the whole of the upper part of the circular nave was taken down, pointed arches placed upon the Norman columns, the triforium destroyed, and a new clearstory built. At the same time a massive west tower, surmounted by a spire, was added, and the present south porch built, the fabric then assuming more or less the aspect it retained till the 19th century. The original chancel had, however, been lengthened some time during the medieval period,[2] but towards the close of the 16th, or beginning of the 17th century, when the fabric was much neglected, the extended east end was demolished, and the outer north aisle was removed.[3]

In 1860-64 a new chancel with north and south aisles, designed by Sir Gilbert Scott, was added to the east of the old one, which then became the nave, and the outer north aisle was rebuilt.[4] The Round was restored in 1868-73, but the general work of restoration was not concluded till 1879, when the chancel was consecrated. In 1887 a vestry and organ chamber were built at the east end of the outer north aisle. The church, therefore, now consists of a modern chancel with north and south aisles, or chapels,[5] nave 46 ft. by 18 ft. 6 in., with north and south aisles respectively 17 ft. 6 in. and 16 ft. 6 in. wide, outer north aisle 17 ft. 10 in. wide, the old circular nave, or 'Round,' now used as a baptistery, south porch, and west tower 11 ft. 10 in. by 14 ft.[6] all these measurements being internal.

The church is built throughout of ironstone, and all the roofs east of the Round are covered with modern slates; the nave and aisles are under separate high-pitched roofs. Before 1860 the old chancel and its aisles extended about 40 ft. east of the Round, with three flush end gables separated by buttresses; the south aisle had been modernised and the tracery of its south windows removed.[7] All the roofs are modern.

Though the Round has suffered many changes, and some of its original features have been destroyed, it remains in plan substantially unaltered and its general proportions can be readily detected. It consisted of two stories, the upper, or clearstory, supported on an octagonal arcade of eight massive cylindrical piers which divided the central space from a circular groined aisle or ambulatory 10 ft. 6 in. wide. The internal diameter of the Round is 58 ft. 10 in.[8] and the outer wall, which is about 25 ft. high and 4 ft. 4 in. thick above the plinth, was pierced by two tiers of round-headed windows, the lower lighting the ambulatory and the upper opening into a triforium above its groined roof. In all probability there were smaller round-headed windows in the circumference of the original clearstory, which would be covered with a conical roof. Of the lower tier of windows only one, on the south side to the west of the present porch, is still in use, but there are remains of three others, two on the north side, and one to the east of the porch. The perfect window is about 9 ft. above the present ground level, its sill resting on a simple stringcourse which ran all round the building. The opening is 4 ft. in height and 15 in. wide, with plain jambs, hoodmould, and wide internal splay, the head of which has a band of cheveron ornament on the edge of the plaster soffit. Of the upper windows two remain on the north side, immediately over a second stringcourse 10 ft. 4 in. above the first. These windows are without hoodmoulds and differ in proportion from those below, being 3 ft. 9 in. high by $20\frac{1}{2}$ in. in breadth. Above them a third stringcourse forms the base of a plain parapet. The wall was strengthened by a series of wide shallow buttresses of which seven still remain, three on the north and two on the south being in an almost perfect condition, while two others on the south are cut away below for the porch walls. These buttresses are from 4 ft. to 4 ft. 6 in. in width, with a projection of 8 in. and die into the wall just below the topmost stringcourse, the two lower strings being carried round them. The main story of the Round was thus divided horizontally into three stages and vertically into a series of bays, that

---

[98] The following description is based upon the account of the church in Cox and Serjeantson's *Hist. of Ch. of the Holy Sepulchre, Northampt.* (1897).

[99] Or five, if the ruined chapel in Ludlow Castle is included.

[1] From the fact that in the gift of the churches of Northampton to the monks of St. Andrew's recorded in the confirmatory charter of 1108 the church of St. Sepulchre is not mentioned, it has been assumed that the building was not then finished. Begun about 1100, the work may have been interrupted by civil war and not completed until after 1108: Cox and Serjeantson, op. cit. 23-25.

[2] 'In extending the church in 1861 a tile pavement was discovered outside the then east end, showing that the church had formerly extended further eastward': ibid. 54.

[3] The outer aisle may have been taken down in 1634, the churchwardens' accounts showing that a considerable amount of work was done in that year, and a vestry resolution indicates that it was chiefly on the north aisle. All east of the Round fell into disuse except for parochial purposes of a quasi-civil nature. The communion table was brought into the Round, which ultimately became filled with seats and pews: ibid. 54.

[4] The restoration of the church was first considered in 1845, but nothing was done till 1851, when it was undertaken as a memorial to the second Marquis of Northampton, though the work of enlargement was not begun until 1860. The building was re-opened in August 1864. The pews and galleries in the Round were removed at this time: ibid. 70-71.

[5] The north aisle is now used as a morning chapel, and the south aisle is the Warriors' Memorial Chapel.

[6] The greater dimension is from west to east.

[7] Probably in 1739: Cox and Serjeantson, op. cit. 61. Before 1860 there were only two windows in the south wall with a doorway between, the position of which may still be seen below the middle window.

[8] The church of the Holy Sepulchre, Jerusalem, is 67 ft. in diameter, the Temple Church, London, 58 ft., Cambridge 41 ft., and Little Maplestead 26 ft. Garway, in Herefordshire, where only the foundations remain, was 43 ft. 9 in.

facing west being probably occupied by a doorway and shallow porch. During the restoration the foundations of a south porch were found, slightly exceeding the present porch in dimensions, which may have been a later 12th century addition covering a doorway then inserted.[9]

The piers of the arcade are plain masonry cylinders averaging 3 ft. 9 in. in diameter, but their capitals and bases differ. The four western piers have circular scalloped capitals, with plain circular chamfered abaci and moulded bases on low square plinths. In the two easternmost piers the abaci are square, the capitals merely shaped, with plain angle ornaments, and the high square plinths are of two stages, while the intermediate piers (at the north-east and south-east angles of the octagon) have divided square abaci and capitals with scalloping on each face. Nearly all traces of the groined roof of the aisle were removed during the alterations at the end of the 14th century, but there is evidence of the general direction of the sustaining ribs, whilst a single Norman wallshaft, with capital, still remains to the north of the west entrance.[10] Of the original round arches of the arcade and the triforium above them, nothing is left, the present acutely pointed arches of a single chamfered order and the wall above them being part of the late 14th century reconstruction. A stone bench originally ran all round the circumference of the Round, but, save for a small portion to the north of the entrance to the chancel, it has now disappeared.

The 12th century chancel was placed somewhat irregularly with its axis about 2 ft. to the north of that of the circular nave, and inclining slightly to the south. Considerable portions of its north and south[11] walls, about 36 ft. in length, through which the later arcades have been cut, have been retained, and in the north wall over the later arches, are the remains of three original round-headed windows, uncovered during the restoration. Of these the westernmost is the least injured, its west jamb being still in position as well as eight of the voussoirs,[12] but of the others only portions of the heads remain. The chancel, therefore, appears to have been lighted by three windows on each side placed high in the wall in the usual way, and there was probably a small doorway in the south wall.[13] Considerable portions of the original external corbel tables still remain at the top of the walls facing the aisles, consisting of moulded stones and grotesque heads, though that on the south side has been raised and the position of the heads changed.[14] Sufficient evidence came to light during the restoration to prove that the 12th century chancel was not square ended, though the exact position of the apse could not be definitely traced.[15] At the west end the walls are built up against the Round without bonding.[16]

About 1180-90 a pointed[17] doorway of two unmoulded orders and hoodmould, on single nook-shafts with water-leaf capitals and moulded bases, was inserted in the north wall of the Round, necessitating the removal of one of the windows, and a lancet was substituted for the one next to it on the west, the splay of which is directed obliquely to the east in order to light the doorway. The addition of an aisle, or chapel, to the chancel was effected about the same time by the piercing of its north wall[18] with two pointed arches of two chamfered orders, which spring from a cylindrical middle pier to which is attached on each of its cardinal faces a cluster of small circular shafts, and from half-round responds, with small flanking shafts to the outer orders. The arches have hoodmoulds on both sides, and the character of the pier and its moulded capital and base is fairly well advanced, but the separate carved capitals of the responds are of earlier transitional type with incurved volutes and foliation. The chapel was dedicated to St. Thomas of Canterbury[19] and St. John Baptist, and on each side of its east window was a carved image bracket supported respectively by the heads of a bearded king and a bishop with low mitre. These, in a more or less mutilated state, are now at the east end of the north chancel aisle, to where also the window has been moved. It consists of three plain graded lancets beneath a containing hoodmould and appears to be rather later in date than the arcade; in the same wall, south of the altar, is built a 13th century round-headed piscina, which no doubt formerly belonged to the original north chapel.[20]

The outer north aisle appears to have been added about 1275, the new arcade consisting of three arches of two chamfered orders with hoodmould on each side, on clustered piers and half-round responds with moulded capitals and bases.[21] Attached to the eastern respond is a pillar piscina the marble shaft and basin of which are copied from 13th century fragments found during the restoration.

It has been suggested that the nearness of occupied secular buildings on the south side of the 12th century

---

[9] The position of the buttresses, which formerly were continued to the ground, preclude the idea that the porch was part of the original design of the Round: Cox and Serjeantson, op. cit. 40.

[10] The original wall-shafts were double: a sectional stone of this double-shafting, as well as a double capital, is preserved amongst the Norman fragments in the church. During the restoration a considerable number of fragments of these shafts, capitals and ribs came to light: ibid. 36.

[11] This was the opinion of Cox and Serjeantson, but the decreased thickness of the south wall (30 in. as against 45 in. on the north side) may indicate that the original wall was removed when the aisle was added.

[12] The bottom of the jamb is about 8 ft. above the floor, some 2 ft. below the springing of the later arch.

[13] This is suggested by a small sculptured stone shaped like a tympanum now preserved in the Round, which may have formed the head of this doorway. It is too small for the west entrance of the Round. The sculpture is of the ruder sort of Norman work and apparently is intended to represent the contest between good and evil for a human soul. A reptile-headed demon with long tail lays hold of the right arm of a human figure, on whose left is a smaller and younger figure. The tympanum is figured in Cox and Serjeantson, op. cit. 39.

[14] On the north side the corbel table is in its original position 21 ft. from the ground: ibid. 39.

[15] Ibid. 39.

[16] Ibid. 40.

[17] Internally it is round headed.

[18] The arcade begins about 7 ft. east of the Round, as does also the later south arcade. Before the enlargement there was an approximately equal length of wall at the east end.

[19] From this it has been conjectured that the chapel was added, or begun to be built, by the second Simon of Senlis earl of Northampton who died 1184, in order to provide a fit altar for the commemoration of the murdered archbishop: Cox and Serjeantson, op. cit. 42.

[20] There is a 13th-century image bracket built into the wall at the west end of the outer north aisle, the mouldings of which are worked diagonally on to a foliated support: its original position was probably in an angle of the original north aisle: ibid. 43, where it is figured.

[21] When the outer aisle was pulled down in the 17th century the arcade was built up and covered over. It was opened out at the time of the restoration.

Northampton: Church of the Holy Sepulchre: The Round

Northampton: Church of the Holy Sepulchre, from the South-East

chancel was the reason of the addition of the outer north aisle,[22] but however that may be a south aisle was thrown out in the 14th century, when an arcade of two pointed arches of two orders was made, the inner order with a half-round moulding and the outer chamfered, springing from a square pier chamfered at the angles and from responds of similar type with moulded capitals and high chamfered plinths. Eighteenth century repairs and modern restoration have left little original work in the south aisle,[23] but a piscina niche with plain pointed head remains in the usual position at the east end of the south wall, and an image bracket supported by a human head is now built into the east wall of the new south chancel chapel.

The late 14th century alterations to the Round included not only the rebuilding of its upper part, but the destruction of the original west doorway and the wall on either side consequent on the erection of the tower, the insertion of three large three-light pointed windows, two on the south side and one on the north,[24] the strengthening of the north wall by two large buttresses, the rebuilding of the south porch and insertion of a new doorway, and the reconstruction[25] of the arches from the Round into the eastern part of the church. The main structural change, however, was the rebuilding of the clearstory in its present octagonal form, the disappearance of the triforium, and the removal of the groined roof of the ambulatory and of the round arches of the arcade. The clearstory has a square-headed two-light window on each of its cardinal faces, plain parapet and pyramidal leaded roof.

There is an ascent of five steps[26] from the Round to the present nave, the arch to which consists of two chamfered orders, the inner springing from half-round responds with moulded capitals and bases, the outer continuous. The arches opening to the aisles are of three chamfered orders, with half-octagonal responds, the two outer orders being continuous. The nave appears to have been re-roofed at this time[27] and a small three-light square-headed window[28] placed in the west gable over the entrance to the Round. Six wooden corbels supporting the new roof principals have survived, three on each side, carved with figures playing musical instruments—on the north rebec, bagpipe, and portative organ, on the south hurdy-gurdy, kettle-drums, and panpipes. Another with harp player is now above the chancel arch on the south side.[29]

The south doorway of the Round is sharply pointed and of three continuous unmoulded orders, with plain segmental rear-arch, and the outer doorway of the porch of two continuous chamfered orders with hoodmould. There is a descent of three steps from the porch to the floor of the Round, and of two steps from the Round to the tower. The tower arch is of four chamfered orders, the inner on half-octagonal responds with moulded capitals and bases, the others continued or dying into the wall.

Cut into the wall on the south-east of the Round and probably contemporary with the late 14th century alterations, is a banner-stave locker nearly 11 ft. in height,[30] the upper part of which, with pointed head, is carried on through one of the blocked triforium windows. On the outside of the wall, to the west of the porch, is an arched sepulchral recess 8 ft. 5 in. wide, probably constructed for some benefactor at the time of the erection of the tower. The two-centred arch is without hoodmould and consists of a single ornamented chamfered order.[31]

The tower is divided externally into six stages by stringcourses which run round and mark the beginning of each set-off of the diagonal buttresses. Owing to the fall of the ground the western buttresses are of unusual size, having a projection of 10 ft. and a width of over 3 ft. At the south-east angle is a vice turret, which is carried up to the level of the base of the bell-chamber windows where it slopes back behind an embattled parapet. The west doorway is of four continuous moulded orders, with hoodmould, and above it is a two-light window. The deeply-recessed bell-chamber windows are of two trefoiled lights with quatrefoil in the head, round which the upper stringcourse is taken as a hoodmould. The tower finishes with a battlemented parapet and had originally pinnacles at the angles: on the north and south sides respectively are two gargoyles. The octagonal spire has plain angles and three tiers of pointed lights in the cardinal faces.[32]

At the enlargement in 1860-64 the nave and aisles were increased in length some 6 ft. and an additional arch added at the east end of the main arcades. The new chancel is of two bays, with projecting semi-circular east end and moulded arches on shafted piers to the side chapels,[33] all the work internally being of a rather elaborate character in the style of the late 13th century. There is a turret at the junction of the south chapel and aisle with a stair leading on to the roof. A new altar was erected in 1882.[34]

The font is modern and stands on three circular steps in the middle of the Round; it is a memorial to Canon James, who took an active part in the restoration, and is copied from the 13th century font in the cathedral of Hildesheim, save that the figures supporting the bowl are knights in mail. The font replaced a small circular stone basin, probably dating

---

[22] Cox and Serjeantson, op. cit. 43.

[23] The windows have been restored in the style of the 14th century, the middle one being entirely modern.

[24] The mullions and tracery of these windows were removed during the 18th century, probably about 1781 (Cox and Serjeantson, op. cit. 61), and in their present form are modern.

[25] It is possible that the entrances to the aisles may have been now first constructed.

[26] The difference of level is 2 ft. 8 in.

[27] Cox and Serjeantson were of opinion that the south wall of the south aisle was also then reconstructed and that a new five-light window was placed in the east end of the chancel: op. cit. 46. This window, with vertical tracery, is shown in a south-east view of the church, 1761. The east window of the south aisle was then square-headed and of three lights.

[28] The middle light contains some 14th century glass brought from the destroyed Hospital of St. Thomas, including a scroll inscribed, 'Ave Maria gratia plena.' This is the only ancient glass in the church.

[29] Cox and Serjeantson, op. cit. 47-49, where the corbels are figured.

[30] The width is 12 in. and the depth at the base 2 ft. 3 in. The opening has a rebate all round of about 3 in.

[31] The recess seems never to have been used for burial: reasons for ascribing its construction to Sir Thomas Latimer, who died in 1401, are given by Cox and Serjeantson, op. cit. 124.

[32] The total height of tower and spire is 116 ft.

[33] The arches are filled with wooden screens erected in 1880.

[34] Designed, as were the screens, by Mr. J. Oldrid Scott.

from 1660, the shaft of which is preserved in the churchyard.[35] The wooden pulpit is modern, on a stone base.

A number of fragments of 12th and 13th century ornamented coffin lids have been preserved; four of these are in the Round, and others are built into the walls at the west end of the outer north aisle and in the east wall of the north chancel chapel.

In the Round, now against the north wall, is a floor slab[36] with five quadrangular brass plates and border inscription,[37] in memory of George Coles (d. 1640) and his two wives. In the upper plate he is represented standing between them giving a hand to each, and is bareheaded, with falling collar, doublet and hose, and a short cloak; the wives are in bodiced gowns and wear wide neck ruffs and high crowned hats. Below are smaller plates with two groups of children, three by the first wife and nine by the second, and under these again an emblem of clasped hands, explained in eight lines of verse below.

Amongst a large number of mural monuments[38] are memorials to members of the families of Fleetwood (1676-1747), Churchill (1750-1803), Woolston (1705-1775), Thompson (1786-1893), and others.

A wall painting in the Round exposed in 1843 has since disappeared, the walls having been stripped, but there are traces of another on the splay of the blocked westernmost window of the 12th century chancel.[39]

There is a scratch dial built bottom upwards into the south-east angle of the porch about 7 ft. from the ground.[40]

An oak lych gate was erected in 1888 at the west entrance to the churchyard in Sheep Street.

There is a ring of eight bells, seven of which were recast in 1927 by Gillett and Johnson, of Croydon; the old bell (now seventh) was cast by Henry Bagley of Chacomb in 1681.[41] A clock is first mentioned in 1634; the present clock was erected in 1882.

The plate is all modern with the exception of a 17th century pewter flagon, and four pewter plates made by Thomas King of London in 1675.[42]

The earliest registers are as follows: (i) baptisms 1571-1574, 1577-1600, 1606-1722, marriages 1566-1722,[43] burials 1571-1722,[44] (ii) baptisms and burials 1723-1778, marriages 1723-1754. The churchwardens' accounts and vestry books begin in 1634.

Built into the wall of a house[45] at the south-west corner of the churchyard is a stone of cruciform shape, with a rudely carved figure of our Lord on the Cross, probably a gable termination on some part of the church at the time of the building of the tower.[46]

The church of *ALL SAINTS* stands in the centre of the town on an island site bounded on the north by Mercers' Row, on the south by George Row, on the west by the Drapery, and on the east by Wood Hill. It was originally a cruciform structure consisting of aisled chancel, central tower, north and south transepts, and clearstoried nave with north and south aisles, the oldest parts of which appear to have dated from the 12th century. The destruction of the medieval fabric in the fire of 1675 was so complete that only the tower and a small crypt below the chancel were preserved. These are incorporated in the present building, erected in 1676-80 in the Renaissance style of the day, which consists of chancel, rectangular nave, and west tower flanked by north and south transepts. It stands on the site of the chancel of the medieval church, the whole of which west of the tower was destroyed, a small churchyard being there formed and the rest of the space thrown into the roadway.

There is no authentic drawing of the church as it was before 1675, but Speed's map (1610) shows a cruciform building with central tower, and a picture made in 1669 by one of the artists accompanying Duke Cosmo III of Tuscany indicates a long nave of seven bays with west gable flanked by turrets or pinnacles.[47] In a description of the old and new churches by Henry Lee, town clerk in 1675, the writer states that the old chancel was 'very large with great stalls and large desks before them on the north and south sides, and on the west side very gentile pews with desks before them to lean upon,' and he quotes a saying that the church was 'as large as some cathedrals.' At its west end were 'very stately gates at the entrance and a very high and large window.' There were 'three aisles,' and in 26 Henry VIII (1534-5) 'the middle roof was made and raised very high and lofty.' On the middle of the church wall was a chapel erected by Mr. Neale (mayor in 1539), 'very finely built with white stone,' and there was 'a south porch very great and large and over it was a large room in which the spiritual court was held.' There is also mention of a tomb and vault built in 1585 'in the place called the Lady Chapel in the chancel,' and of 'an old strong building adjoining to

---

[35] The basin is buried beneath the present font.

[36] The slab 'has been moved several times within the memory of man, so that it is difficult to say what was its original position': Cox and Serjeantson, op. cit. 88.

[37] The inscription reads, 'Here resteth ye body of Mr. George Coles of Northampton wth his 2 wives Sarah and Eleanor by whom he had 12 children. He gave to pious uses xi^l yearely for ever to this towne and deceased ye first of January 1640.'

[38] 'At the time of the restoration of the church the mural monuments were all taken down, and much carelessness and thoughtlessness characterised the refixing.' Cox and Serjeantson, op. cit. 89, where all the inscriptions are given.

[39] Ibid. 67.

[40] It is a complete circle, with a perpendicular and a horizontal line cutting across it, and radiating lines in three of the right angles thus formed.

[41] Till 1898 there were six bells, of which Bagley's remaining bell was the fourth, two trebles by Mears and Stainbank in commemoration of Queen Victoria's Jubilee, and dated 1897, being then added. In the 1927 recasting Bagley's bell, then sixth, became the seventh. Another of the old bells was dated 1681, the tenor 1733, the treble 1739, and two others 1805 and 1857 respectively. The inscriptions are given in North, *Ch. Bells of Northants*, 349.

[42] The modern plate consists of a silver chalice parcel gilt, and a silver paten of 1879, and a silver gilt chalice and paten of 1884. Of the plates two are inscribed 'Saintse Pulkers,' and the others 'Saint Seplkers' and 'Saint Sepulkers' respectively.

[43] October 1648–November 1651 missing, a leaf being torn out.

[44] No entries for 1575 and 1576.

[45] In north end wall of no. 68 Sheep Street, facing the churchyard.

[46] Cox and Serjeantson, op. cit. 120, where it is figured. The sculpture is repeated on the other side of the stone-(*Northants N. and Q.* ii, 240), which measures 19 in. across the arms and about 20 in. in height.

[47] A sketch of this drawing is reproduced in Rev. R. M. Serjeantson's *Hist. of Ch. of All Saints, Northampt.* (1901), 160, but its architectural veracity is open to question, especially as regards the tower, which is shown with open arches. Mr. Serjeantson's book has been used in the following description of the church.

Northampton : All Saints' Church : The Interior, looking East

Northampton : All Saints' Church from the South-east

BOROUGH OF NORTHAMPTON

the south side of the chancel reported to be formerly a chapel,' in which were the stairs to the crypt.[48]

No evidence has been found of pre-Conquest work, and though no architectural remains or fragments of 12th century date have come to light, there seems some reason to believe that the core of the pillars supporting the tower is of that period.[49] From the Bishop of Lincoln's grant in 1232 of an indulgence of twenty days to contributors to the work of All Saints[50] it may be assumed that a considerable amount of the building was mainly of this period,[53] the changes in the 15th century being those already mentioned, together with the introduction of pointed arches below the original tower openings. The church was 'greatly in decay' in January 1594–5, and in the following March much damage was done by a storm, 'many large stones being blown on to the leads' and through the roof 'just over the mayor's seat.'[54] In 1617 considerable repairs were done to the tower,[55] and either then or a few years later the 15th century

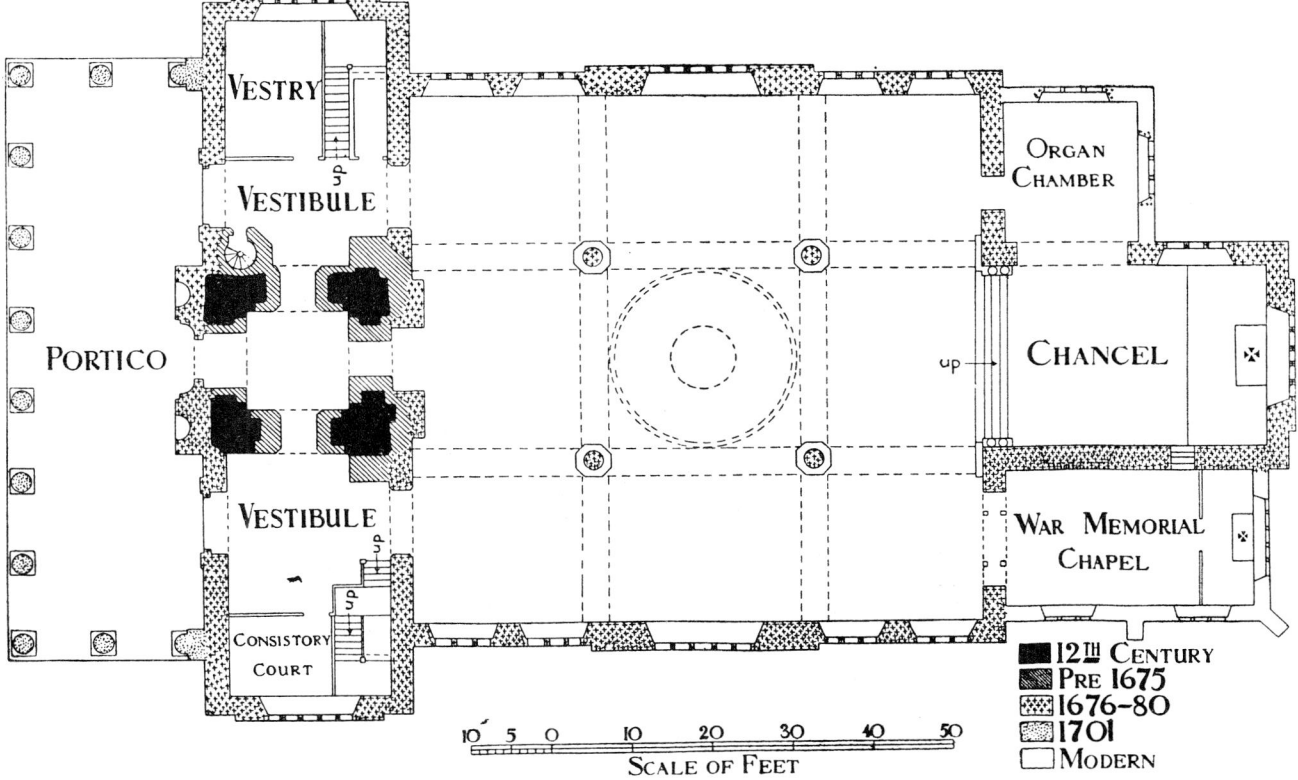

PLAN OF ALL SAINTS' CHURCH, NORTHAMPTON

building was at that time in progress, perhaps the reconstruction of the Norman church; but whatever the nature of the work then done it probably continued for many years after Bishop Wells's death in 1235, though no remains of distinctly 13th century masonry have been found. The church, however, appears to have undergone a variety of alterations and adaptations during the 14th and two succeeding centuries.[51] The existing crypt, below the western part of the chancel, is of the early 14th century, and the upper part of the tower seems to be very little later. Pieces of jamb and mullion stones recovered from crypt excavations[52] were all of the 14th century, and it is not unlikely that at the time of its destruction

arches were built up and the existing narrow arches on the north, east and south sides constructed.[56] There were repairs at the west end in 1624, in the chancel in 1632, and of a more general character in 1633–5[57]; in 1667 the roof of the south aisle of the chancel was 'very ruinous and out of repair.'

The new church was opened in September 1680, but was not completed in its present form till the beginning of the 18th century.[58] The great west portico was erected in 1701, and the cupola and vane added to the tower in 1704. A gallery was erected on the north side of the nave in 1714, but it was not until 1815 that the south gallery was set up.[59] The church was partially restored in 1840,[60] and more extensively

[48] Serjeantson, op. cit. 245–6.
[49] Ibid. 236. [50] Ibid. 16. [51] Ibid. 236.
[52] During alterations in 1886.
[53] This was the opinion of Mr. Matthew Holding, architect, quoted by Serjeantson, 239.
[54] Serjeantson, op. cit. 243: 'A great part of the church is fallen down by means of the great wind that happened on Thursday last (March 20).'
[55] Ibid. 244.
[56] Mr. Holding dated these arches from about 1619, when it is recorded that 'this year the congregation of All Saints was afraid the church would have fallen in sermon time.'
[57] Serjeantson, op. cit. 244. In November 1658 it was ordered that the churchwardens 'do take and weigh the lead that came off the chapel of the Lady Mary and other the materials thereof except the walls and what else may be useful for the church, and make sale of them.'
[58] Ibid. 247.
[59] At the west end a gallery was erected in 1806 on each side of the organ, which had been placed there in 1700.
[60] It was closed for five weeks: the tower was restored 'in a substantial manner.'

in 1865–6 when the galleries were reduced in width,[61] the seating cut down 15 in. in height, and made to face wholly east, the chancel screen removed and the position of the pulpit altered.[62] In 1883 an organ chamber was built on the north side of the chancel,[63] and in 1920 a War Memorial Chapel [64] was erected on the south side. The tower was restored and refaced in 1928.

Of the older parts of the fabric something has already been said about the tower, the lower part of which appears to incorporate much 12th century masonry, though no architectural features of that period are now visible. Internally, the tower is 12 ft. 11 in. square on the ground floor, with walls 5 ft. 6 in. thick, except on the west side where the thickness is increased by the 17th century facing. There is a vice in the north-west angle. The original openings appear to have been 11 ft. 3 in. wide, and there is some reason to believe that the four lofty semi-circular arches in the upper part of the ringing chamber are ancient.[65] The inserted 15th century arches spring from half-octagonal responds with moulded capitals at a height of about 24 ft. above the floor,[66] but in their turn are filled on three sides by the existing low and narrow 17th century arches of four orders. The levels of the different floors have been altered from time to time. The vice projects as a half-octagonal turret to the level of the bell-chamber stage, and has a pointed doorway now giving on to the roof of the transept.[67] The bell-chamber has on each side a pointed window of two trefoiled lights with elongated quatrefoil in the head[68] and low transom, the windows being recessed within wide two-centred moulded arches. The top of the tower with its balustraded parapet belongs to the 17th century rebuilding.

The crypt is under the western part of the present chancel and extends about 4 ft. below the nave. It was originally 22 ft. 10 in. square internally, covered with a vault of four quadripartite compartments, with longitudinal and transverse chamfered ribs forming pointed arches, springing from a central octagonal pier and responds with moulded capitals and bases. The ribs spring at a height of about 6 ft. above the floor, the total height of the crypt having been about 14 ft., but the floor is now considerably raised. In the east wall are two small rectangular windows, now blocked, and the diagonal angle buttresses show that the medieval chancel ended here, the 17th century chancel being erected about 16 ft. eastward. The crypt has undergone considerable alteration and has long housed the heating apparatus. Many of its original features are mutilated or destroyed, and its size is reduced to about 18 ft. by 19 ft.[69]

As rebuilt in 1676–80[70] the church may be said to follow the Greek cross plan used by Wren at St. Mary-at-Hill, the area enclosed being here a rectangle 72 ft. 2 in. long by 68 ft. 9 in. in width, the superstructure of which is formed into a cross by the grouping of vaulted ceilings round a central dome. Four tall stone columns with enriched Ionic capitals,[71] standing on high pedestals, carry a dentilled cornice, above which spring segmental plaster vaults spanning the four arms of the cross, but, instead of intersecting in a groin, they are treated as arches and carry a cupola or dome resting on pendentives. The four compartments at the angles of the building have flat ceilings, which form abutments to the arched roofs, or vaults, covering the arms of the cross. The dome is lighted by a lantern. Above the capitals of the pillars the whole construction is of wood, with elaborate plaster ceilings, the general effect being of much dignity and beauty.

The chancel measures internally 33 ft. by 24 ft., and was lighted by a large five-light east window and by two windows in the side walls. The east window is now blocked by a classic reredos erected in 1888, occupying the whole of the end wall, the principal feature of which is a large painted panel of the Crucifixion[72] flanked by coupled Corinthian columns supporting an entablature and lofty semicircular canopy. One of the windows on the north side has been displaced by the organ chamber, and those on the south have been shortened so as to clear the roof of the War Memorial Chapel. The elaborate moulded plaster ceiling of the chancel is contemporary with the rebuilding, but the ornament on the walls dates only from 1888, in which year also the arch to the nave was remodelled, its curve improved, and supporting Ionic columns and entablature introduced.[73]

Externally, the 17th century work is faced with ironstone ashlar, with plinth and cornice, and the windows are all round-headed, with pseudo-Gothic tracery. The north and south arms of the cross and the east end of the chancel are slightly advanced and have large five-light windows and curved pedi-

---

[61] They originally extended the full width of the aisles, in line with the pillars: they were set back 5 ft.

[62] The church was re-opened in October 1866. There had been much intra-mural burial: before the seats were reconstructed the floors were taken up, the graves arched over or covered with stone slabs, and the whole area within the walls laid with a bed of concrete: Serjeantson, op. cit. 252. A small crypt, or bonehouse, under the middle part of the south aisle, was filled up at this time: ibid. 242.

[63] In the angle formed by the nave and chancel the walls of which were advanced and the windows re-used. The organ was at this time moved from the west gallery.

[64] Designed by Arthur C. Blomfield and A. J. Driver, architects, London. It is entered from the east end of the south aisle of the nave.

[65] This was the opinion of Mr. Holding. The arches are about 30 ft. to the springing. Portions of late 12th century moulding in the angles of the tower, 10 ft. from the ground, were thought by Sir Henry Dryden to be the impost mouldings of low arches. The difficult problem of the tower is discussed at length in Serjeantson, op. cit. 237–240.

[66] Ibid. 239.

[67] A small fragment of weather moulding against the turret indicates the height of the roof of the old north transept: ibid. 240.

[68] The tracery is modern, but is said to reproduce the old design.

[69] Serjeantson, op. cit. 241, where there is a lengthy description of the crypt by Sir Henry Dryden, from notes taken during the alterations in 1886. The vault is mutilated at the west end to make room for the pavement of the east end of the 17th century nave. The entrance seems to have been originally from the outside, on the south of the chancel.

[70] It is said to have been designed by Henry G. Jones, architect, of Northampton.

[71] The capitals bear the emblems of the four Evangelists in the hollows of the abaci.

[72] The panel is let into the recess of the window. Two large paintings of Moses and Aaron, together with the Decalogue, Creed, and Lord's Prayer, formerly at the east end of the chancel, were removed to the west gallery when the reredos was erected. The paintings are attributed, probably erroneously, to Sir Godfrey Kneller: Serjeantson, op. cit. 264.

[73] It was originally quite plain; the pilasters in the nave also date from this period.

BOROUGH OF NORTHAMPTON

ments, the other windows in nave and chancel being of three lights. There are elliptical windows in the nave pediments, and the roofs are leaded. The dome sits on a square base.

The transepts are internally about 31 ft. long by 20 ft. in width, and have straight dentilled pediments and five-light end windows. They contain the gallery staircases and vestries,[74] and in the south transept the Consistory Court: they also form vestibules, with lofty round-headed outer doorways opening on to the portico. The smaller west doorway of the tower is flanked externally by semicircular wall recesses. The great octastyle portico covers the west end of the building to within about 8 ft. of the ends of the transepts: it is two columns deep and the Ionic order is used. The entablature is surmounted by a balustrade with urn ornaments, in the centre of which are the Royal Arms and a statue of Charles II in Roman costume and long flowing wig, added in 1712. Along the frieze is the inscription: 'This statue was erected in memory of King Charles II, who gave a thousand tons of timber towards the rebuilding of this church, and to this town seven years' chimney money collected in it. John Agutter, mayor, 1712.'

The white marble chalice font was the gift in 1680 of Thomas Willoughby.[75]

The carved 17th century pulpit stood from 1815 till 1866 in front of the altar below the chancel arch, but was then removed to its present position on the north side: it was altered in 1888 and a new base provided.[76] The removal of the 17th century chancel screen is to be deplored: its carved pilasters, pediment and Royal Arms have been worked up in the three western doorways of the nave.[77] The mayor's seat has a carved and panelled back surmounted by the arms of the town and is inscribed 'Anno Majoratus 20 Ricard White. Anno Dom. 1680.'

The only monument apparently[78] older than 1675 is a marble tablet at the west end of the south aisle in memory of John Travell (d. 1669). The later monuments include tablets to Dr. John Conant, vicar (d. 1693); Dr. Daniel Danvers (d. 1699); John Bailes (d. 1706), who 'was above 126 years old and had his hearing, sight, and memory to the last'; Isabella Stewart, daughter of John Haldane of Lanrick and widow of the Jacobite leader Charles Stewart of Ardsheal, who died at the Peacock Inn, Northampton, 8 April 1782; Sir John Stonhouse, bart., founder of the County Infirmary (d. 1795), and others.[79] A record of the monument of Francis Samwell, erected in 1585, has been preserved, and also of upwards of a hundred coats of arms taken from stained glass or from monuments in the church at the beginning of the 17th century.[80]

There is a ring of eight bells by Chapman and Mears, of London, 1782.[81] In 1829 the corporation presented a clock and new set of chimes by John Briant of Hertford.[82]

The plate consists of a set of two cups and cover patens, two breadholders, two flagons and two alms dishes of 1677, given in that year by 'Mrs. Mary Reynolds, relict of Edward, late Lord Bishop of Norwich'; a cup and strainer spoon of 1718; a cup of 1740; two cups of 1888, and a small plain paten. There is also a plated set of seven pieces.[83]

The registers before 1812 are as follows: (i) baptisms 1560-1722, marriages 1559-1721, burials 1559-1722, (ii) baptisms and burials 1721-1812, marriages 1721-1754, (iii) marriages 1754-1812. There is also a series of Vestry Books from 1620.

Interments in the churchyard west of the portico were prohibited in 1857, and in 1871, with a view to widening the lower end of The Drapery a portion of the yard was cut off. Originally enclosed by low fence walls on the north and south and by an iron grille on the west, the churchyard was afterwards bounded by a low wall and chains; these remained until 1926, when the whole space was added to the roadway and the existing steps to the portico formed. An octagonal conduit, which stood at the south-west angle of the churchyard, was taken down in 1831; it is said to have been of 14th century date.[84] A war memorial in the churchyard, designed by Sir Edward Lutyens, was unveiled by Gen. Lord Horne on 11 Nov. 1926.

The church of ST. GILES consists of chancel 42 ft. by 25 ft. 6 in. with north and south chapels, central tower 17 ft. 6 in. by 16 ft. 6 in., clearstoried nave of five bays 68 ft. 6 in. by 21 ft., north and south aisles respectively 14 ft. 6 in. and 15 ft. 8 in. wide, outer north aisle of four bays 14 ft. 9 in. wide, and north and south porches, all these measurements being internal. The tower is flanked on the north and south by continuations of the aisles representing former transepts. Including the outer north aisle the total internal width of this building is 74 ft. 6 in. The south chancel chapel is now the organ chamber, and the vestry is in the space south of the tower.

The building is faced with dressed ironstone and has plain parapets throughout; the porches are tiled, but elsewhere the roofs are leaded.

The architectural history of the building may be briefly summarized as follows: as originally built early in the 12th century it was an aisleless cross church with central tower, the lower part of which remains. Early in the 13th century the chancel was rebuilt, lengthened and increased in width on the north side, and later in the same century the south arcade of the nave was begun, with the intention of adding aisles, but was temporarily abandoned. The tower was strengthened at the same time by blocking up its four arches and building narrower

---

[74] In the north transept a clergy vestry on the ground floor with choir practice room above, in the south transept a temporary choir vestry.
[75] It is inscribed 'Donum Thomae Willoughby armigeri Ecclesiae Omnium Sanctorum in Northon.'
[76] Serjeantson, op. cit. 261.
[77] Ibid 252.
[78] It is possible that this monument may have been erected after the fire.
[79] Serjeantson, op. cit. 277-297, where the inscriptions on all the monuments are given. Certain of the tablets were removed from the chancel to other parts of the church in 1888.
[80] Ibid. 278-280, where the Samwell monument and some pieces of heraldic glass are figured, taken from the Belcher MS. in the Bodleian Library (Lansd. MSS. 213, col. 379).
[81] North, Ch. Bells of Northants, 344, where the inscriptions are given. Before 1782 there were six bells, which appear to have been by Bagley.
[82] Serjeantson, op. cit., 273. The date 1829 is on the west face of the tower above the clock; chimes had been presented by the Corporation in the reign of Elizabeth, and a 'new pair of chimes' was erected in 1628. The chimes were renewed in 1651 and 1680: ibid. 275-6.
[83] Markham, Ch. Plate of Northants 199.
[84] Serjeantson, op. cit. 302.

A HISTORY OF NORTHAMPTONSHIRE

arches within, of which those on the north and south still remain. In the first half of the 14th century the chancel was repaired, its east wall rebuilt, a chapel added on the north side, and the aisles and arcades of the nave (of three bays) completed; the aisles were afterwards continued eastward on the site of the transepts,[85] the work being finished about 1350-60. The chapel south of the chancel was finished in its present form later in the century, the church then assuming the plan it retained till the middle of the 19th century. In 1613 the tower fell, demolishing outer order, the greater part of the hoodmould, and the moulded bases of the shafts only are original, the rest being a modern reconstruction. The doorway is of three orders all with cheveron ornament, the two outer on shafts with enriched cushion and scalloped capitals, the inner continuous: the hoodmould is enriched with a reticulated pattern. The smaller round-headed north doorway is of two un-moulded orders, but the jambs and imposts are modern. The new east and west arches of the tower represent the original openings in dimensions if not

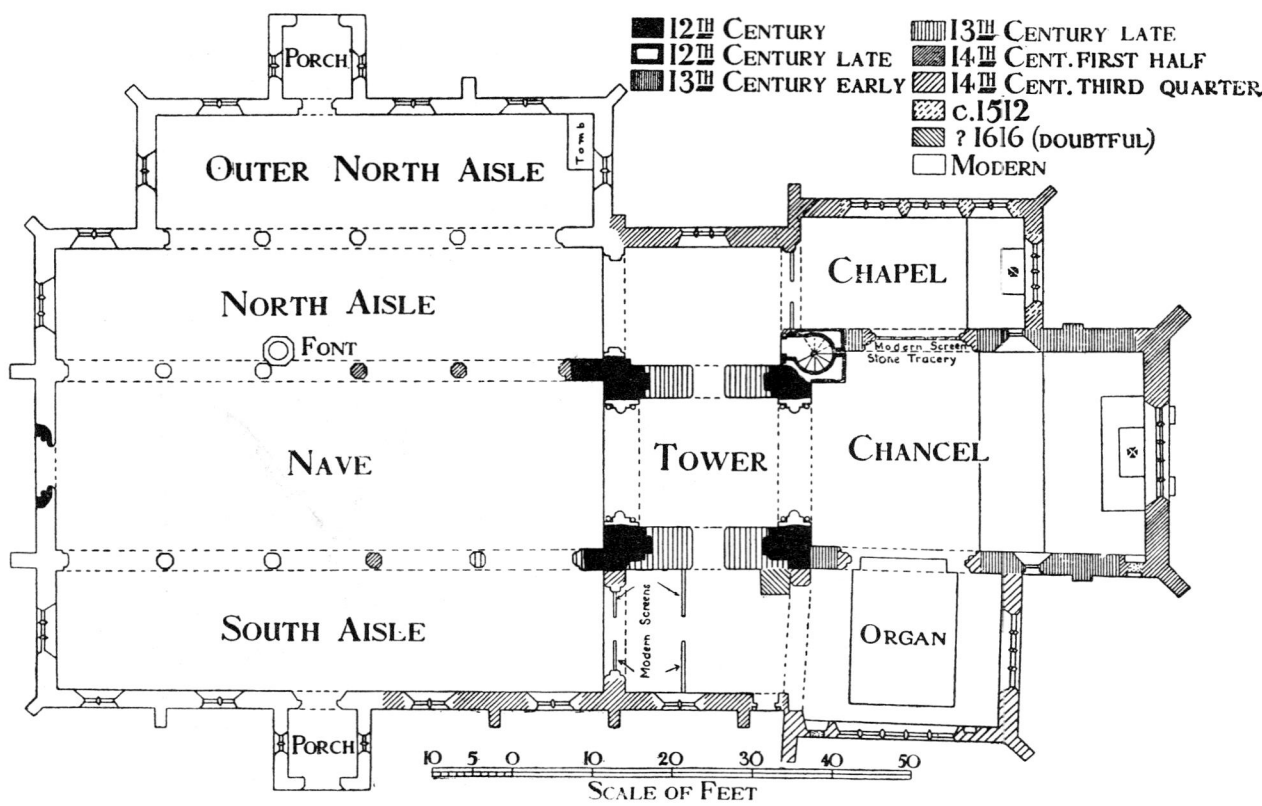

PLAN OF ST. GILES' CHURCH, NORTHAMPTON

or seriously injuring the north arcade of the nave, but both were rebuilt three years later.[86] In 1853-5 the nave and aisles were restored and extended westward two bays,[87] an extra north aisle added, the 13th century fillings removed from the east and west tower arches, the whole of the church west of the tower re-roofed, its windows renewed and the porches rebuilt.[88] The chancel was restored in 1876.[89]

Of the 12th century church little remains but the lower part of the tower and the west and north doorways, both very much restored, which were re-erected in their present positions at the time of the extension. In the west doorway some stones in the in details,[90] but several voussoirs and the line of the eastern jamb of the blocked 12th century north arch have been exposed towards the aisle.

The projecting staircase turret at the north-east angle of the tower, entrance to which was from the transept, appears to have been added later in the century,[91] after the completion of the cross-plan and may at first have been intended to be external. On its east face are three narrow windows, the lowest round-headed, now overlooking the chancel, and the stairway is vaulted with a winding barrel vault of plastered rubble. The round-headed doorway on the west side is of a single square order with quirked

---

[85] The transepts probably stood till this time: if the width of the aisles was conditioned by the length of the transepts they must have been very short.

[86] Nothing is known of a clearstory until this time: Serjeantson, *Hist. of Ch. of St. Giles, Northampt.* 124. Prof. Hamilton Thompson's account of the fabric has here been used.

[87] Before its extension westward, the nave was 49 ft. in length.

[88] The restoration, begun in August 1853, was carried out under the direction of Mr. E. F. Law, architect, after a report by Sir Gilbert Scott. The church was re-opened in November 1855.

[89] Begun in summer of 1875, re-opened Oct. 1876. The tower was repaired in 1914.

[90] Serjeantson, op. cit. 109. They are of three orders, the two inner with cheveron moulding on shafts and the outer square with hoodmould. The tower has a flat wooden ceiling immediately above the arches.

[91] Mr. Serjeantson's conclusions are here followed, op. cit. 110.

52

Northampton: St. Giles' Church from the South-east

Northampton: St. Giles' Church: The Interior, looking East

hoodmould, moulded imposts[92] and slightly chamfered jambs. The 12th century chancel appears to have been little shorter than at present, as traces of a blocked doorway of that period occur *in situ* in the south wall some 12 ft. from the east end.[93] There is also a small round-headed doorway, also blocked, at the eastern extremity of the wall, which if of 12th century date must have been originally elsewhere.

In the 13th century rebuilding of the chancel the north wall was advanced 4 ft. and built as a continuation of the north face of the staircase turret,[94] but the line of the south wall was retained. The new chancel appears to have consisted of three bays divided by buttresses, with a lancet window in each, and probably three lancets in the east wall. Of these windows two remain entire: one in the south wall still lights the chancel, but the other immediately opposite is now covered by the north chapel. West of this, also in the north wall, is the upper part of a third lancet, the lower portion of which was cut away when the arch between the chancel and chapel was pierced. These windows have rather broad external chamfers, and hoodmoulds which are continued along the walls and round the buttresses as strings; there is also a string at sill level. Internally the openings are widely splayed and moulded all round.

The addition of aisles to the nave towards the close of the 13th century was begun on the south side, the first arch being cut through the wall and its eastern respond built about 2 ft. 6 in. west of the tower. The intention evidently was to proceed westward with an arcade of pointed arches of two chamfered orders on octagonal piers with moulded capitals and bases. Only one arch, with the pier west of it, was, however, completed, probably on account of fears for the safety of the tower, the tall round-headed openings of which were therefore filled with masonry. The existing filling on the north and south sides is pierced by narrow acutely pointed arches of three chamfered orders, the outer chamfer in each case being continued down the jambs and the middle order dying out. On the north side the inner order also dies out, but on the south it springs from moulded corbels supported by sculptured human heads,[95] the south arch has also a fourth order towards the aisle where the wall is thickened,[96] and strengthened at its east end by a massive buttress of uncertain date,[97] which blocks the north jamb of the arch between the aisle and the south chancel chapel.

The 14th century repair of the chancel included the rebuilding of the east wall in its present form with diagonal angle buttresses of two stages and two dwarf buttresses below the window, and of about 3 ft. of the east ends of the north and south walls.[98] The east window is of five trefoiled lights with reticulated quatrefoil tracery, double chamfered jambs, and hoodmould ending in head-stops. A new string-course was taken round the whole chancel below the sills of the side windows and continued round the 13th century buttresses, which were perhaps rebuilt,[99] though a keel-shaped string forming a continuation of the hoodmoulds of the lancets and taken round the upper part of the old buttresses was retained as far as the old material would go, and re-used on the east wall, until broken by the hoodmould of the window. During these alterations the gable and roof of the chancel were reduced to their present pitch and the parapet erected. With the refashioning of the chancel went the building of the north and south chapels, though the latter seems only to have been begun. The north chapel (28 ft. by 14 ft.) opens from the chancel by a wide arch of three continuous chamfered orders with hoodmould, which has the appearance of having been rebuilt or completely finished at a later period,[1] and from the transept by a lesser arch of two continuous chamfered orders the inner of which is stopped near the ground by mouldings, while the outer, dying into the wall on the north side, is stopped on the south by a small broach.[2] The windows of the chapel are later insertions:[3] that at the east end is four-centred, of four cinquefoiled lights with vertical tracery, and in the north wall are three closely-placed windows, one of two lights and the others of three lights each, the sill of the two-light easternmost window being raised considerably in order to clear a 14th century triangular headed aumbry, opposite to which, in the usual position in the south wall, is a restored trefoiled piscina, with modern canopy. The north chapel appears to have been the Lady Chapel, and was planned simply as a north aisle to the chancel,[4] but the plan of a corresponding chapel, which was begun on the south side, seems to have been modified, and the work of completing the arcades and aisles of the nave proceeded with. The south arcade was first continued two bays westward, after which the north arcade was begun from the east end, starting about 4 ft. 6 in. from the west face of the tower. The eastern respond is thus some 2 ft. further west than that on the south side, with the consequence that the positions of the piers of the two arcades do not exactly correspond. Both western responds were removed when the nave was lengthened, but

---

[92] The south impost and hood have been restored, and the north impost and spring of the arch cut away in the 14th century when the adjoining arch to the chapel was made.

[93] These traces consist of the four eastern voussoirs of a round-headed arch below the lancet window. There has been much disturbance in the masonry which blocks the doorway towards the west, but the spring of the arch is in its original position: it is figured in Serjeantson, op. cit. 114.

[94] The turret was thus brought wholly within the church, and in order to admit light to the stair windows, which otherwise would have been blocked by the new north wall the inner corner of this wall, at its west end, was chamfered off at the level of each opening: ibid. 112.

[95] The carving is rather rough, but the date is obviously about 1300: Serjeantson, op. cit. 117. Drawings made in the middle of the 19th century indicate that the inserted east and west openings were like that on the north.

[96] The thickness of the south wall is 5 ft. 3 in., of the other 4 ft. 1 in.

[97] It 'may have been added as a precaution by the 14th century builders, or it may represent a 17th century addition': Serjeantson, op. cit. 127.

[98] The junction of the old and new work is very noticeable, a rough and irregular joint being formed on both sides: ibid 119.

[99] Ibid. 120.

[1] Ibid. 118: 'At the base, however, of the east jamb there remains a projecting moulding of early 14th century character, and a similar moulding has been restored on the west side.' The arch is now completely filled with a traceried stone screen erected in 1896.

[2] This arch, as already stated, cuts into the hoodmould of the 12th century stair doorway, the north impost of which seems then to have been renewed.

[3] An allusion to 'the new work in our Lady Chapel' fixes the date of the insertion of these windows at 1512: Serjeantson, op. cit. 128.

[4] Ibid. 121. It is now used as a Morning Chapel.

the octagonal 14th century pier on the south side, dividing the two original western bays, remains. It differs from the earlier eastern pier, and from the evidence of its masonry appears to have been heightened or repaired at some subsequent date.[5] The capital is moulded with an ogee and a swelled chamfer,[6] and the base is of ogee section projecting from a high plinth of two plain chamfers.

The north arcade is all of one build and is contemporary with the additions on the south side, but its octagonal piers are lower and the arches do not reach a corresponding height. Like those opposite, they are of two chamfered orders and the hoods are connected by horizontal mouldings. In its present form the arcade is as rebuilt in 1616, with high chamfered plinths to the piers, but the mouldings of the capitals suggest a conservative reconstruction or copy of the old work.

After the completion of the nave aisles the transepts[7] seem to have been taken in hand and rebuilt in their present form as eastward extensions of the aisles, engaging the tower. The spaces thus formed are divided from the aisles and chancel chapels by pointed arches, and on the south side the outer wall is a continuation of that of the aisle and contemporary with it. East of the porch the wall is of 14th century date, but the windows have been renewed and their tracery is modern: they are of two trefoiled lights with a quatrefoil in the head. On the north side the aisle wall west of the transept was removed when the outer aisle was built, but the portion immediately north of the tower remains and contains a 14th century window of three trefoiled lights with elongated quatrefoil tracery.

The south chapel of the chancel appears to have been first planned as an aisle like that opposite and of somewhat similar dimensions, but when the walls reached a certain height and its western arch was pierced in the then existing transept wall fears for the stability of the tower seem to have arisen, and as the nave aisles approached completion a newer and stronger arch was substituted for the earlier one, slightly to the east of it, affording direct abutment to the tower and itself abutted by a strong buttress on the outside.[8] At the same time the plan and elevation of the chapel were altered and it became a kind of transept (24 ft. by 20 ft.), with a lofty arch of three chamfered orders[9] opening to the chancel and occupying the whole height of the wall. The chapel roof is at right angles to that of the chancel, with a plain gable at the south end, below which is a large pointed window of five cinquefoiled lights with vertical tracery.[10] The chapel is also lighted on the east side by a square-headed window of four trefoiled lights with quatrefoil tracery. In the usual position in the south wall is a piscina with trefoiled ogee head and fluted bowl, and west of it a plain rectangular aumbry. In the east wall, north of the window, is an image bracket supported by a carved head, and at the west end of the south wall is a blocked low side window with ogee head and hoodmould terminating in a finial.[11]

Above the roof the tower is of two stages and finishes with a battlemented parapet and angle pinnacles. No portion of a 12th century superstructure remains, but the square turret at the north-east angle and a large portion of the masonry on the east and south sides of the lower stage are old. A large part of the north and almost all the west side fell in 1613 and at the rebuilding the new work was bonded into the old masonry. In this stage there is a doorway on the east side to the roof, and a window of two trefoiled lights on the north and south.[12] The whole of the upper stage belongs to the 17th century rebuilding, and the nave clearstory of two-light four-centred windows was either rebuilt or added. The bell-chamber is lighted by double two-light pointed windows on each side, with transoms, cinquefoiled heads to each light and quatrefoil above, the hoodmoulds of which are joined by strings, and there is also a stringcourse at sill level and another some 5 ft. below, where the walls are slightly gathered in.

Set in the wall of the north arcade of the nave are three inscriptions[13] on framed panels, recording the 17th century reconstruction in these terms: (1) 'Rob. Sibthorpe's care to God's true feare, This downefalne church got helpe to reare 1616. Will. Dawes, mason'; (2) 'Bp., Chanc[lor] and Clergie, nobles knights & gent: the countrie parishes, All Sts. North[ton.] St. Sepulchers gave . . . without breefes'; (3) '1616 John Pattison, Humf: Hopkyns, churchward when this buil[ding] began.'

The octagonal stone font is said to be partly of 15th century date,[14] but nearly all the carving is modern.

The oak pulpit belongs probably to the second quarter of the 17th century. It is hexagonal in shape, with carved upper and moulded lower panels. The balustraded stair appears to be an early 18th century addition and the stem is modern.

There is a brass candelabrum given under the will of Samuel Pennington, who died in 1745.

There is no ancient glass,[15] but two chained books

---

[5] Serjeantson, *Hist. of Ch. of St. Giles, Northampt.* 121: 'It seems very likely that the masons abandoned, on renewing their work, their previous plan of a tall arcade, and built a low arch next the high one already constructed, or, taking a new centre for the western curve of their new arch, dropped that curve upon the capital of a lower column and so made their western bay altogether lower in elevation than in their original scheme. The heightening, then, must have taken place in the 17th century, when so much was done to the building; the pillar would have been continued a few feet higher, and the old capital, which is of the same type of masonry as the lower part of the column, would have been replaced at the higher level.' The churchwardens' accounts show that something was done to a 'piller' in the nave in 1628.

[6] 'Probably fifty years later than the carefully grouped and geometrically drawn mouldings of the eastern column and respond': ibid. 122.

[7] No trace of the 12th century transepts remains, and their extent is purely conjectural.

[8] Serjeantson, op. cit. 126. This buttress covers a portion of an earlier buttress (which took the thrust of the first arch) the bottom of which has been cut away to make room for a doorway in the angle of the chapel and tower aisle.

[9] The two inner chamfers are hollowed, and there is a shaft with moulded capital on the jamb face of the innermost order.

[10] The tracery and mullions of this and the east window are modern.

[11] Internally it now shows as an arched recess. The sill is 19 in. above the ground outside and the opening is 4 ft. 1 in. by 1 ft. 8 in.: *Assoc. Arch. Soc. Reports*, xxix, 434.

[12] These windows seem to have been reconstructed on the old lines: Serjeantson, op. cit. 131.

[13] Two of these, one above the other, are over the first pier west of the tower; the third is above the third pier from the east.

[14] Serjeantson, op. cit. 161. An old font had, however, been removed in 1654: ibid. 57.

[15] William Belcher, of Guilsborough, at the beginning of the 17th century noted

54

BOROUGH OF NORTHAMPTON

have been preserved: (1) Calvin's *Commentary on Isaiah*, 1609, and (2) *The Second Book of Homilies*, 1676.

The only medieval monument that has survived is a beautiful 15th century table tomb, 'said to have been erected for one of the Gobion family,'[16] now against the east wall of the new north aisle.[17] It is of white alabaster, with six canopied niches on the long side and two at the south end containing shield-bearing angels and weepers. There is no effigy, and the brass inscription round the verge has disappeared.

The 18th century mural monuments include those of James Keill, M.D. (d. 1719), who 'opened by the surgeon's knife a path for the physician's skill'; Edmund Bateman (d. 1731), Town Attorney of Northampton, 1689-1700; Edward Watkin, vicar 1735-86, and his son John Watkin, D.D., vicar 1786-95. There are also monuments to members of the families of Goodday (1683-1797) and Woolston (1717-1778).[18]

There are ten bells, two trebles having been added in 1895 to a ring of eight cast in 1783 by Edward Arnold, of St. Neots.[19]

The plate is all modern and consists of a set of eight pieces, all silver-gilt, presented in 1883 by Benjamin Vialls: it comprises a cup, two patens and a strainer spoon of 1876, a cup, flagon, and breadholder of 1882 and an alms dish of 1881.[20] There are also a plated cup and five plates. Four pewter basins are exhibited in the church.

The registers before 1812 are as follows: (1) bapisms, marriages, and burials 1559-1747, with gaps 1584-87 and 1613-16;[21] (ii) baptisms and burials 1748-1812, marriages 1748-1766; (iii) marriages 1754-1789; (iv) marriages 1789-1812. There are churchwardens' accounts 1628-39, 1653-70, 1683-1709 and others till 1855.

ADVOWSONS The churches of St. Peter, the Holy Sepulchre and All Saints are all, as we have seen, probably as old as the Norman Conquest. The Priory of St. Andrew, by the charter of Earl Simon I,[22] confirmed by Henry I and Henry II,[23] had the presentation of all the churches in Northampton, and Bishop Hugh of Lincoln's charter[24] specifies nine by name: All Saints', St. Giles', St. Michael's, Holy Sepulchre, St. Mary's (by the Castle), St. Gregory's,[25] St. Peter's, St. Edmund's and St. Bartholomew's, as well as the chapel of St. Thomas. All these churches then were in existence by 1200, and we have records of presentations to all of them by St. Andrew's priory between 1219 and 1247.[26] Other churches mentioned in the records or by Henry Lee are St. George's in the Castle,[27] St. Lawrence's outside the North gate, St. Catharine's in College Lane,[28] St. Martin's in the North quarter,[29] and, outside the liberties, St. Leonard's in Cotton End[30] and St. Margaret's in St. James' End, but it is not likely that all or most of these were parish churches. The inquest for the taxation of parish churches in 1428[31] gives the number of parishes as eight, naming all those of 1200 with the exception of St. Bartholomew's. The Valor Ecclesiasticus[32] also omits St. Bartholomew's as well as St. Peter's, which was not in the gift of St. Andrew's, but St. Lawrence's is described as a chapel attached to the parsonage or rectory of St. Andrew's.[33] Leland says that there were seven parish churches, two being in the suburb. It would appear therefore that the number of parishes was constant from 1200 to the Reformation, though other churches may have been used for parochial purposes.

After the Reformation the ecclesiastical parishes of Northampton were reduced to four. St. Sepulchre's absorbed the parishes of St. Bartholomew's and St. Michael's; St. Giles' that of St. Edmund's; and All Saints' that of St. Mary's by the Castle[34] and St. Gregory's, the latter by the authority of Cardinal Pole, when the site of St. Gregory's was converted to the use of a free school.[35] In a suit as to tithes due to the vicar of St. Giles' in 1598 it was deposed that the parish of St. Edmund's had been deceased for about 60 years.[36] The same record gives the bounds of St. Giles' parish at the same date.[37]

The four ecclesiastical parishes of Northampton remained unaltered till the 19th century. The smallest, St. Peter's, remains unaltered still: but

---

twenty-four shields of arms in the windows, and a later copyist in 1614 noted twenty-three shields on tombs and windows. None of these now remain. Twenty-eight of these coats are figured in Serjeantson, op. cit. 137-143.

[16] Bridges, *Hist. of Northants.* i, 445. The male line of the Gobions became extinct in 1301, but the tomb may have belonged to one of their descendants, the Paynell-Gobions, or the Turpyns: Serjeantson, op. cit. 145.

[17] In Bridges' day it stood 'against the east end of the south cross aisle.' Serjeantson, writing in 1911, says 'it has been moved three times during the last sixty years.'

[18] The inscriptions on all the monuments earlier than the 19th century are given in Serjeantson, op. cit. 146-159.

[19] North, *Ch. Bells of Northants*, 347, where the inscriptions on Arnold's bells are given. The two trebles are by Taylor of Loughborough. Before 1783 there were six bells. Quarter chimes were added in 1845 striking on all ten bells. The earliest reference to a clock occurs in 1633: the present clock was erected in 1865.

[20] Markham, *Ch. Plate of Northants*, 203. The older plate was stolen in 1892: it included a cup and paten presented in 1683, a flagon of 1735, a breadholder of 1756, and a cup of 1878.

[21] No marriages are recorded in 1642, 1644, 1653-4, and no burials in 1642-44, 1647-51, and 1654-59: Serjeantson, op. cit. 184.

[22] Dugdale, *Mon. Angl.* v. 190.

[23] *Cal. Ch. R.* iv. 118.

[24] Dugdale, *Mon. Angl.* v. 191.

[25] For the parochial history of St. Mary's and St. Gregory's see R. M. Serjeantson, *Hist. of the Ch. of All Saints, Northampt.* c. viii.

[26] *Rot. Hug. de Welles* (Cant. and York Soc.), 106, 142, 149, 271; *Rot. Rob. Grosseteste*, 177, 231.

[27] The west window was still there in Lee's time. Lee, Coll. p. 98. The 'St. Miles in Cock Lane' mentioned by Lee, p. 99, is St. Michael's. See *Boro. Rec.* ii, 528.

[28] A chapel of ease to All Saints, demolished in 1631. *Boro. Rec.* ii, 421. See above, p. 21, and Serjeantson, op. cit. pp. 60-62.

[29] In 1274-5 this chapel had been without a chaplain for twenty years, and was ruinous. *Rot. Hund.* ii, 2. But in 1348, Edward III was presenting to it, as in the gift of an alien priory. *Cal. Pat.* 1348-50, p. 247.

[30] The chapel was probably older than the hospital and had all the adjuncts of an ordinary parish church. Serjeantson, *Leper Hospitals of Northampt.* pp. 7-10.

[31] *Feudal Aids*, iv. 504.

[32] *Valor Eccl.* iv. 315-6.

[33] Dugdale, *Mon. Angl.* v, 195. Pat. R. 36 Eliz. pt. 14; 6 Jas. I. pt. 30; 11 Chas. I. pt. 24. Lee says St. Lawrence's was called the lawless church, because marriages were performed there without license (p. 99).

[34] In 1590; see Serjeantson, op. cit., p. 97. In 1549 the communicants in St. Mary's parish numbered 150, as against 62 in St. Gregory's, 1,000 in All Saints', and 1,140 in St. Giles'. Chantry Cert. Roll 35, mm. 1-1 d.

[35] In 1556; *V.C.H. Northants.* ii, 236.

[36] Coram Rege Rolls. 33 Eliz. mm. 22, 81 d. See R. M. Serjeantson, *Hist. of the Ch. of St. Giles, Northampt.*, p. 287.

[37] For an account of the bounds as beaten in 1851 see ibid. p. 228.

A HISTORY OF NORTHAMPTONSHIRE

as the vacant spaces within the old walls filled with houses, and the open fields were first enclosed and then built over, the others had to be subdivided.[38] From All Saints' parish, lying within the old walls, was formed St. Katharine's parish in 1839, subsequently enlarged by an addition from St. Andrew's parish. From St. Sepulchre's, which extended north of the old walls, was formed St. Andrew's parish in 1842, with a church designed by Mr. E. F. Law, architect. From St. Giles' parish, which extended east of the old walls, was formed in 1846 St. Edmund's parish, the church of which, consecrated in 1852, was built from plans by Mr. Matthew Holding and enlarged in 1891. In 1879 St. Lawrence's parish was formed from part of St. Edmund's and part of St. Sepulchre's; the church, built of red brick, was consecrated in 1878. In 1882 St. Michael's and All Angels was also formed from a part of St. Edmund's, a church of red brick being built from designs by Mr. George Vials. The district of Christ Church was formed in 1899, from parts of St. Edmund's, St. Michael's and Abington parishes, and was made a parish in 1907. The transepts and part of the nave of the church were consecrated in 1906, the chancel was subsequently built but the nave has yet to be completed. The architect was Mr. Matthew Holding.

The enlargement of the municipal boundary in 1901 meant the inclusion of the district parish of St. James, formed in 1872 out of parts of Duston and Dallington; the church, of red brick, was consecrated in 1871, enlarged in 1900 with a tower, subsequently completed. St. Mary's (an ecclesiastical district), formed in 1885 out of Hardingstone parish, for Cotton End and Far Cotton, has a church designed by Mr. Matthew Holding. St. Paul's (an ecclesiastical district), formed in 1877 out of the parishes of Kingsthorpe and St. Sepulchre's, the church of which was designed by Mr. Matthew Holding. St. Matthew's, an ecclesiastical parish formed in 1893 out of Kingsthorpe parish; the church built from plans by Mr. Matthew Holding, has a north-west tower with a spire, 170 ft. high. Holy Trinity, an ecclesiastical district, was formed in 1899 (parish 1908) out of Kingsthorpe parish. Northampton thus consists to-day of 15 ecclesiastical parishes.

St. Andrew's priory presented to the church of ALL SAINTS down to the Dissolution. From 1539 to 1616 the Crown had the patronage, after which date it came into the hands of Sir Thomas and Dame Katherine Littleton, who sold the advowson and rectory to the mayor and corporation of Northampton on 24 May 1619. The patronage remained in their hands till 1835, being exercised by such members of the corporation as were parishioners of All Saints'.[39] In 1835 the advowson was sold to Lewis Loyd, from whom it descended to Lord Overstone, whose daughter, Lady Wantage, made it over to the Bishop of Peterborough, the present patron.

The church of All Saints, first mentioned in 1108,[40] stands to the south of the market place, at the centre of the modern as of the medieval town. The congestion of traffic owing to the convergence of main roads and tramways at this point has been relieved by the town's acquiring in 1871 and more recently the land west of the church, formerly the churchyard and before 1675 the site of the nave. The church has been the scene of many events of national importance. Ecclesiastical courts have been held here[41]; the convocation of the province of Canterbury sat here in 1380[42]; 'prophesyings' originated here, and it was the centre of the opposition to Laudian reform, as described in the previous volume.[43] Two political sermons of some interest were preached here in the 17th century, one by Robert Wilkinson on the anti-enclosure riots on 21 June 1607, given before the Lord Lieutenant of the county and the Commissioners[44]; the other—Sibthorpe's Assize sermon on Apostolic obedience—given on 22 Feb. 1626-7.[45] It was the town church in an especial sense. Mass was celebrated here before the elections of town officials under the Act of 1489[46]; from 1553 the town records were kept in the vestry, in a special chest[47]; and special seats were assigned for the mayor and bailiffs both before and after the fire,[48] which is recorded in the register for marriages by the sentence, 'While the world lasts, remember September the 20th, a dreadfull Fire, it consumed to ashes in a few hours 3-parts of our Town and Chief Church.' The Justices of Assize attend service here before the Assizes.

ST. PETER'S church is first mentioned about 1200.[49] Down to 1266 the patronage was in dispute between the priory of St. Andrew's and the Crown. Henry III presented in 1222.[50] The jurors in the eyre of 1253 presented that the Church of St. Peter's had been in the gift of the Kings of England down to Henry II, but was now in the possession of St. Andrew's priory.[51] In 1266 Henry III recovered the advowson from the priory, allowing the prior an annual pension of 15 marks in compensation, which, however, was not being paid in 1334.[52] In 1329 Edward III granted the advowson to the hospital of St. Katharine, near the Tower of London,[53] in whose hands it remained till the middle of the 19th century, though leased out from 1550–1640 to the Morgan family.[54] The last appointment was made in 1873; the patronage has since been exercised by the Queen Consort, the patron of St. Katharine's.

From time immemorial the chapel of ST. JOHN THE BAPTIST, Kingsthorpe, was attached to St. Peter's as a chapel of ease.[55] It only became an independent parish church in 1850.[56] The chapel of St. Michael at Upton has also continued to be appurtenant to St. Peter's as a chapel of ease from the earliest recorded times.[57]

St. Andrew's priory presented to ST. SEPULCHRE'S until the Dissolution. The advowson then

---

[38] See V.C.H. Northants. ii. 66.
[39] Serjeantson, Hist. of the Ch. of All Saints, Northampt. p. 184-5.
[40] Ibid. p. 12.
[41] Gesta Abbatum Mon. S. Albani (Rolls Ser.), p. 332.
[42] Fine R. 4 Ric. II, m. 22.
[43] V.C.H. Northants. ii, 44, 52.
[44] A Sermon preached at North Hampton . . . printed in London for John Flacket, 1607.
[45] Apostolike Obedience . . . by Robert Sybthorpe. . . . London . . . to be sold by James Bowler, 1627.
[46] See above, p. 9.
[47] Boro. Rec. ii, 4.
[48] Serjeantson, Hist. of the Ch. of All Saints, Northampt. pp. 254-8.
[49] Harl. Ch. 44, H. 34.
[50] Cal. Pat. 1216-25, p. 342.
[51] Assize R. 6 15, m. 14 d.
[52] Rot. Parl. ii, 76.
[53] Cal. Pat. 1327-30, p. 420.
[54] R. M. Serjeantson, Hist. of the Ch. o St. Peter, Northampt. p. 105-108.
[55] Ibid. p. 250 (Harl. Ch. 44 H.34.)
[56] Ibid. p. 147.
[57] Ibid. p. 217.

BOROUGH OF NORTHAMPTON

passed to the Crown, and was in the royal hands till 1615, when James I sold it to Edmund Duffield and John Babington of London.[58] From them it passed a month later to Sir John Lambe.[59] His executors sold it in 1653 to Peter Whalley, twice mayor of Northampton, and Ferdinando Archer, headmaster of the grammar school, 1646–96. It passed from the Whalley family to the Watkins,[60] and was sold early in the 19th century to Thomas Butcher and by him to W. Butlin,[61] who sold it to Lord Overstone, whose daughter, Lady Wantage, made it over to the present patron, the Bishop of Peterborough.

ST. GILES' church is first mentioned about 1120.[62] It served as the meeting place of the town assembly down to the time of the Act of 1489, possibly, it has been suggested, because it was equally remote from the Castle and the Priory of St. Andrew's.[63]

St. Andrew's presented to St. Giles' church down to the Dissolution. From that time the advowson went with that of St. Sepulchre's until 1833, when the Rev. Edward Watkin sold it to the Simeon trustees, the present patrons.

Of the eleven newer churches of Northampton, the advowsons of St. Katharine's and St. Andrew's belong to Hyndman's trustees, and that of St. Matthew's, Kingsthorpe, to Pickering Phipps, Esq.; the other eight are in the gift of the Bishop of Peterborough.

GILDS. There were a great number of religious gilds and fraternities in Northampton on the eve of the Reformation. In the church of All Saints there were the following. The Gild of St. Mary, stated in 1388 to have been founded before 1272, supplied three chaplains for the saying of daily masses and other services.[64] The Gild of St. John Baptist, founded in 1347 for the maintenance of one chaplain, and also, if funds permitted, for convivial purposes,[65] was closely connected with the craft gild of the Tailors.[66] The Corpus Christi Gild, founded 1351, was for the maintenance of one (later three) chaplains and the organisation of a Corpus Christi procession.[67] The Gild of the Holy Trinity and the Blessed Virgin Mary, founded in 1392, maintained four chaplains to say mass.[68] The craft gild of the Weavers came to be connected with this gild.[69] The Fraternity of the Rood was for the adornment of the Rood beam.[70] The Fraternity of St. George found a priest to sing mass in St. George's chapel, and was the owner of St. George's Hall, which later became the property of the corporation.[71] The Fraternity of St. Katharine appears to have existed for the purpose of assisting the burials of those who died of the plague and were buried in St. Katharine's churchyard (between College Lane and Horsemarket).[72] The chaplains of these several fraternities formed the college of All Saints, described in the previous volume.[73]

In the church of St. Gregory there was the Gild of the Holy Rood in the Wall, founded by the Hastings in 1473 for the maintenance of chaplains to celebrate mass.[74]

In the church of St. Mary there was the Gild of St. Katharine,[75] founded in 1347 for the maintenance of one chaplain (later two) to celebrate mass, and to keep the gild Feast on St. Katharine's Day, and attend at the funeral of the gild brethren.

In the church of St. Giles there were the Gild of St. Clement, in existence by 1469,[76] for finding one priest,[77] and the Gild of the Holy Cross, mentioned in a will of the year 1521.[78]

In the church of St. Sepulchre's there was the fraternity of St. Martin, mentioned in a will of the year 1500.[79]

RELIGIOUS HOUSES. Besides the parish churches and chapels of ease there were five conventual churches and a hospital chapel within the walls of Northampton in the middle ages as well as several in the suburb.

The *PRIORY OF ST. ANDREW*,[80] founded by Simon I *c.* 1100 for Cluniac monks, was at first, according to the statement of its prior in 1348, located in a house adjoining the chapel of St. Martin, probably on the present Broad Street.[81] Later, at a date to which we have no clue, it was translated to the site in the north-west corner of the medieval borough which it occupied till the Reformation, as shown in Speed's map. The estate map of 1632[82] shows that the priory wall ran from St. Andrew's mill along the site of the present St. George's Street to the Northgate, then west along the present Grafton Street to Grafton Square, where the great gate of the priory probably stood, then south along Lower Harding Street, west along Spring Lane to St. Andrew's Road and thence north to St. Andrew's mill.[83] The priory church stood between Brook Street and Lower Priory Street, and Monks' Pond Street runs across the site of the fish pond. The cemetery lay across Upper Harding Street, Priory Street and Francis Street, where stone coffins were found in 1838, 1852, and 1880, some architectural fragments are now in the Northampton Museum.[84]

ST. JAMES' ABBEY,[85] was a house of Austin Canons, founded at the beginning of the 12th cen-

---

[58] Pat. R. 12 Jas. I, pt. 15, m. 24.
[59] *Cal. S. P. Dom.* 1611–1618, p. 274.
[60] For the descent see the family tree in Serjeantson, *Hist. of the Ch. of St. Giles, Northampt.* p. 289.
[61] Whellan, *Hist. of Northants* (1874), p. 135.
[62] Cott. MS. Vesp. E. xvii, f. 17 d.
[63] Serjeantson, *Hist. of the Ch. of St. Giles, Northampt.* p. 15.
[64] Certif. of Gilds, Chan. No. 383.
[65] Ibid. Chan. no. 381.
[66] Boro. Rec. i, 266, 281.
[67] Cert. of Gilds, Chan. no. 380.
[68] Pat. R. 16 Ric. II, pt. 2, m. 32; Chan. Inq. a.q.d. 151, pt. 2 a.
[69] Boro. Rec. i, 332.
[70] Serjeantson, *Hist. of the Ch. of All Saints, Northampt.* p. 56.
[71] Ibid. pp. 56–9.
[72] Court of Augm. Proc. bdle 27, no. 4. Aug. Off. Bks. vol. 132, no. 173.
[73] *V.C.H. Northants.* ii, 189–1.
[74] Pat. R. 12 Ed. IV, pt. ii, m. 8.
[75] Chan. Inq. p.m. 16 Ric. II, pt. i, 103.
[76] Serjeantson, *Hist. of the Ch. of St. Giles, Northampt.* p. 33.
[77] Ibid. p. 36. [78] Ibid. p. 33.
[79] Cox and Serjeantson, *Hist. of the Ch. of the Holy Sepulchre, Northampt.* p. 238.
[80] *V.C.H. Northants.* ii, 102–8; R. M. Serjeantson in *Northants Nat. Hist. Soc.* vol. xiii.
[81] *Cal. Pat.* 1348–50, p. 247. This reference seems to have escaped the observation even of Mr. Serjeantson.
[82] Original in Messrs. Markham's offices; copy in Northampt. Public Library.
[83] See plan; *Northants Nat. Hist. Soc.* xiii, 136.
[84] See *Journal of Brit. Arch. Assoc.* viii, 67. They are of the 12th and 13th century, and include an enriched Norman shaft. There are also two tiles, one with arms of Fitzwalter of Daventry (possibly for Sir Thomas Fitzwalter, M.P. for Northampton, d. 1381) and the other with a lion rampant (possibly for Sir John Lyons, sheriff, 1381).
[85] *V.C.H. Northants.* ii, 127–30; Serjeantson in *Northants Nat. Hist. Soc.* vol. xiii.

A HISTORY OF NORTHAMPTONSHIRE

tury by William Peverel. It lay outside the liberties, but in the suburb, and owned much property in the town. The only trace remaining to-day is the name Abbey Street; a small part of the Abbey wall on the Weedon Road, near the point where the roads to Duston and Upton divide, was entirely taken down in 1927.[86] The great barn of the abbey was described by Henry Lee (1715) as 'one of the greatest and stateliest barns of England. A carriage with grain could stand in one of its southern porches, as I have seen, before it was shaken down and the material sold.'[87] He adds that the abbot of St. James' entertained travellers coming from the west, as the prior of St. Andrew's entertained those coming from the north, the town inns being often 'very ordinary.' From early in the 13th century the two houses were much used for monastic gatherings. Twenty at least of the triennial general chapters of the Austin Canons were held at St. James' between 1237 and 1446, and thirty-nine of the forty general chapters of the Benedictine order between 1338 and 1498 were held at St. Andrew's, though a Cluniac house.[87a]

ABBEY OF ST. JAMES, NORTHAMPTON. *Party argent and gules a scallop or.*

THE FRANCISCANS[88] first settled in Northampton in 1226. Valuable details as to the foundation of the house are to be found in the Phillips MS. of Eccleston, not yet in print when the previous volume of this history was written, which contains a number of marginal notes specially bearing on Northampton. The first two friars arriving in the town in 1226 were received by Sir Richard Gobion, 'who settled them outside the east gate on his own hereditary estate near St. Edmund's Church.'[89] The knight's own son John was one of the first to take the habit, and in consequence the angry parents ordered the friars to depart. The humble acquiescence of the brothers and their poverty, however, so touched Gobion's heart that he relented and allowed them to stay. About 1235 the friars moved into the town, where the townsfolk had given them a site in St. Sepulchre's parish, and thenceforward a series of grants from their devoted patron Henry III of timber for building are found on the Close Rolls.[89a] By 1258 the friary was complete, and the brothers began building a house for their schools. The Greyfriars' site, 'the best builded and largest House of all the places of the freres,' according to Leland,[90] was almost due north of the market place, near the present Greyfriars Street. Traces of interments were found in 1849, 1887 and 1889,[91] in Princess Street, showing conclusively that the cemetery lay between Newland and the south side of Princess Street, on the site of the present Temperance Hall and Masonic Hall. The well also was discovered, and is under the present Masonic Hall.

A house of *POOR CLARES* or *SISTERS MINOR*, the first in England, existed for a short time in Northampton. From 1252 to 1272 the sheriff of Northants is ordered to provide the sisters with five tunics of russet every two years. They are described as dwelling near the Friars Preachers, that is, not far from the Mayorhold. Nothing is known of the house beyond the references on the Close and Liberate Rolls, first noted by Mr. Serjeantson in 1911.[92]

The *FRIARS OF THE SACK*[93] also had a house in Northampton, founded by Sir Nicholas de Cogenhoe in the reign of Henry III. In 1271 they received a grant from the king for the building of their church.[94] From the returns to the inquest of 1274–5 it appears that their house was in the south-east quarter, between the Derngate and 'Dandeline's court,' wherever that was.[95] The friary came to an end before 1303,[96] and the order itself was suppressed in 1307.

THE DOMINICANS[97] first settled in Northampton about 1230, and began building about 1233, assisted by a series of grants from Henry III, from 1233 to 1270.[98] The house was large enough for a provincial chapter to be held there in 1239.[99] The building of 'studies' is mentioned in 1258.[1] Building continued through the reigns of Edward I and Edward II, and in 1310 the friars obtained a license from the bishop to have six superaltars in their church.[2] The royal chancery was established in the Blackfriars' Church from 31 July to 6 August 1338.[3] No traces of the house are left; it was situated on the east side of the Horsemarket and its precincts came down to Gold Street.[4]

If the later tradition can be trusted,[5] by which Simon de Montfort was one of their first benefactors, *THE WHITE FRIARS*[6] must have settled in Northampton by 1265; they were certainly here by 1270, when Simon de Pateshull was bestowing lands on them.[7] An inquest of 1278[8] shows that their house was near the town wall, and they were making additions to it both at that date and in 1299.[9] In 1310 they obtained leave to have six altars in their church,[10] and four provincial chapters were held in it in the course of the 14th century. The site of their house was in the parish of St. Michael,[11] near the top of Wood Street, formerly called Whitefriars Lane,

---

[86] Ibid. p. 262. The position indicated by Dr. Cox in his map, *Boro. Rec.*, vol. ii, is definitely incorrect.
[87] Lee, Coll. p. 92.
[87a] H. E. Salter, *Chapters of the Augustinian Canons* (Oxf. Hist. Soc.), pp. xiii–xli; W. A. Pantin, *Trans. Royal Hist. Soc.* 4th Ser. x, 251–5.
[88] *V.C.H. Northants.* ii, 146–7; Serjeantson, *Hist. of the Six Houses of Friars in Northampt.* (1911).
[89] Eccleston, *De Adventu Fratrum Minorum*, ed. A. G. Little (Paris, 1909), p. 29.
[89a] Serjeantson, op. cit. pp. 4–7, gives full references.

[90] *Itinerary*, i, 10.
[91] *Assoc. Arch. Soc. Reps.* 1887–8, pp. 121–4, contains a full account of the excavations, by Sir H. Dryden.
[92] Serjeantson, *Hist. of the Six Houses of Friars in Northampt.*
[93] Ibid.
[94] Close R. 56 Hen. III, m. 10.
[95] *Rot. Hund.* ii, 3.
[96] Close R. 31 Ed. i, m. 10.
[97] *V.C.H. Northants.* ii, 144–6; Serjeantson, op. cit.
[98] Ibid.
[99] Liberate R. 23 Hen. III, mm. 5, 8.
[1] Close R. 42 Hen. III, m. 2.

[2] Linc. Epis. Reg. Dalderby, Mem. fo. 162.
[3] Close R. 12 Ed. III, pt. 2, m. 20 d.
[4] Serjeantson, op. cit. The position indicated by Dr. Cox upon the map in *Boro. Rec.* vol. ii, is incorrect.
[5] Tanner, *Notitia Monastica*; cf. *Boro. Rec.* i, 360.
[6] *V.C.H. Northants.* ii, 148–9; Serjeantson, op. cit.
[7] *Rot. Hund.* ii, 2.
[8] *V.C.H. Northants.* ii, 148.
[9] Pat. R. 27 Ed I, m. 32.
[10] Linc. Epis. Reg. Dalderby, Mem. ff. 162, 171.   [11] *Boro. Rec.* i, 360.

Northampton: Master's House of St. John's Hospital (now destroyed)

BOROUGH OF NORTHAMPTON

lying between Newland, Ladies' Lane, and the Upper Mounts of to-day.[12] The foundations of the church were uncovered in 1846, under the road now known as Kerr Street[13]

The house of *THE AUSTIN FRIARS*[14] was founded by Sir John Longevile in 1322,[15] and was situated on the west side of Bridge Street, opposite St. John's hospital, on the site now occupied by Augustine Street. No traces of it remain.

THE HOSPITAL OF ST. JOHN,[16] founded by William de St. Clare, Archdeacon of Northampton, about 1138, is the only one of the religious houses of Northampton still standing.[17] It is on the east side of Bridge Street, within the line of the town wall, near to the site of the south gate, and now covered with blue slates: the interior is in a bad state of repair. The west end,[18] with its gable to the street, is apparently of early 14th century date, its chief feature being a wide and lofty recessed pointed arch of two moulded orders, the inner springing from shafts with moulded capitals and bases, within which is set the continuous moulded west doorway, and over it the remains of a niche with bracket for a statue. In the gable above the arch is a large circular window of four pairs of trefoiled lights radiating from a quatrefoil, the spaces between having sexfoil cusping: the window is surrounded by a hood-mould which dies into the apex of that of the great arch. Probably no other part of the building is contemporary with the west front, but parts of the north

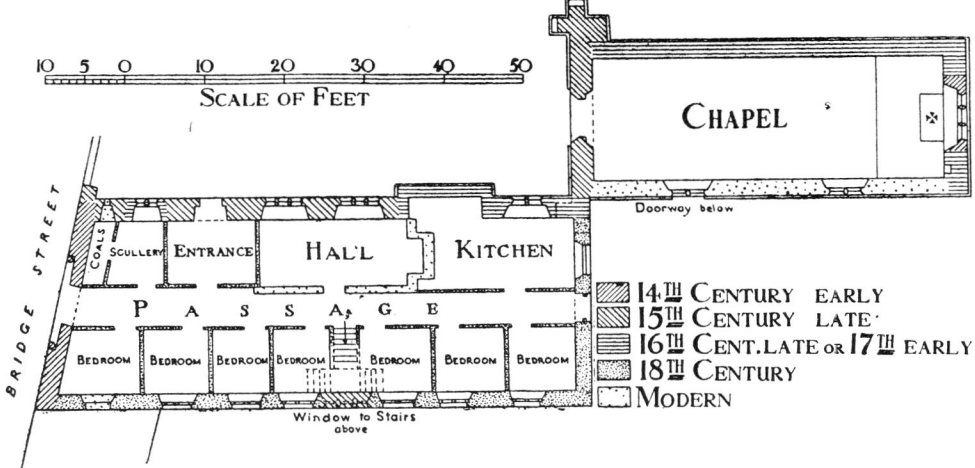

PLAN OF ST. JOHN'S HOSPITAL, NORTHAMPTON

consisted originally of an almshouse and chapel, with a master's house about 60 yards to the north-east. The site of 3¼ acres was bounded on the north by St. John's Lane, on the south by the town wall, and on the west by Bridge Street. The master's house has been pulled down, but the chapel and almshouse, or domicile, still stand. In 1871 the property was sold to the Midland Railway Company, and the master's house was demolished to make room for the Midland Station. The infirmary and chapel were resold to Mr. Mulliner, from whom they were purchased in 1877 for a Roman Catholic community, in whose possession they now are. The inmates of the hospital were transferred to a new building at Weston Favell, opened in 1879.

The almshouse is a building of red sandstone standing east and west, in plan a parallelogram, measuring internally 62 ft. 6 in. by 22 ft., except that the west wall is slightly skewed in order to accommodate itself to the direction of the street, and it is attached by its north-east angle to the south-west angle of the chapel. The building is of two stories, but has been a good deal rebuilt and altered.[17] The roof is wall and the middle part of the south wall, which contain pointed windows, are apparently of late 15th century date, and the square-headed windows on the north side are perhaps a century later. The greater part of the south wall and the whole of the east wall were rebuilt in the 18th century, when wooden-framed windows were introduced on both floors and alterations made in the interior arrangements. A 4 ft. passage runs down the middle of the building from the west to the east door, with staircase and a series of bedrooms on the south, and four larger rooms on the north side. There is reason to believe that originally the building did not extend so far to the east.[19] the buttresses of the south-west angle of the chapel having been cut away to allow for the erection of the east end of the north wall of the almshouse, which appears to be not earlier than the end of the 16th century. The side walls are about 16 ft. to the eaves, and in the middle of the south side is a window of three cinquefoiled lights with depressed head and hollow chamfered jambs, lighting the staircase, its sill about 6 ft. above the ground. This window contains the figure of a man and the name of 'Richard

---

[12] The positions indicated by Dr. Cox upon his map in *Boro Rec.* vol. ii, for the White Friars' and the Grey Friars' houses should be exchanged.

[13] G. N. Wetton, *Guide-book to Northampt.* p. 48.

[14] *V.C.H. Northants.* ii, 147; Serjeantson, op. cit.

[15] Inq. a.q.d. 16 Ed. ii, 160-2.

[16] *V. C. H. Northants.* ii, 156-9; Serjeantson in *Northants Nat. Hist. Soc.* vols. xvi and xvii.

[17] Bridges early in the 18th century states that it had been 'altered in some parts by modern reparations': op. cit. i, 457.

[18] The elevation towards the street is 29 ft. in length, inclusive of a later buttress at the north-west angle. The ground level has been raised outside.

[19] *Assoc. Arch. Soc. Reps.* xii, 233, in a paper by Sir Henry Dryden, 1875, use of which has been made in the present description.

Sherd,' who was master in 1474,[20] and it formerly contained also fragments of painted glass, including shields of Grey, Hastings and Valence, but these have been lately taken out. The stairs are not centrally placed, being slightly nearer the east end: from a landing below the window they lead east and west to two large upper rooms, one at each end of the building, said to have been for the ' co-brothers ' or chaplains.[21] On the north side of the ground floor passage is a room at the west end with a square-headed two-light window, and next to it one with a small pointed external doorway. Next to this is a larger room, or hall, lighted by two three-light windows similar to that on the staircase, and open to the roof, and at the east end the kitchen, which has a large projecting fireplace and a two-light square-headed window in the north wall. The roof of the building is of six bays. Although the division of hall and kitchen is apparently modern the construction of the two bays of roof over the hall seems to imply that this part of the building alone was always open its full height.[22] Of the two upper rooms, which are 22 ft. by 20 ft., that at the west end is lighted by the circular window and by two square-headed mullioned windows on the north, and two wooden-framed ones on the south side, and has a fireplace in the south-west angle. The eastern room has also mullioned windows on the north and wooden ones on the south side, and a fireplace with moulded jambs. Both rooms extend the full width of the building, and occupy two bays of the roof.

The chapel is in plan a plain rectangle, 16 ft. wide internally by 44 ft. long, built of local red sandstone, and the roof covered with blue slates. The three-light east window is of the early 14th century with cusped intersecting tracery and moulded mullions and jambs, and the chapel was probably wholly rebuilt in that period. The entrance is at the west end. The north wall is blank. The west wall is of the 15th century and has coupled buttresses at the angles standing wholly beyond the face of the north and south walls, i.e., the west end is nearly 6 ft. wider than the body of the chapel, and it is possible that the whole of the north, south and east walls have been rebuilt on a narrower plan, leaving the west end as it was and re-using the east window.[23] The building was extensively restored in 1853–4 by the Charity Commissioners, the whole of the south wall being then taken down and rebuilt in its present form with two two-light windows in the 14th century style,[24] below the westernmost of which is a small pointed doorway.[25] The roof of five bays and the wooden bell turret are modern. The building was renovated in 1882, to which date the present fittings belong. The buildings are now undergoing further repair.

The moulded west doorway has an almost semicircular two-centred head under a square label, the spandrels of which contain quatrefoils with square-leaf flowers. The original double doors remain. Above is a large four-centred five-light window with Perpendicular tracery and moulded jambs and mullions. The two-armed cross on the gable is said to be original. The doorway and west and east windows are of oolite. In the east windows are considerable remains of 15th century glass, including saints, a head of the Blessed Virgin, an angel holding a shield, and a kneeling figure.

The Master's House, now demolished, is said to have contained work of every century from the 13th to the 19th, and its architectural history was complicated.[26] It was rectangular in plan with a south porch and north-west wing, and had a frontage of about 87 ft. The hall, 26 ft. 3 in. by 19 ft. 2 in., had been divided in the 18th century. The kitchen and offices were at the west end.

THE HOSPITAL OF ST. LEONARD,[27] founded by Richard de Stafford in the 11th century, was in Hardingstone parish, outside the liberties, on the west side of the road leading to Queen's Cross. The hospital buildings, of which no description is extant, included a chapel and churchyard which served the inhabitants of Cotton End as a parish church. The Lazar House is mentioned in the Assembly Books from 1623 to 1823, when it was finally pulled down; it can have been little more than a cottage at this time, when there was only one recipient of the charity.

THE HOSPITAL OF ST THOMAS,[28] founded apparently in the 15th century, stood on the east side of Bridge Street, just outside the south gate. In 1834 the residents removed to a new house in St. Giles' Street, and the buildings were used for a carriage-builders' shop until, in 1874, they were pulled down to make room for a road to the new cattle market.[29] It was a rectangular 15th century stone building, consisting of a large hall, 22 ft. 3 in. wide internally with upper floor, and a chapel at its east end 15 ft. wide by 16 ft. 9 in. long, the south wall of which was continuous with that of the hall. The roofs were covered with Collyweston slates. At the time of demolition the hall, or domicile, was 54 ft. 8 in. long internally, but it had been shortened some 3 ft. or 4 ft. at the west end, probably for street-widening purposes. The original west elevation facing Bridge Street, as shown in Bridges' *History*, had a central arched doorway, with window on the south side, and above these a row of quatrefoils containing blank shields. Over the doorway was a four-light window and on each side of it a canopied niche containing a figure. The hall was, no doubt, formerly divided by screens in the usual way, with cubicles arranged round the walls: several lockers[30] remained in both the north and south walls, but some had been converted into windows. In the middle of the north wall was a large fireplace, one jamb only of which was

---

[20] This may give the approximate date of the 15th century alterations.

[21] Bridges, *Hist. of Northants.* i, 457.

[22] *Assoc. Arch. Soc. Reps.* xii, 233.

[23] Ibid. 232. There are no buttresses at the north-east and south-east angles, and except at the west end, where it is chamfered, the plinth is a mere set-off.

[24] They are said to have been indicated by fragments found in the wall, but the windows previously in the south wall were round-headed and probably of 18th century date: ibid. 230.

[25] The doorway is probably in its original position, but the form of the previous one is not known: ibid. 230.

[26] *Assoc. Arch. Soc. Reps.* xii, 225, where there is a lengthy description by Sir Henry Dryden. His measured drawing of the building is in the collection of the Northampt. Arch. Soc. in the rooms of the Ladies' Club.

[27] *V.C.H. Northants.* ii, 159–161; Serjeantson, *Northants Nat. Hist. Soc.* Vol. xviii.

[28] *V.C.H. Northants* ii, 161–2; Serjeantson, *Hospital of St.Thomas, Northampt.* (1909).

[29] The following description is based on a paper by Sir Henry Dryden in *Assoc. Arch. Soc. Reps.* xiii, 225–231.

[30] They were 3 ft. 3 in. high, 2 ft. 2 in. wide, and 16 in. deep. There were no lockers in the upper room.

Northampton : St. Thomas' Hospital (now destroyed)

BOROUGH OF NORTHAMPTON

original, and two square-headed two-light windows. There was no arched wall opening to the chapel at the east end of the 'domicile' and no trace of any division between the chapel and the lower room, though probably a screen had existed.[31] The upper room had several windows. The chapel had an east window of four cinquefoiled lights with vertical tracery and a canopied niche on either side within : in the south wall was a piscina and a window of three lights. Both chapel and domicile had open timber roofs, the former of two, the latter of five bays, with wind braces under the upper and lower purlins.

After its vacation in 1834 the building was used for business purposes.[32]

Two hospitals stood outside the north gate of the town in Kingsthorpe parish; the Leper hospital of Walbeck[33] and the hospital of St. David and the Trinity,[34] founded in 1200 by the prior and convent of St. Andrew's on the petition of Peter, son of Adam.

THE COLLEGE OF ALL SAINTS,[35] founded in 1460, stood on the west side of College Lane, opposite the end of College Yard, and consisted of a priest's house for the warden and fellows and a garden. It was used as a hospital for the sick during the plague of 1603 to 1605, being then the property of Abraham Ventris.[36]

There were two HERMITAGES, one on the west and the other on the south bridge.

THE CASTLE HILL MEETING is probably older in origin than 1662,[37] though it was augmented by secessions from St. Giles' and St. Peter's in that year. In 1672 licenses were granted for worship in 6 houses in Northampton, of which three were Presbyterian and two Congregational.[38] The definite history of the Castle Hill congregation begins with the ministry of Samuel Blower in 1674; and his meeting house was one of the few that escaped the fire. The present Castle Hill Chapel was built in 1695 and is now known as Doddridge Chapel. It is a rectangular building with hipped roof. On the south side is a sundial on which was originally the motto, 'Post est occasio calva, 1695.' Within, the roof was propped inside by two great wooden pillars, and there was a heavy white pulpit with sounding-board and galleries. In 1852 the building was enlarged and newly roofed, the pillars removed and new galleries put up. A spacious vestibule was added on the south side in 1890 covering the doorways. There are five other Congregational chapels, of which one was built in the 18th, three in the 19th, and one in the 20th century.

NONCONFORMIST CHAPELS.

COLLEGE STREET CHAPEL is the second oldest Free Church centre. In its origin it was a secession from Castle Hill Meeting, though friendly relations were maintained between the two, and the members met for some seventeen years at Lady Fermor's house in the south quarter. The 'Church Covenant' at the time of the formal establishment of a Baptist church is dated 27 October 1697,[39] and the chapel in College Street was built in 1712. Beginning as an Independent, it became a Baptist community. As Castle Hill is associated with Doddridge (1729–53) so College Street is connected with the Rylands, father and son, the elder famous for his ministry (1759–86) and his school; the younger (minister 1786–93) for his friendship with Carey and share in founding the Baptist Missionary Society (1792).[40] There are eight other Baptist chapels in Northampton besides the College Street Chapel, which was rebuilt in 1863. Of these one, Providence Chapel, Abington Street, was built in the eighteenth and the rest in the 19th century.

There are six Wesleyan chapels, four Primitive Methodist chapels, two chapels of the Plymouth Brethren, one Unitarian chapel, and two Salvation Army barracks.

The Friends were early persecuted in Northampton, and several died in Northampton gaol. They have a meeting house in Wellington Street.

The cathedral of the Roman Catholic diocese of Northampton, opened as ST. FELIX CHURCH in 1844, now the church of St. Mary and St. Thomas of Canterbury, is in the Kingsthorpe Road. The chapel of St. John's hospital in Bridge Street is also used as a Roman Catholic place of worship. There is a Jewish synagogue in Overstone Road.

SCHOOLS.

To the account of the early schools of Northampton in the previous volume[40a] should be added a reference of the year 1232. John de Duston, presented in that year to the church of St. Bartholomew's, Northampton, by the prior and convent of St. Andrew's, and being examined by the archdeacon of Northampton, was ordered to frequent the schools of Northampton and study there, and at the end of the year to present himself to the archdeacon for re-examination.[41] In 1258 the Grey Friars of Northampton were granted ten oaks from Silverstone Forest for the building of their schools.[42] In the same year the Black Friars were given six good oaks for their study rooms (studia).[43] Possibly these buildings are to be associated with the transitory university of Northampton, whose history was given in the previous volume.[44]

The Grammar School[45] endowed by Chipsey in 1541 and housed first at 'The Lamb' in Bridge Street and later on the site of St. Gregory's Church, in the modern Free School Street, was moved in 1867 to new buildings in Abington Square, and in 1911 to the

---

[31] 'The part of the east wall of the domicile outside the chapel roof was wooden framework, covered with lath and plaster,' except a small piece of stone work covering the wall over a doorway at the east end of the hall north of the chapel: Assoc. Arch. Soc. Reps. xiii, 227.

[32] The chapel and the east part of the hall were used as a carriage house, double doors being inserted at the east end below the window. After the rebuilding of the west wall, probably early in the 19th century, a small house had been constructed in the north-west part of this hall, and a large doorway made in the south end of the new west wall to admit carriages. Some 14th-century glass from the Hospital is now in the Church of St. Sepulchre: Cox and Serjeantson, Hist of Ch. of Holy Sepulchre, Northampt. 50.

[33] V.C.H. Northants. ii, 162; Northants. Nat. Hist. Soc., Vol. xviii.

[34] V.C.H. Northants. ii, 154–6.

[35] Ibid.

[36] Serjeantson, Hist. of Ch. of All Saints, Northampt., p. 72.

[37] V.C.H. Northants. ii, 69; T. Gasquoine, etc., Hist of Castle Hill Ch. Northampt. 1896.

[38] Cal. S. P. Dom. 1671–2, p. 306; ibid. 1672, 238, 379; ibid. 1672–3, 178, 259, 261.

[39] J. Taylor, Hist. of College St. Ch. (Northampt. 1896), p. 3.

[40] V.C.H. Northants. ii, 74; Dict. Nat. Biog.

[40a] V.C.H. Northants. ii, 15, 16.

[41] Linc. Rec. Soc. vi, 170.

[42] Close R. 42 Hen. III, m.6.

[43] Ibid. m. 2.

[44] V.C.H. Northants. ii, 15–17.

[45] Ibid. ii, 234–41.

present buildings in the Billing Road, just outside the municipal boundary. It is now known as the Town and County School, and has some 530 pupils.[46]

In the 18th century Northampton became a centre of Nonconformist higher education, by the presence here, from 1729 to 1751, of Philip Doddridge's academy, a training college for the Free Church ministry. This academy, opened in July 1729 at Market Harborough under Doddridge's headship, came to Northampton with him and was originally in No. 34 Marefair, at the corner of Pike Lane.[47] In 1740 it was removed to a large house in Sheep Street opposite the Ram.[48] Formerly the Rose and Crown inn, it later became the town house of the Earl of Halifax, and later still was divided into tenements. The course of instruction was based upon that of Doddridge's tutor at Kibworth, John Jennings,[49] and included Hebrew, Greek, psychology, ethics, divinity, natural philosophy, civil law and some mathematics. All had to learn Doddridge's special system of shorthand.[50] The full course occupied five years, and some two hundred pupils passed under his care, of whom 120 entered the ministry,[51] and several had careers of distinction.[52] After his death, the academy removed to Daventry, and was carried on by Caleb Ashworth, one of his own former pupils. The elder Ryland also had an academy; but this was no more than a boarding school (1769-1786); it moved with him to Enfield when he resigned the ministry of College Street Chapel to his son.[53]

The three charity schools, namely, Dryden's Free School, or the Orange School, founded in 1710, the Blue Coat School, founded by the Earl of Northampton in 1755, and combined with Dryden's, and the Green Coat School, founded by Gabriel Newton in 1761, were amalgamated in one, known as the Corporation Charity School, and survived until the 20th century. In April 1923 the school having been closed, the endowments of the charity were, under a scheme of the Board of Education, devoted to educational purposes, forming a fund known as the Blue Coat Corporation Charity School Foundation for the provision of scholarships.[54]

Becket and Sargeant's (Blue) Girls' School, founded in 1738 for 30 girls,[55] is still in existence at 13 Kingswill Street. On the Sunday next after 29 May, following the practice of the 18th century,[56] the school girls attend a special service at All Saints' Church, wearing their distinctive dress.

In 1738, owing to the efforts of Doddridge, a free church charity school was established for instructing and clothing twenty boys which seems to have come to an end about 1772.[57]

In 1812 British and National Schools were set up by Lancaster and Bell respectively. A number of Church of England schools were set up in the course of the 19th century, five being founded between 1839 and 1858, and nine more before the close of the century. There are now 22 elementary schools, of which two are Church of England; and in addition one special school for mentally deficient children and two Roman Catholic elementary schools.

There are two girls' secondary schools: namely, the Girls' High School, Derngate (165 pupils), and the County Borough Secondary Girls' School, in St. George's Avenue, opened in 1915 (270 pupils). There are also a number of private schools, including a convent school, a large and imposing building in Abington Street, under the Sisters of Notre Dame.

The Northampton School of Arts and Crafts, Abington Street, now under the control of the county borough, was established in 1871; the Technical School in Abington Square was opened in 1894; a Domestic Economy School, under the Northants County Council, in Harleston Road, was established in 1896, and there is a housewifery centre, under the Northampton Education Committee.

CHARITIES. Cleveland Henry James Butterfield, by a declaration of trust dated 12 April 1923, gave £100, the interest to be applied in granting a prize to the most deserving mother during the year. The endowment, known as the Catherine Anne Butterfield Memorial Charity, now consists of £124 8s. 1d. 3½ per cent. Conversion Stock with the Official Trustees producing £4 7s. 2d., which is distributed by the Town Clerk and four other trustees appointed under the provisions of the declaration of trust.

Mrs. Mary Clark, by her will proved 9 March 1907, gave £200, the income to be distributed among the poor members and attendants at the Doddridge Congregational Chapel. The money was invested in £300 15s. Consols and is with the Official Trustees producing £7 10s. 4d. yearly which is distributed by the deacons amongst the poor members of the congregation.

Emma Pressland, by her will proved at Northampton 24 Feb. 1911, gave £100 to the trustees of the Doddridge Congregational Chapel, to apply the income for providing coal for the poor members of the chapel. The money was invested on mortgage producing approximately £7 annually.

William Jeffery, by his will proved 14 March 1896, gave £200, the income to be distributed among the poor members of the Doddridge Congregational Chapel. The endowment of the charity now consists of £211 13s. 10d. 5 per cent. War Stock 1929-47 with the Official Trustees; the dividends amounting to £10 11s. 8d. yearly are distributed by the trustees among the poor members of the chapel.

Mary Jeffery, by her will proved at Northampton on the 4 March 1864 bequeathed £150, the interest to be equally divided between the Coal Club, Sunday School and Bible Mission in connexion with the Doddridge Congregational Chapel. The endowment of the charity now consists of £284 Northampton Gas Light Company Consolidated Stock; the dividends are distributed annually.

---

[46] A. P. White, *The Story of Northampt.* pp. 109, 112, 150.
[47] T. Gasquoine, *Hist. of Castle Hill Ch., Northampt.*, p. 22.
[48] Ibid, p. 19.
[49] Jennings' Lectures, printed at the *Northampton Mercury* office in 1721, are in the Taylor Collection in the Northampt. Public Library. [Author J.J.]
[50] The Rules of the Academy, from a MS. Book at New College, Hampstead, are printed Gasquoine, op. cit. pp. 63-71.
[51] Job Orton, *Life of Doddridge* (ed. D. Russell), p. 115.
[52] E.g. Dr. Aiken, Dr. Kippis, J. Orton, T. Urwick, Samuel Merivale, Stephen Addington, Benjamin Fawcett, etc.
[53] Ibid. p. 269.
[54] Information from the Town Clerk.
[55] See tombstone of founders, with figure of Charity school girl, in All Saints' Church, west end of north aisle.
[56] The children then wore gilded oak apples.
[57] Gasquoine, *Hist. of Castle Hill Ch.* p. 24-5.

BOROUGH OF NORTHAMPTON

Rebecca Clifford, by her will dated 19 Jan. 1719, gave a yearly payment of £10 issuing out of premises No. 24, in the Drapery, Northampton, for the wives or widows of poor members of the Corporation of Northampton. This charge was redeemed in 1915 and the endowment now consists of £333 6s. 8d. India 3 per cent. stock with the Official Trustees producing £10 annually. The charity is administered by five trustees appointed under the provisions of the scheme of the Charity Commissioners, dated 8 May 1903.

The same donor, by her will dated as above, gave a yearly payment of £10 charged upon her messuage and liquorice ground in Northampton, to be distributed annually to the poor of Northampton. This charge was redeemed in 1901 and the endowment of the charity now consists of £400 Consols with the Official Trustees producing £10 annually. The charity is administered by five trustees appointed under the provisions of the scheme of the Charity Commissioners dated 14 March 1902.

John Shortgrave, by his will dated 27 November 1775, gave a sum of £350, the income thereon to be applied in the purchase of clothing for poor men of Northampton. The endowment now consists of £428 10s. 3d. Consols with the Official Trustees producing annually £10 14s., which are applied in accordance with the trusts by the Vicar of All Saints' and three others as trustees.

Susannah Elizabeth Jones, by her will proved at Northampton on 13 Feb. 1909, gave to the Mayor of Northampton for the time being, £1,100 for the benefit of poor widows and spinsters. The endowment now consists of £1,310 14s. 8d. Consols with the Official Trustees producing £32 15s. 4d. annually.

Jonathan Warner, by will dated 17 July 1725, gave £60, the income to be applied in providing coats for four poor men of Northampton. To this sum a further £65 16s. 10d. was added by Christopher Smyth in order that better coats might be provided. The endowment now consists of £200 Consols with the Official Trustees producing £5 annually which is expended by four trustees.

Georgiana Sophia Worley, by her will proved 18 May 1907, gave to her trustees the residue of her estate (after payment of debts, legacies, etc.) to be sold, the proceeds to be invested and the interest thereon to be expended in providing pensions for poor widows. The endowment of the charity now consists of sums of £93 9s. 6d. Consols, £1,316 5s. 5d. Cape of Good Hope 3½ per cent. stock, £1,300 Natal 3½ per cent. stock, £1,800 London Midland and Scottish Railway 4 per cent. preference stock, and £1,032 London Midland and Scottish Railway 4 per cent. preference stock, with the Official Trustees, producing approximately £207 annually. The charity is administered by the Vicar and Churchwardens.

George Coles, by an indenture dated 1 Sept. 1640, conveyed to trustees properties situate at Northampton, the rents and profits to be distributed among the poor. The charity is now administered by trustees appointed by a scheme established by the Charity Commissioners dated 11 July 1919. The endowment consists of messuages known as Nos. 37 and 39, Gold Street, Northampton; £4,714 15s. 10d. Consols, and £524 17s. 7d. 5 per cent. War Stock 1929–47, with the Official Trustees, the whole producing approximately £436 per annum.

Julia Ellen Rice, by her will dated 25 Nov. 1922, gave a sum of £400 as a fund for providing pensions for two poor old persons in Northampton. The endowment now consists of £400 5 per cent. War Stock 1929–47, with the Official Trustees, producing £20 annually. The charity is administered by the trustees of George Coles' Charity.

John Friend, by his will dated 29 Jan. 1683, gave to trustees his messuage called the Black Boy and 2 acres of garden ground, the rent to be appropriated to such charitable purposes as the trustees and the Mayor and Justices of Northampton should think fit. The properties were sold, and the endowment now consists of £3,811 2s. 4d. Consols, £4,387 6s. 1d. Consols, £250 13s. 9d. 3½ per cent. War Stock, £400 5 per cent. War Stock 1929–47, held by the Official Trustees and producing £233 14s. 6d. annually. The charity is now administered by trustees appointed by a scheme of the Charity Commissioners dated 2 May 1922.

Henry Green, by his will proved at Northampton on 26 Oct. 1922, gave to the trustees of Kettering Road Free Church, Northampton, £100, the income thereof to be applied by the trustees to such purposes in connection with the church as they think fit. The endowment of the charity consists of £180 1s. 3 per cent. stock, standing in the names of T. T. West, B. Nelson and John Sale, producing £5 8s. annually.

The Royal Victoria Dispensary, to which charity the Charitable Trusts Acts 1853 to 1914 were extended by an order of the Charity Commissioners of 21 June 1921, is now regulated by a scheme of the Commissioners dated 9 Feb. 1923. The endowment consists of £1,367 7s. 3d. 3½ per cent. Conversion Stock, £250 India 3½ per cent. stock, and £623 14s. 9d. Natal 3½ per cent. Inscribed Stock, with the Official Trustees, producing £78 11s. 4d. annually, which is administered by the members for the time being of the Board of Management of the Northampton General Hospital as trustees towards providing convalescent treatment for patients or ex-patients.

By a declaration of trust dated 6 Mar. 1920 Sir Henry Edward Randall gave £5,000, the interest to be applied in granting annuities of £25 per annum to poor widows or spinsters of not less than 55 years of age. The endowment now consists of £5,949 5s. 11d. 4½ per cent. Conversion Stock with the Official Trustees, producing £267 14s. 4d. yearly. This is distributed by the trustees appointed under the provisions of the declaration.

The endowment of the charity of Jane Porter consists of £96 19s. 2d. India 3½ per cent. stock with the Official Trustees and is administered by trustees appointed by deed. The income, amounting to £3 8s. annually, is distributed to poor members of the congregation of the Protestant Dissenting Chapel, in accordance with the provisions of the deed dated 16 July 1901. The origin of the charity is unknown.

The endowment of the charity of Mary Holmes and the charity for the Minister consists of £305 14s. 3d. Consols with the Official Trustees, producing £7 12s. 10d. yearly, which is paid to the minister of the Protestant Dissenting Chapel by the trustees appointed by deed. The origin of the charities is unknown.

John Driden, by his will dated 2 Jan. 1707, among

A HISTORY OF NORTHAMPTONSHIRE

other bequests, gave £1 per annum for a sermon to be preached one day at Christmas in remembrance of the donor of the charity.

Daniel Herbert, by his will dated 9 Nov. 1696, gave £10 per annum, charged upon his farm at Burton Latimer, for the purpose of apprenticing poor boys resident in the borough. By an order of the Charity Commissioners dated 6 July 1906 it was determined that the sums of £400 and £40 Consols with the Official Trustees should be set aside to form the endowments of the above mentioned charities. The income, amounting to £10 and £1 respectively, is applied by the trustees.

The Almshouse adjoining St. Thomas's Hospital was erected by Sir John Langham about the year 1682. By an indenture dated 14 June 1797 £300 stock was given by Juliana Lady Langham for the benefit of the two women inmates. The endowment of the charity now consists of £923 3s. 3d. Consols with the Official Trustees, producing £23 1s. 4d. annually, which is distributed to the two almswomen. By an order of the Charity Commissioners dated in 1870, the Vicar and Churchwardens of All Saints' were appointed trustees *ex officio* of the charity.

St. John's Hospital, formerly regulated by a scheme of the High Court of Chancery of 15 June 1875, is now regulated by a scheme of the Charity Commissioners dated 5 Dec. 1913. The endowment of the hospital consists of considerable properties in Northampton and various sums of stock held by the Official Trustees in trust for the charity, as set out in the schedule of the scheme of 1913. In accordance with the provisions of the scheme, the income is applied in the payment of the stipends of the Master and of the out-pensioners of the charity, and in supporting and maintaining the hospital and the inmates therein. The trustees consist of 14 persons, among whom the Master and the Mayor for the time being of Northampton are included *ex officio*. The hospital has now been moved to Weston Favell and the building in Bridge Street sold.

William Rae, by his will proved in the Principal Registry 13 Aug. 1906, gave £500 to the Weston Favell Convalescent Home connected with the St. John's Hospital, the income to be devoted to the purchase of newspapers, periodicals and books for the use of the patients. The endowment now consists of £497 9s. 3d. New South Wales 3½ per cent. Inscribed Stock and £104 14s. 8d. 3½ per cent. Conversion Stock with the Official Trustees, producing £21 1s. 6d. yearly, which is applied by the trustees of St. John's Hospital. The same donor by his will gave £5,000 and the residue of his estate to the Northampton Town and County Nursing Institution, to be invested and the income devoted to the services of the Queen's District Nurses in Northampton. The endowment now consists of various sums of stocks invested in private names, producing in 1925 approximately £640, which is applied by the trustees of the Queen Victoria Nursing Institution.

The endowment of the Margaret Spencer Home of Rest consists of £20,000 5 per cent. War Stock 1929-47 held by the Official Trustees, and forming part of the endowments of the Northamptonshire Regimental Prisoners of War Fund, as provided by a scheme of the Charity Commissioners dated 26 Nov. 1920. The income, amounting to £1,000 yearly, is paid by the trustees to the Board of Management of the Northampton General Hospital towards the maintenance of the Home.

The following charities are applied to the General Hospital:—

The Rev. John Henry Smith, by his will proved at Northampton 29 Feb. 1884, gave to the Governors of the General Hospital £100 for investment. The endowment now consists of £99 2s. 8d. Consols with the Official Trustees, producing £2 9s. 4d. yearly.

William Dash, by his will proved at Northampton 12 April 1883, gave £100 to be invested for the general purposes of the hospital.

George Charles Benn, by his will proved in the Principal Registry 14 Nov. 1895, gave his farm and lands situate at Bozeat to the Governors for the benefit of the hospital. The property was sold in 1896 and the net proceeds, amounting approximately to £1,287, invested.

The John Putley Bequest, founded by will proved at Taunton 17 June 1899, bequeathed to the treasurer of the hospital £100 for investment.

Mrs. Margaret Webster, by will dated 11 Oct. 1759, bequeathed £130 to be applied to the payment of a chaplain to the hospital to the extent of £30 a year for 4 years, and gave certain directions for the performance of the duties of the chaplain.

Sir Edmund Isham, Bart., by a codicil to his will dated 3 Jan. 1865, bequeathed £1,000 stock, the income to be applied to the support of the chaplain.

Sarah Edwards, by will proved in the Principal Registry 11 Mar. 1919, bequethed the sum of £1,000 to the treasurer of the hospital for the endowment in perpetuity of a bed to be named the 'Sarah Edwards" bed.

Louisa Mary Lady Knightley of Fawsley, by will proved in the Principal Registry 3 Feb. 1914, bequeathed to the treasurer a sum of £1,000, the interest to be applied for the endowment of a bed to be called 'The Rainald Knightley' bed.

Thomas Faucott Sanders, by will proved in the Principal Registry 3 June 1921, bequeathed the residue of his estate for the general purposes of the hospital.

Francis Clarke, by will proved at Northampton 27 July 1910, gave a third of the residue of his estate to be disposed of and the proceeds invested for the same purpose. The endowment now consists of a sum of £1,866 17s. 4d. Consols, standing in private names.

Mary Augusta Scott, by will proved in the Principal Registry 15 Mar. 1913, bequeathed £1,000 to the treasurer for endowing a bed in memory of her parents, William and Sophia Scott.

Edwin Ellard, founded by will proved in the Principal Registry 17 Mar. 1925, whereby he devised certain real estate in the County of Northampton, subject to a life interest to his widow, upon trust for the hospital. The widow of the testator is still living.

The following charities comprise the Municipal (Church) Charities, and are regulated by a scheme of the Charity Commissioners dated 15 Aug. 1899:—

St. Thomas's Hospital is supposed to have been founded and endowed by the citizens and burgesses of Northampton about the year 1450 for the benefit of the poor of the town, and was dedicated to the

BOROUGH OF NORTHAMPTON

memory of St. Thomas of Canterbury. By the original foundation twelve poor people were maintained in the hospital upon a small weekly allowance besides clothing and fuel, arising from bequests made by Edward Elmar, Agnes Hopkins, Thomas Hopkins, John Bryan, Thomas Craswell and others. In 1654 and 1680 John Langham and Richard Massingberg made further bequests, and in 1683 James Bales devised considerable estates for the use and yearly relief of the poor people of the hospital, the rents of which were first received in 1748. In 1833 the present hospital was erected. The income of the charity is derived from various properties in Northampton (the donors of which are in most cases unknown) and considerable sums of stock held by the Official Trustees. In 1925 the income was approximately £3,000. The number of pensioners has varied from time to time, and in 1925 amounted to 9 in-pensioners and 141 out-pensioners.

Sophia Danner, by will proved at Peterborough 15 July 1925, gave £250 for the benefit of St. Thomas's Hospital. The endowment now consists of £255 2s. 11d. Funding Stock 1960–90 with the Official Trustees, producing £10 4s. 1d. yearly.

William Parbery Hannen, by will proved at Northampton 3 Feb. 1921, gave to the trustees £25, the interest to be applied in providing warm garments for the oldest widow of St. Giles Street Almshouses. This sum is now represented by £34 11s. 6d. Local Loans 3 per cent. stock with the Official Trustees, producing £1 0s. 8d. yearly.

James Henry Clifden Crockett in 1924 gave £1,000, the interest to be used for the benefit of in and out pensioners of St. Thomas's Hospital. This sum was invested in £1,134 12s. 4d. 4 per cent. Funding Stock 1960–90 with the Official Trustees, producing £45 7s. 8d. annually.

The endowment of Wades' Charity, the origin of which is unknown, consists of a payment of £2 out of the revenues of the town council, whereof £1 is paid to the minister of All Saints' for a charity sermon, 13s. 4d. to the churchwardens for distribution in bread to the poor, 3s. 4d. to the clerk, and 3s. 4d. to the sexton.

Robert Ives, by will dated 16 Sept. 1703, bequeathed £100 to the corporation upon trust to purchase freehold land, the rents of which to be applied as follows :—20s. yearly to the minister of All Saints' to preach a sermon in the church on New Year's Day, and the residue to be applied by the mayor and minister of All Saints' for clothing poor old men and women. The endowment now consists of a rent charge of £5 issuing out of Mill Holme Meadow.

The charities are administered by a body of trustees consisting of 6 representative trustees and 14 co-optative trustees.

The following charities comprise the Municipal (General) Charities, and are regulated by a scheme of the Charity Commissioners dated 30 July 1915 :—

John Ball bequeathed to the corporation £50, and directed that the interest be applied in clothing six poor widows of the parish of All Saints on St. Thomas's Day. The endowment now consists of £50, invested on mortgage, the interest of £2 being distributed in money to six poor widows.

The Bugbrooke Charity, formerly the Corporation Charity School and the Earl of Northampton's Gift, was founded by indentures dated 1 and 2 Jan, 1755, whereby the estate at Bugbrooke was conveyed to the mayor, bailiffs and burgesses upon trust that they should apply two-thirds of the rents and profits to poor freemen of Northampton. The endowment of the charity now consists of a yearly sum of £100, payable out of income of land at Bugbrooke containing about 67 acres, also land and cottages at Bugbrooke containing about 12 acres, which is applied in clothing and donations to 15 poor freemen.

Thomas Crasswell in 1606 bequeathed to the corporation £50, the interest to be given yearly towards the preferment of a poor maid of Northampton in marriage.

The endowment now consists of £50 invested on mortgage, producing £2 annually, which is paid to the mayor, and distributed as above.

Matthew Sillesby by will dated 18 April 1662 gave to the mayor, bailiffs and burgesses a messuage, tenement, garden, and a close of ground all in Northampton, the rents and profits to be distributed between two poor widows or widowers of Northampton, more especially of the parish of All Saints. The endowment now consists of £1,994 15s. 1d. Consols with the Official Trustees—£333 6s. 8d. Consols in the High Court of Justice, producing £58 4s. annually, which is distributed to three poor widows in annuities, together with residence at 35, Horsemarket.

Richard White, by will dated 1 June 1691, gave to the mayor, bailiffs and burgesses two closes of land at Duston, also garden ground at St. Peter and All Saints, the rents and profits to be distributed between two poor widows, one of whom to be of the parish of St. Peter. The land has since been sold, and the endowment now consists of £1,313 10s. 2d. Consols with the Official Trustees, £2,178 13s. 4d. Consols with the High Court of Justice and £150 National War Bonds (1927), the whole producing £94 16s. annually, which is distributed in annuities to poor widows.

Sir Thomas White, by an indenture dated 26 July 1552, conveyed certain estates in Coventry and the County of Warwick to the mayor, bailiffs, and commonalty the rents and profits of the estates to be lent out in free loan to young men of Northampton. The rents are received from the Coventry trustees every 5 years, and lent out to young men of Northampton in sums of £100 each for 9 years without interest. In 1922 the sum of £3,152 15s. was received from the Coventry Corporation, and the total amount of the loans outstanding on 31 December 1925 was £42,900. These charities are administered by 10 representative trustees and 11 co-optative trustees.

Ann Camp, by her will proved at Northampton 19 April 1899, directed that the whole of her real estate should be sold and the proceeds after payment of certain expenses and debts, invested, the income to be applied in granting pensions to poor widows or spinsters possessing the qualifications mentioned in the will. The endowment of the charity now consists of £3,300 invested on mortgage, £5,155 3s. 6d. 5 per cent. War Stock, and £5,333 3s. Corporation Redeemable Stock. The income is distributed in annuities of £20 per annum to poor widows and spinsters. The trustees of the charity are the

A HISTORY OF NORTHAMPTONSHIRE

trustees for the time being of the Municipal General Charities.

The endowment of the charity of Samuel Wollaston consists of a rent charge of £2 10s. a year issuing out of premises in Royal Terrace, Northampton, for the benefit of the poor of Northampton. The income is administered by the minister of All Saints' and the mayor of the borough.

The charity of George Phillips, founded by will proved at Northampton on 21 December 1899, is now regulated by a scheme of the Charity Commissioners of 23 March 1910. The income of the charity is applied by the trustees for the benefit of indigent blind persons belonging to the town and county of Northampton.

The Northamptonshire and Peterborough Prison Charities, consisting of the charities of Rebecca Hussey, Margaret Countess of Lucan, and John Hall, are regulated by a scheme of the Charity Commissioners dated 1 Nov. 1889. The endowment consists of £1,714 13s. 9d. Consols and £150 National War Bonds 1928, with the Official Trustees, producing £50 7s. 4d. annually, which is applied for the benefit of discharged prisoners, preference being given for the County of Northampton and the Liberty of Peterborough. The trustees of the charities are the Visiting Committee of H.M. Prison of Northampton.

Whiston's Gift is a lost charity. No account can be given of a payment of £4 a year in respect of this gift, mentioned in Gilbert's Returns. It has not been received for many years, nor is it known from whom it was received.

Parish of All Saints.—William Parbery Hannen, by will proved at Northampton 3 Feb. 1921, bequeathed to his trustees properties known as Nos. 144 and 146, High Road, and No. 1A, Villiers Road, Willesden Green, London, the income thereof to be distributed among the aged poor of the parishes of All Saints and St. Katherine. The properties were sold in 1921 and the proceeds invested in £869 5s. 4d. 5 per cent. War Stock 1929-47, in the name of the Official Trustees of Charitable Funds. By a scheme of the Charity Commissioners dated 2 Jan. 1923 the sum of stock was apportioned between the two parishes, each receiving £434 12s. 8d. 5 per cent. War Stock, 1929-47. The income, amounting to £21 14s. 8d. yearly in dividends in each case, is applied by the churchwardens of the respective parishes. The same donor also gave the sum of £28 to the churchwardens of All Saints' to provide the choir boys with a new shilling each on Christmas Day.

Edward Whitton, in or before 1774, bequeathed a legacy consisting of £100 4 per cent. Annuities, the income to be applied in providing bread for poor persons of the parishes of All Saints, St. Giles, St. Peter and St. Sepulchre. The endowment now consists of £100 Consols, with the Official Trustees, producing £2 10s. yearly, each parish receiving 12s. 6d. a year. By an order of the Charity Commissioners, dated 1 August 1905 the incumbents' churchwardens of each parish were appointed trustees for the administration of the charity.

William Stratford, by will dated 16 July 1753, gave £500, the income to be applied for the benefit of poor housekeepers and other poor. This sum was expended in the purchase of an estate at Helmdon, which was sold in 1920, and the proceeds invested in £3,113 8s. 5d. Local Loans 3 per cent. Stock, in the name of the Official Trustees. The income amounts to £93 8s. annually.

Francis Clarke, by will proved at Northampton 27 July 1910, gave to the vicar and churchwardens of All Saints' £500 London and North Eastern Railway 4 per cent. Guaranteed Stock, and £250 London and North Eastern Railway 4 per cent. Guaranteed Stock, the interest to be distributed among the sick and aged poor of the parish. The stock has been transferred into the name of the Official Trustees, and the dividends, amounting to £30 annually, are distributed by the vicar and churchwardens.

Mrs. Dorcas Sargeant, as appears by an entry in the vestry book of the parish of All Saints, gave the rents of a small plot of ground in Cow Lane, Northampton, for the clothing of two poor widows. The land was sold in 1877, and the endowment now consists of £627 12s. 5d. Consols, with the Official Trustees, producing £15 13s. 8d yearly in dividends, which are applied by the vicar and churchwardens. In the year ending 31 March 1926, 16 widows received clothing.

The Beckett and Sargeant Sermon Charity was founded by Dorothy Beckett and Anne Sargeant, by deed dated 20 Sept. 1735. The deed (among other things) directed the trustees to pay the yearly sum of £1 to the vicar of All Saints' to preach a sermon yearly on the Feast of St. Andrew in All Saints' Church, for which purpose £40 Consols with the Official Trustees has been set aside.

James Bracegirdle, by will dated 24 March 1633, gave an annual rent charge of £2 issuing out of land at Bugbrooke to be distributed among the poor of All Saints and St. Sepulchre.

Each parish receives 16s. annually for distribution, 8s. being deducted from the charge in respect of land tax. The vicar and churchwardens of All Saints' and St. Sepulchre's are the Trustees.

Under the charity of Sir Edward Nicholls, founded by will dated 12 August 1708, the vicar of All Saints' receives from the trustees £30 per annum for the augmentation of the vicarage.

Parish of St. Andrew.—The charity of Miss C. E. Hyndman was founded by deeds dated in 1836 and 1842 which provided that the interest on £272 3 per cent. Annuities should be applied towards the cost of the repair of St. Andrew's Church. The endowment now consists of £272 Consols with the Official Trustees producing £6 16s. annually. The charity is administered by the churchwardens of St. Andrew's.

Parish of St. Giles.—The Feoffment Estates comprises the following:—The charity of Edward Watson founded by deed dated 2 Edward VI, 1548, which provided that the income of the charity should be applied for the benefit of the poor of the parish. The endowment consists of property known as 'The Chequers' Inn, 4 cottages and 6 closes of land at Rothersthorpe containing about 45 acres. The charity of George Coldwell, founded by deed dated 22 Mar. 1553, which provided that the income of the charity should be applied for the use and relief of the poor and for other pious and charitable uses within the parish of St. Giles. The endowment consists of two shops and houses known as Nos. 40

BOROUGH OF NORTHAMPTON

and 40a, Abington Street, together with the rent of £1 per annum received from the 'Vine' Inn. The charity of Thomas Stone was founded by deed dated 31 Eliz., 1589. The endowment consists of 5 houses known as Nos. 20, 22, 24, 26 and 28, Wood Street. The trusts of the charity were similar to those of George Coldwell's charity.

Owen Dodden, by will dated 26 July 1615, gave £100, the income to be given to the poor of the parish of St. Giles. The money was invested in the purchase of a dwelling house known as No. 64a, Abingdon Street, Northampton. The house was sold in 1913 and the proceeds invested in £533 4s. 8d. Consols in the name of the Official Trustees.

Nicholas Rothwell in 1658 gave the sum of £100 to the Mayor of Northampton, the interest to be distributed among the poor of the parish of St. Giles and for placing out poor boy apprentices. The money was invested in the purchase of land at Duston containing about 32 acres.

By a deed dated 6 Apr. 1802 the several properties comprised in the before-mentioned charities were conveyed to 15 trustees or feoffees. Under the trusts of this deed the income of the Feoffment Estates is to be applied as follows :—To the vicar of St. Giles the annual sum of £15 ; to the clerk and sexton the annual sums of £2 and £2 3s. 4d. respectively ; to apply the residue for the benefit of the poor of the parish and for such other pious and charitable uses within the parish as the trustees should think proper. The gross income of the charities in the year ending 1925 was about £620. It was distributed in accordance with the directions contained in the deed, the trustees giving a donation of £50 to the funds of the General Hospital and sums of £15 each to the funds of St. Giles', St. Edmund's, St. Michael's and St. Gabriel's Sunday Schools.

The charities are administered by 15 trustees appointed under the provisions of the deed of 6 Apr. 1802. When their number is reduced to 7 or less new trustees are appointed by the surviving trustees.

Arthur Goodday, by will dated 13 Jan. 1692, gave a close of garden ground at Northampton and a rentcharge of £5 per annum issuing out of No. 2, Ambush Street, Northampton. The garden ground was sold in 1859, and the endowment now consists of £1,841 4s. 2d. Consols with the Official Trustees producing £46 0s. 4d. annually, and the rentcharge of £5. Under the directions contained in the will the rentcharge is paid to the vicar of St. Giles and the remainder of the funds distributed to the poor of the parish in clothing and bread. The charity is administered by the trustees of the Feoffment Estates.

William Brooks Gates, by will proved in the Principal Registry 16 May 1876, gave £200 upon trust, the income to be given towards defraying the expenses of the parish church of St. Giles and schools. The endowment of the charity for the church now consists of £106 4s. 10d. Consols with the Official Trustees producing £2 13s. annually, which is applied by the vicars and churchwardens as above.

The Northamptonshire Orphanage for Girls stands in St. Giles' Street. It originated in the Northamptonshire Servants Training Institution which was founded at Wootton in 1858, removed to St. James' Street, Northampton, in 1861, and to the Horse Market in 1867. In 1868 it was merged into the Northamptonshire Orphanage for Girls, then in process of formation, and in 1870 moved to the premises in St. Giles Street which it now occupies—291 girls have been trained at the home.[58]

William Stratford, by will dated 16 July 1753, gave a sum of £500, which was laid out in the purchase of an estate at Denton in 1755. The estate was sold and the proceeds invested in £794 13s. 7d. Victoria Government 3 per cent. Consolidated Inscribed Stock in the name of the Official Trustees, and forms the present endowment of the charity. The income, amounting to £27 16s. 2d. annually, is distributed to the poor of the parishes of St. Giles, St. Peter and St. Sepulchre. Each parish receives about £9 5s. yearly, which is distributed by the minister and churchwardens of each respective parish.

The charity of Miss C. E. Hyndman was founded by deeds dated in 1836 and 1842, which provided that the interest on £224 13s. 3d. Consols should be applied towards defraying expenses in connexion with the repair of St. Katherine's Church. This amount is now with the Official Trustees, and produces £5 12s. 4d. yearly, which is applied by the churchwardens towards church expenses.

The Rev. Robert William Stoddart, by will proved 16 Aug. 1898, gave to the rector and churchwardens of St. Peter's £100 for investment, the income to be distributed among the poor of the parish. The endowment now consists of £92 9s. 8d. Consols with the Official Trustees, producing £2 6s. annually.

The origin of the Church Estate Charity is unknown. By an indenture dated 20 Dec. 18 James I (1620) properties in Northampton were conveyed to the churchwardens, the rents to be applied towards the repair and expenses of the church. The properties were sold in 1911 and the proceeds invested in £1,156 1s. 8d. India 3½ per cent. stock in the name of the Official Trustees. The interest amounts to £40 9s. 4d. yearly.

Nicholas Rothwell, who died in 1658, gave by his will £100, the income to be applied towards the relief of the poor of the parish of St. Sepulchre. This sum was invested in the purchase of a close of land at Northampton which was sold in 1875 and the proceeds invested in £1,168 13s. 3d. Consols with the Official Trustees, the present endowment of the charity. The charity is regulated by a scheme of the Charity Commissioners dated 8 Mar. 1918, and the income, amounting to £29 4s. 4d. annually, is applied by the trustees (of whom the churchwarden of St. Sepulchre is a trustee *ex officio*) for the benefit of the poor.

[58] Inf. from Miss L. H. Wake, late Hon. Sec.